# GENDER INEQUALITIES IN SOUTHERN EUROPE:
## WOMEN, WORK AND WELFARE IN THE 1990s

# Books of Related Interest

**Immigrants and the Informal Economy in Southern Europe**
Martin Baldwin-Edwards, Mediterranean Migration Observatory,
Athens, and Joaquin Arango, Instituto Universitario Ortega y Gasset,
Madrid (eds)

**The Politics of Immigration in Western Europe**
Martin Baldwin-Edwards, Mediterranean Migration Observatory,
Athens, and Martin A. Schain, Center for European Studies,
New York (eds)

**Southern European Welfare States**
*Between Crisis and Reform*
Martin Rhodes, European University Institute, Florence (ed.)

**Politics and Policy in Democratic Spain**
*No Longer Different*
Paul Heywood, University of Nottingham

# Gender Inequalities in Southern Europe
## Women, Work and Welfare in the 1990s

*Editors*

María José González
Teresa Jurado
Manuela Naldini

FRANK CASS
LONDON • PORTLAND, OR

First published in 2000 in Great Britain by
FRANK CASS PUBLISHERS
Newbury House, 900 Eastern Avenue, London IG2 7HH

and in the United States of America by
FRANK CASS PUBLISHERS
c/o ISBS
5804 N.E. Hassalo Street
Portland, OR 97213-3644

Website www.frankcass.com

British Library Cataloguing in Publication Data

Gender inequalities in southern Europe: women, work and
welfare in the 1990s
1. Women – Europe, Southern  2. Women – Employment
– Europe, Southern  3. Family – Europe, Southern
4. Europe, Southern – Social policy
I. Gonzalez, Maria Jose  II. Jurado, Teresa  III. Naldini,
Manuela
305.4'2'094
          ISBN 0 7146 5028 5 (cloth)
          ISBN 0 7146 8084 2 (paper)

A catalogue record for this book is available from the
Library of Congress

This group of studies first appeared in a Special Issue on 'Gender Inequalities in
South Europe: Women, Work and Welfare in the 1990s' of South European
Society & Politics, 4/2 (Autumn 1999) ISSN 1360-8746, published by
Frank Cass.

Printed in Great Britain by
Antony Rowe Ltd., Chippenham, Wilts.

# Contents

Foreword     Ann Shola Orloff    1

Introduction: Interpreting the Transformation of Gender Inequalities in Southern Europe     María José González, Teresa Jurado and Manuela Naldini    4

Women's Flexible Work and Family Responsibilities in Greece     Nota Kyriazis    35

Development and Equality Between Women and Men in the Portuguese Labour Market     Isabel Margarida André and Paulo Areosa Feio    54

The Family Paradigm in the Italian Welfare State (1947–1996)     Franca Bimbi    72

Social Rights of Women with Children: Lone Mothers and Poverty in Italy, Germany and Great Britain     Elisabetta Ruspini    89

Gender in the Reform of the Italian Welfare State     Elisabetta Addis    122

To What Extent does it Pay to be Better Educated? Education and the Work Market for Women in Italy     Francesca Bettio and Paola Villa    150

Is the Male Provider Model Still in Place? Partnership Formation in Contemporary Spain     Marta Luxán, Pau Miret and Rocío Treviño    171

Separation and Divorce in Spain     Montserrat Solsona, René Houle and Carles Simó    195

Political Participation: Exploring the
Gender Gap in Spain                **Laura Morales**   223

Abstracts to Articles                                 248

Biographical Notes                                    252

Index                                                 255

# Foreword

Only a few years ago, one could say (as many of us did in critiques of the mainstream comparative literature on social policy regimes) that we needed more comparative work on the gendered dimensions of systems of social provision. Happily, the 1990s have seen a host of new research on gender and social policy filling this gap in the literature. However, until recently, little of the new work (in English) has attended to southern Europe. Pioneering work by scholars such as Chiara Saraceno, Laura Balbo, Rossana Trifiletti and Celia Valiente, and also by the senior scholars represented in this collection, has brought insights based on southern European realities to English-speaking audiences. This special issue represents a significant joint contribution to the literature from the perspective of southern European academics, who address questions which have concerned all interested in gender and the state. To what extent does social policy depend on and reinforce a male breadwinner-female care-giver model of the family? How do women reconcile employment and family life and what are the sources of the changed life patterns that are observed among younger women? How does gender inequality in the southern European cases compare in character and strength with patterns seen in other western countries?

To the extent that studies of gender relations and welfare states have considered the southern European countries, there has been a tendency to consider them 'backward'. This has been particularly because overall labour-force participation rates for women are low in a cross-national perspective, but also because of the legacy of authoritarian regimes or their conservative political descendants and the Catholic Church, which have exalted traditional gender roles and subsidiarity (that is, the family must be the first defence in cases of need, rather than the welfare state). Most feminist analysts would agree that the possibilities for women's economic independence are a good criterion for judging the gendered effects of a given system; by this standard, the southern European cases are less advanced than some, but not all, northern European ones.

But while we might agree on how systems should progress with regard to gender equality, it is not so easy to see what is the way forward. Scandinavian approaches to promoting gender equality through social policy are only one possibility, and one unlikely to be replicated in other political contexts. The editors choose to measure their cases with respect to an ideal type of post-industrial, gender-egalitarian policy — the 'universal care-giver' model championed by Nancy Fraser. This model postulates that to realize gender equality, both men and women must be equally involved in care giving and paid work. This model is used as a reference point for contrast with current realities, and to assess positive and negative aspects of change with regard to the situation of women. Younger women in southern Europe do seem to aspire to greater involvement in paid work than their mothers' generation, and in other ways are breaking with older patterns of behaviour. At present, it appears that the constraints that make it difficult for women to be involved in both employment and care giving (particularly the lack of services provided either by state or market and the lack of employment opportunities for women) vary in degree, rather than kind, from those present in other European countries. There is certainly a great reliance on the family in southern Europe, which has, in fact, allowed many younger women to be employed and protected others from poverty, but whether there is a distinctive familist culture that would last beyond the necessity of such reliance is less clear.

This book comprises of case studies of four southern European states (Greece, Italy, Portugal and Spain), touching on the themes of change and continuity across systems of social provision, family and household forms, gender divisions of labour, women's employment patterns and women's political participation. The editors argue that the relationships among welfare states, families and labour markets provide an explanation for the prevailing 'gender cultures' in southern Europe. This approach echoes similar analyses that have been applied productively to other western welfare states in attempting to understand gender relations.

Most significant for those of us less familiar with the southern European cases is the thoroughgoing attempt to deconstruct the monolithic image of southern European society. Some authors highlight the importance of sub-national differences (across regions or autonomous communities) on issues such as family change or women's involvement in the labour force. Indeed, it is striking for those who have looked only at aggregate statistics to see the important differences across cohorts uncovered by a number of the contributors. While older women are attached to traditional gender values, and have organized their lives around a traditional division of labour and marriage, younger women are at the forefront of challenging an oppressive 'gender order' in terms of their educational attainment, labour-force participation, household formation, fertility, political participation and values.

The authors are able to provide this generationally differentiated picture by doing detailed empirical analyses using new statistical data sources. For example, two of the Spanish contributions exploit a very rich retrospective Spanish socio-demographic survey conducted by the National Statistical Office in 1991 (with 160,000 respondents), which provides unpublished information on Spanish conditions. Spanish opinion surveys from 1994 were analysed for the first time using multivariate methods to test current theories of political participation that emerged from comparative studies which excluded southern Europe. The new European Household Panel of 1994 and three extensive national panel studies were used for a cross-sectional and dynamic analysis of lone mothers in Germany, Italy and the UK. Lastly, new qualitative information collected in Greece in 1996 was analysed in order to obtain a comprehensive picture of the relationship between employment flexibilization and family life. These rich empirical studies will provide a strong basis for future comparative work on gender relations, markets, families and welfare states, incorporating southern European cases along with northern European ones.

Ann Shola Orloff

Professor of Sociology, Women's Studies and Political Science,
Northwestern University, USA,
and Jean Monnet Fellow,
European University Institute, 1998–99

# Introduction: Interpreting the Transformation of Gender Inequalities in Southern Europe

MARÍA JOSÉ GONZÁLEZ, TERESA JURADO
and MANUELA NALDINI

Recent years have been very productive for the literature of comparative studies on gender roles and gender relations in western Europe. Some scholars, for instance, have studied the effects of state social provisions on gender relations, from which they have elaborated certain typologies of *gender regimes* and *diverse worlds of European patriarchy* (Orloff 1996; Duncan 1995, 1996; Lewis 1992). Another strand of research has looked at the new role of women in accelerating certain aspects of demographic change, such as increasing divorce rates (Daly 1996), declining fertility (Pinnelli 1995; Bettio and Villa 1998) and the transformation of the traditional patterns of family formation from a cross-national perspective (Boh, Bak, Clason *et al.* 1989; Blossfeld 1996). Lastly, other studies have incorporated regional divisions in their comparative framework with the understanding that national states conceal heterogeneous configurations of *gender cultures* (Perrons 1998; Garcia-Ramon and Monk 1996; Mingione 1994; Duncan 1991).

There is also a group of political scientists (Leibfried 1992; Castels 1994; Ferrera 1996; Sarasa and Moreno 1995) that has specifically defined the features of the Mediterranean welfare state, which can be summarized as: high transfer payments (especially pensions); national health care (with near universalism and an extended scope for private provision); and low penetration of the welfare state and low degree of 'stateness' (Ferrera 1996). These authors have, however, conducted a gender-blind analysis. Southern European countries also share common traits in the way in which gender roles and responsibilities are embedded in social policies and law.

This book attempts to fill some of the gaps left in the existing literature on comparative gender studies. On the one hand, southern states have often been neglected in comparative frameworks, and, on the other, generalizations about the nature of gender inequalities have been formulated in the name of southern Europe when only a single case study was analysed, normally Italy and seldom Spain, Portugal or Greece.

The present compilation presents studies of the recent situation of gender inequalities in southern states (Greece, Italy, Portugal and Spain). An effort has been made to encompass the main ways in which gender inequalities are reproduced or ameliorated, namely, the state, the family and the labour market. This triad of institutions interact together, shaping the specific *gender orders* (that is, the cultural or legal assumptions about the rules, rights and obligations differently attributed to women and men) by which the relationships between women and men are constructed.

Some of our authors have made an effort to compare their case studies with central and northern European states. They do not thereby aspire to estimate differences in the degree of gender inequality between these countries, a rather difficult task. On the contrary, they illustrate the fact that gender inequalities take different forms in the south. Let us mention, as an example, the archetypal association made between a high level of gender inequality and a low level of female participation in the labour force, which is typical of most southern states. Participation does not necessarily measure higher or lower degrees of gender inequality. It is only one aspect through which gender inequalities are manifested. According to Perrons (1995), for instance, in Mediterranean countries, regulations operating on the formal labour markets have secured more equal conditions for working women than in many other EU states.

Lastly, the limitations of our study have also to be mentioned. This collection is biased toward contributions focusing on Italy and Spain. In these countries, the links between the welfare state, the labour market and the family system have been more extensively explored. As a result, it has been easier to assess the similarities and differences between them. For Portugal and Greece, a more limited picture is offered, although the authors provide a broad introduction before going into their particular case studies.

As for the content of this monograph, we would like to summarize in a few words the main lines of research. First, the Greek contribution, by Nota Kyriazis, provides a rich qualitative analysis of the difficulties of combining family and employment for women working in the retail sector in Athens. The author argues that employer-induced flexibility facilitates women's entry into paid employment, but it strengthens traditional gender relations within the family. A similar perspective is taken by the Portuguese study of Isabel Margarida André and Paulo Areosa Feio, which pays particular attention to gender inequalities in the labour market and to the role of education in women's professional careers. In addition, they provide an explanation for the extraordinarily high level of women's labour-force participation in Portugal.

The specific interaction between the Italian welfare state, the family and the labour market is explored by three of the four Italian contributions. Franca Bimbi analyses the extent to which the absence of family policies and the meagre development of services in the Italian welfare state have contributed to the permanence of the 'family paradigm', that is, that care is a matter for the family, and the care of the family is the responsibility of women. Elisabetta Ruspini illustrates the strong differences in the single mothers' poverty rate in Italy, Great Britain and Germany and shows how in the Italian case the family plays the chief role in protecting lone mothers against poverty. Elisabetta Addis discusses gender inequalities in the Italian welfare state and argues that recent reforms in the area of cash transfers reinforce the male breadwinner-female housekeeper model. Lastly, she proposes new criteria for evaluating and taking into account gender equity in welfare state policy. The final Italian contribution (Francesca Bettio and Paola Villa) describes the impact of rising female education on the differentiated labour-force patterns of poorly and highly educated women. It shows that the growing participation and performance of women in education increases their individual employment chances, but also increases the aggregated unemployment rate of women.

The Spanish authors Marta Luxán, Pau Miret and Rocío Treviño conduct a longitudinal analysis to reconstruct recent patterns of family formation in Spain. They explore whether the male-provider model is still in place and they find important signs of change as regards women's behaviour. The contribution of Montserrat Solsona, René Houle and Carles Simó highlights precisely how the new economic role of women in Spain facilitates their options for exiting marriages. Yet, they show that there are important regional variations. Laura Morales, instead, offers an analysis of women's political involvement and participation in Spain. She applies, for the first time, current theoretical approaches to the Spanish case.

In the remainder of this introduction, we aim to make some general reflections on the recent transformation of gender inequalities in southern Europe. We partly base this approach on the main findings of the contributions included in this monograph. In order to carry out this task, we define, in the first place, our notion of *gender equity* or what we consider to be the ideal model of a *gender equity system*.

Frequently, it is taken for granted that those contexts in which gender equity is achieved to a relatively significant extent are good normative models. This occurs when Scandinavian countries are, implicitly or explicitly, taken as a reference. Instead of resorting to foreign models, we choose a theoretical ideal-type with which to contrast reality and to assess present obstacles and achievements. We then proceed with a general description of the main transformations of gender inequalities and the main legacies of the traditional gender order.

## FEMINIST VIEWS ON GENDER EQUITY: TWO EARNERS OR TWO CARERS?

During this century, in most advanced countries, the male-breadwinner model, which requires the man to be the breadwinner and the woman to be the carer and reproducer, has been the main principle concerning gender relations embedded in social policies and law. In most welfare states, this model was historically developed through the idea of a 'family wage': a wage or a supplementary wage (in terms of tax advantages, family allowances and so on), or both, which should enable the worker to support a dependent wife and children. Such ideas required at least two necessary conditions: first, full male employment and economic growth as a normal economic phenomena; second, family stability and an accepted idea of a hierarchical division of labour and power within the family. Consequently, the idea of a family wage and that of a male-breadwinner model underwent cross-national and historical variations according to the different degree of male employment rates and the intensity of gender inequalities within the family (compare Lewis and Ostner 1994).

The post-industrial phase of capitalism, the changing age structure of the population and the growth of unemployment rates in most advanced countries, which resulted in the crisis of the welfare state, together with a widening of family forms and a new determination on the part of women to enter into the labour market, have undermined the bedrock of the male-breadwinner model. In other words, if a new world of economic production and social reproduction is emerging, the old gender order is destined to crumble.

Among feminists the main question still discussed at the theoretical level is: what should people of different gender do, think and be? The issue remains whether feminists want women to become more like men are now (which means allowing women to go into the labour market, as men do) or whether they want to make women's difference cost less (for example, attaching rights to unpaid work). A third possibility would be to make men become more like women. Clearly, all call for gender equity. But, there is no common view of what gender equity means.

Many feminists have associated gender equity with two different notions: equality and difference. In short, it can be said that 'equality' means treating women like men. In this regard, supporters of the 'difference' approach have critically stressed that such treatment has the fault of considering 'the male as the norm'. They have argued that women should be considered differently because they differ from men. In their turn, egalitarians have criticized the 'difference' approach because it relies on 'essentialist' notions of femininity, which therefore reinforce the gender division of roles. Clearly, these two different notions also imply that different strategies should be put into practice and a different role given to the state to achieve gender equity. Using Lewis' words (1992), the fundamental question is 'what can be hoped for from the state?' In policy terms, different strains of feminist scholarship have never shared a 'unique' vision either of what should be the basis for women's social rights (their worker or mother (or wife) citizenship status) or of the role of the state in shaping gender relations.

Recently, feminist historical research has challenged the assumption that, in the past, all feminists demanded 'equality'. For instance, some historians have shown that women reformers in the period between the two world wars called for the attachment of greater value to the role of women as carers and reproducers. As shown by Susan Pedersen's research on the 'endowment of motherhood' (Pedersen 1993), other historians have preferred to define such ideas and discourses as the 'maternalism' approach (Koven and Michel 1993) (for a discussion on this issue, compare Orloff 1996).

As far as the role of the state is concerned, most Scandinavian feminists and social democrats, for instance, have given support to a state vision (that of a 'women-friendly state'), although they have added that this development has to be interpreted in terms of a 'transition from private to public dependence' (Hernes 1987). By contrast, other analysts have emphasized the role of the state in reproducing 'patriarchy' and in reinforcing pre-existing (traditional) gender roles and gender inequality (Sassoon 1987; Pateman 1989) or have highlighted how the state's policies themselves constitute and construct gender roles and inequalities

(Saraceno 1996). As the long-lasting disputes over the choice between the difference and the equality approaches have shown, to choose between them is probably impossible (Lewis and Amström 1992).

Given the equality/difference theoretical impasse, and since the main approaches to the study of gender inequalities and strategies to attain greater gender equity are mainly based on northern experiences, we have, rather, chosen to present a normative ideal-type. In this way, the normative idea becomes explicit and more accessible to discussion, and provides a reference category to which reality can be contrasted.

Nancy Fraser (1997) has proposed a set of evaluative standards for social policy which should be seen as alternative pictures of a post-industrial welfare state. The notion of gender equity she sets up is multidimensional. Gender equity should be considered as a compound of various distinct normative principles (Fraser 1997: 45). These principles include: (1) anti-poverty and anti-exploitation principles, in particular to prevent three kinds of exploitable dependencies, which are dependency on an individual family member, on employers and supervisors, and on the personal whims of state officials; (2) equality of resources and leisure time; (3) the equality of respect principle; (4) the anti-marginalization principle; and (5) the anti-androcentrism principle.

Alternative feminist visions of possible post-industrial welfare states are then put forward by the author. With the aim of deconstructing the male-breadwinner model, as it has been incorporated in social policy, Fraser defines three alternative models of gender equity (described below). They serve to dismantle the sexual division of gender roles and their cultural coding in order to reduce the persistence of gender inequalities by encouraging a set of 'optional' and alternative state interventions. An illustrative example of alternative state interventions is, for instance, to be found in the field of childcare facilities, where the state's options are to expand childcare services or to pay parents to stay at home for parental leave.

The first vision of Fraser is named the Universal Breadwinner Model, that is, a model that aims to foster gender equity by supporting women's employment. This model is implicit in the politics of most US feminists and liberals. The core of this model is state provision of employment-enabling services for women, such as day care (so that most of the care work is provided outside of the family either by the market or the state). This scenario is not far away from the one provided by Esping Andersen in revisiting his analysis on welfare state regimes through the lens of the family, although the author's analysis does not have gender equity as a goal (Esping Andersen 1996). In short, the author looks at the US model (characterized by a low cost of services and a high level of job mobility across the life cycle and between different types of jobs) as a solution to western Europe's main economic and social problems: high unemployment rates and low fertility rates. According to Esping Andersen, the main answer to these problems is to foster post-industrial families (especially in countries such as Spain and Italy with a high level of unpaid work) in order to externalize most services still performed within the family. This externalization of 'family services' would result in the creation of new jobs, allowing women to enter the labour market in greater numbers and thus become more like men are now.

The second model that Fraser describes is called the Care-giver Parity Model, which is implicit in the politics of most European feminists and social democrats. This model prefers to promote gender equity by supporting informal care work. Its centrepiece is state provision of care-giver allowances. According to this model, the bulk of caring work has to be kept in the household and supported by public funds. Although both models would produce a major improvement over the current situation, there are still too many shortcomings. According to the author, neither the first nor the second model would be able to achieve full gender equity.

A third possibility is to 'induce men to become more like most women are now, namely people who do primary care-work' (Fraser 1997: 60), thereby deconstructing the gender order. This could mean dismantling the gendered opposition between bread winning and care giving, to break down those separated roles and their cultural coding and to move toward a gender model that she calls the Universal Care-giver Model, meaning that some women's current life patterns should become the norm for everyone. Most women today combine both unpaid reproductive and domestic work and paid work, although with huge difficulty given the unbalanced division of labour. All jobs would be created for workers who are care-givers; all would have a shorter weekly working time; some unpaid reproductive work would be performed in the household by parents, relatives and friends publicly supported. Other domestic and caring work would be located outside the household, in civil society, overcoming both the 'workism' of the first model and the 'domestic privatism' of the second. The Universal Care-giver Model constitutes the normative ideal-type that guides the following summary of transformations and continuities in gender inequalities in southern Europe.

## TRANSFORMATION OR CONTINUITY?

A common trait in southern Europe is the rapid transformation of the role of women in society that has taken place during the past two decades. As a result, the gap between old and young female generations has enormously broadened. This situation defines, as it were, a transitional phase in between two different gender orders, when elements of tradition and modernity continue together. For the sake of clarity, the following sections are precisely divided into these two dimensions of change and continuity of gender roles.

### Emerging Patterns of Greater Gender Equity

The traditional family based on the spouses' rigid division of labour appears to be cultural and economically speaking weak, unattractive or unbearable for most of the young generation, at the very least in its more extreme expression (that is, a full-time female home-maker who is married for life to a male breadwinner). Nowadays, there is a transition toward a new gender order, mainly performed by young adult women. The evidence of change can be summarized in the following points.

(1) *Weakening the Figure of the Male Provider.* Most western societies have moved away from Fordist economies to enter into a post-Fordist regime characterized by a reduction of industrial employment and an expansion of wage labour (in both the private and public sectors) in decentralized enterprises, and a deregulation of labour markets. Bettio and Villa, for instance, describe the decline of the industrial sector, which produced a stagnation in male employment in the 1980s while female employment expanded.

Hence, even if in southern Europe the figure of the male provider is still to some extent well regarded not only culturally, but also in law (see below), the general trend signals an increase in the flexibilization of employment practices. Consequently, single-earner families (a model still prevalent among the oldest generations) create too much uncertainty for newly constituted partnerships, as the analysis of women's family formation in the Marta Luxán, Pau Miret and Rocío Treviño's contribution shows. In short, even if some young men would prefer a traditional gender division of labour, their role as breadwinners (that is, a full-time and lifelong, stable occupational career) is no longer guaranteed.

(2) *Improving Women's Education and their Attachment to the Labour Force.* The access of women to higher education represents one of the most impressive changes in contemporary western societies, and southern Europe is not an exception. In the 1980s, the proportion of young people in higher education (that is, any level above secondary school) was favourable to men in Italy, Spain and Greece, and very similar for both genders in Portugal. In the 1990s, only ten years later, women became a majority in universities in Portugal, Greece and Spain and reached a similar proportion to that of male students in Italy (Bonke 1995). It is not only that more women than men are now entering higher education, but, as Francesca Bettio and Paola Villa show for the Italian case, that women's performance in the educational system is systematically better than men's. In addition, the segmentation of curricula by gender is also diminishing.

The implications of rising educational attainment for women are manifold. Education tends to increase women's occupational expectations. Highly educated women also tend to have a long-term attachment to the labour market in order to capitalize on their investment in human capital, as is demonstrated by the Italian, Spanish and Portuguese studies included in this special issue.

If the traditional model of female occupation meant a definitive withdrawal soon after marriage or childbearing, highly educated women (especially from the younger cohorts) tend to break with this pattern. The novelty, then, is the progressive increase in the number of women who remain permanently in the labour force, regardless of their family circumstances. This means that more women are able to consolidate their position as paid workers and, consequently, secure their economic independence in the long run (for example, through social security, pension schemes and so on). Portugal is a pioneer in southern Europe with regard to the appearance of a large proportion of women in continuous occupational careers. Participation on a permanent basis by Portuguese women has been apparent since the 1970s and 1980s, as described by Isabel Margarida André and Paulo Areosa Feio.

Figure 1 shows a cross-sectional snapshot of the proportion of women in the labour force according to their age (25–34 and 45–54) and region of origin in 1995.[1] These figures illustrate that the proportion of young women in the labour force is much higher in the younger age group (aged 25–34) than in the older (aged 45–54), albeit with important regional dissimilarities. Of course, it is as yet unknown whether they will all remain or withdraw from the labour force as the first child arrives.

FIGURE 1
GEOGRAPHY OF THE FORMAL FEMALE LABOUR FORCE IN SOUTHERN EUROPE:
ACTIVITY RATES IN 1995

## Young Adult Women Aged 25–34
### Greece

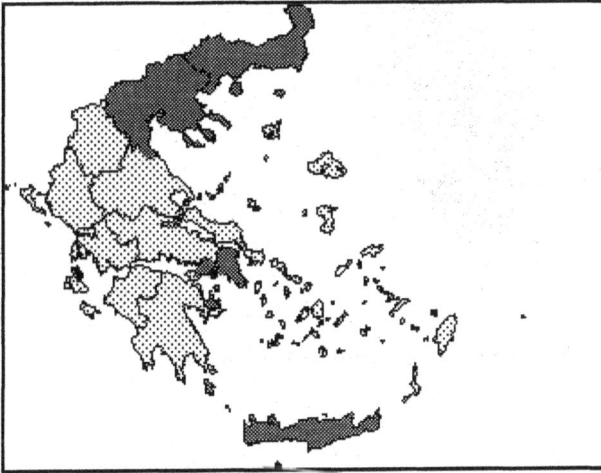

### Italy

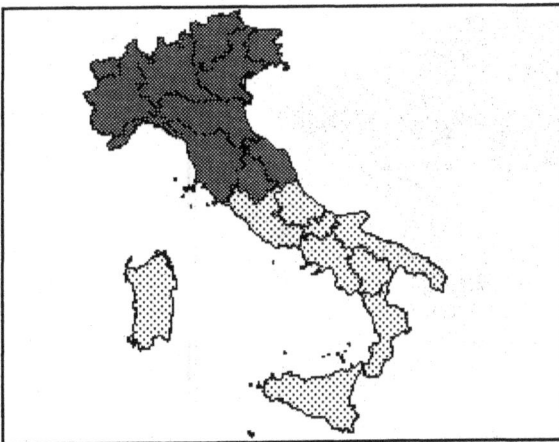

**Portugal**

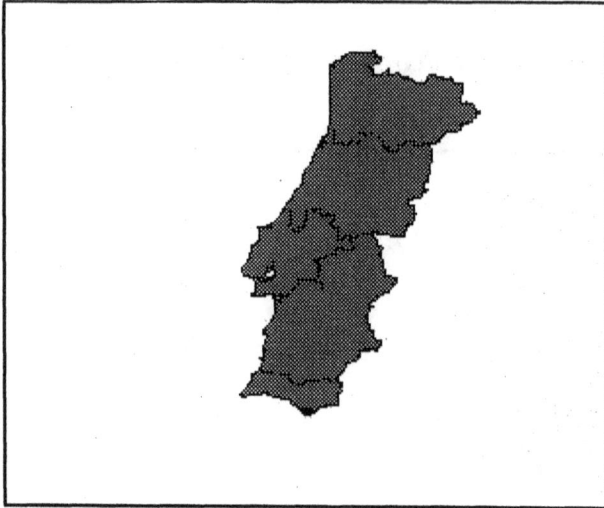

**Spain**

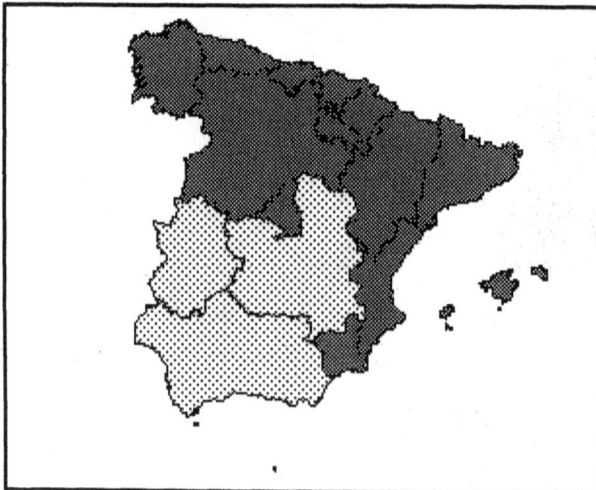

# Adult Women Aged 45-54

## Greece

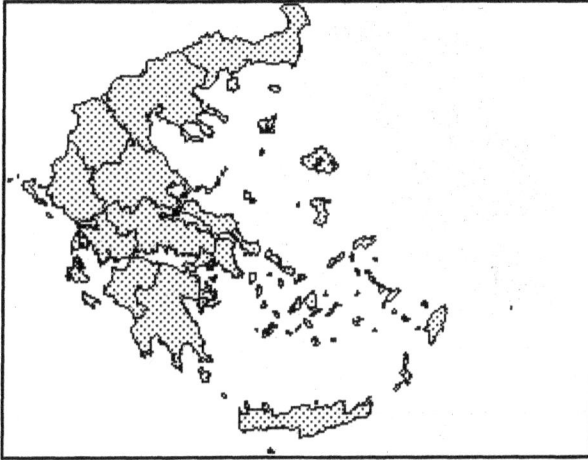

## Italy

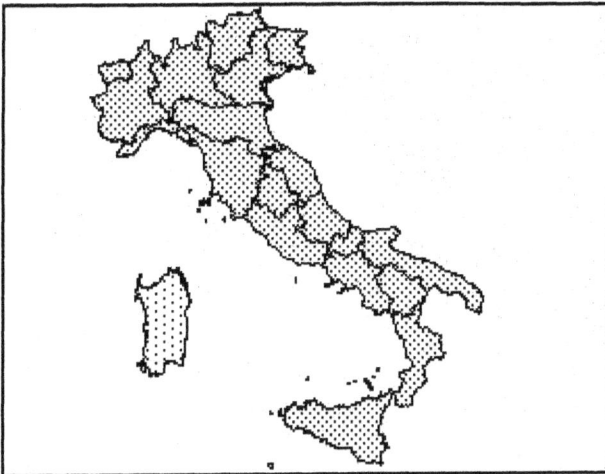

## Portugal

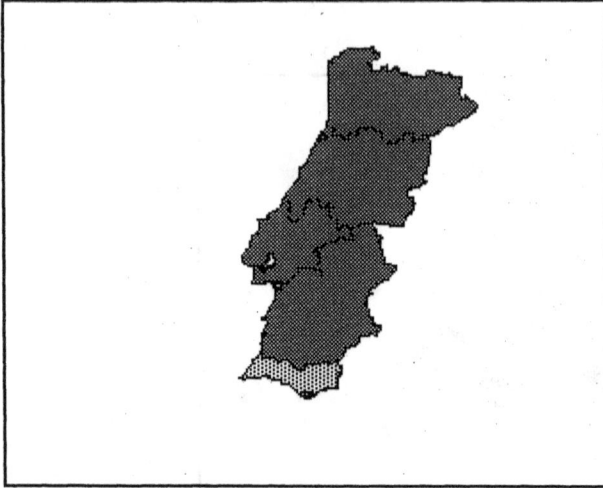

## Spain

Key:

| | | | | | |
|---|---|---|---|---|---|
| ☐ | < 30% | ▨ | 30.01% – 60% | ■ | >60.01% |

Nevertheless, the fact that female employment is scarce (that is, they face the highest unemployment rates) and that returning to full-time employment after a long interruption is rather difficult supports the belief that the younger age group will tend to keep their position in the labour force regardless of their family life.

On the other hand, rising educational attainment has brought about a rescheduling of women's family life. The common adjustment consists of delaying marriage (see Figure 2) and the birth of the first child (Blossfeld 1996). In 1996, Italian women aged 30–34 with primary education had their first child at the age of 23.9 as compared with those with higher education who had it at the age of 33.1; the respective age of these two educational groups in Spain in 1994 was 24.8 and 31.1 (Beets 1997). The fact that highly educated women have to wait until the moment they have consolidated their career entails, eventually, less time for procreation and a reduction in family size. Hence, controlling fertility to a low level seems to be a strategy for women to reconcile paid work and family life. This may partly explain the very low total fertility rates (sum of age-specific fertility rates) of southern European states as compared with other states such as France or Denmark (see Figure 3).

Lastly, education has an emancipating effect, as shown by Montserrat Solsona, René Houle and Carles Simó, insofar as it is associated with greater opportunities for women to initiate a divorce or dissolution of a consensual partnership. Actually, the large proportion of mature women economically dependent on their husbands (that is, many mature women who are full-time home-makers in Italy, Greece and Spain) may be primarily related to the current low levels of divorce.

(3) *The Gradual Inclusion of Gender Equity Principles and Expansion of the Welfare State.* Although gender interests have not played a central role in the political agenda of Mediterranean states, recent decades have witnessed some positive achievements, such as the trend toward the progressive individualization of social rights. The way in which the wife's and husband's income is treated in the taxation system may encourage or discourage women's employment. It has been said that the joint taxation system tends to favour the single-earner couple. By contrast, the individual taxation system tends to be gender neutral and to support women's employment, although the system of tax reliefs for married couples, in the form of tax allowances or tax credits, have also to be taken into account. In 1977, Italy adopted an individual taxation system with exemptions for dependent partners, which are reduced if the spouse

FIGURE 2
MEAN AGE OF WOMAN AT FIRST MARRIAGE IN SOUTHERN EUROPEAN STATES
FOR 1980, 1985, 1990 AND 1995

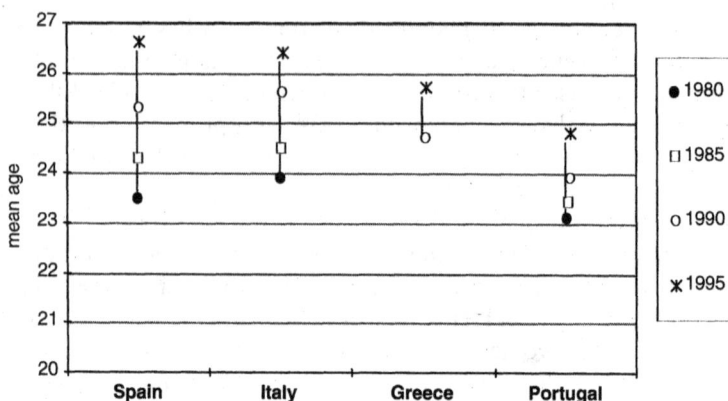

*Source:* Eurostat, 1997.
*Note*: Last data for Spain and Italy refer to 1994. There were no data for Greece in 1980 and 1985.

is economically active. In Spain, married couples have been able to choose either joint or separate taxation since 1989. In Greece, married couples file joint returns, but are taxed separately, while Portugal adopted joint taxation (income splitting) in 1989, which tends to favour either single-earner couples or couples with one high and one low earner (compare Leilièvre and Gauthier 1996).

There has also been an enforcement of policies on equal pay, a further recognition of maternity rights for employed women (that is, a guaranteed return to the same job after maternity leave, protection against dismissal for pregnant women and so on), and liberalization of the legislation on abortion on demand, which is completely legal in Italy (1978) and Greece (1986), but permitted only on restricted grounds in Portugal (1984) and Spain (1985). In the latter country, abortion is permitted in the case of rape, malformation of the foetus or of danger to the mother's physical or mental health.

Maternity policies currently in force have occurred as part of the expansion of the welfare state. In the first place, it should be noted that maternity leave (mainly conceived as a health measure for mothers) is

FIGURE 3
TOTAL FERTILITY RATE, SOUTHERN EUROPEAN STATES,
DENMARK AND FRANCE, 1960–1995

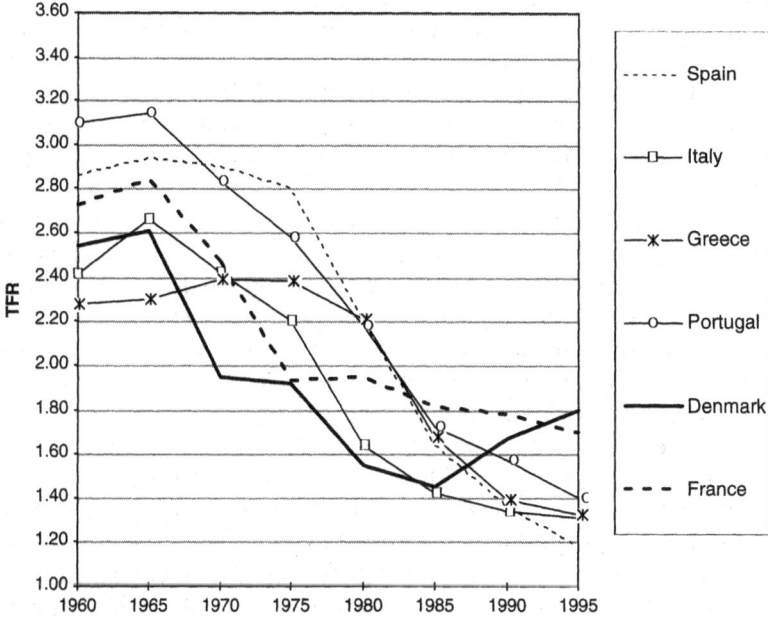

*Source:* Eurostat, 1997.

quite generous in all countries both in terms of length and payments. The
EC statutory minimum of 14 weeks paid maternity leave is attained in all
these countries (remunerated on an earnings-related basis). Only Portugal
had 90 days paid maternity leave for all insured women until recently, but
this was extended to 14 weeks in 1995. In Spain, women have the right
to 16 weeks paid maternity leave on condition that they have had six
months of social security contributions in previous years; in Greece, there
is 16 weeks leave for all insured women; and Italy has the longest paid
maternity leave in all 12 EU countries, consisting of 22 weeks which are
granted to all employed and self-employed women. Furthermore, leave
arrangements tend to be more generous in the public sector, that is, civil
servants are additionally allowed a year-long career break for family
purposes (Ditch *et al.* 1996).

As far as paternity leave is concerned (solely for fathers and usually around the birth of a child), only Spain allows fathers to take two days of paid leave (100 per cent of earnings). Additionally, mothers can opt to transfer up to four weeks of maternity leave to the father. Parental leave (taken by either partner, usually while children are of preschool age) is granted for different lengths of time in every state, but it is usually unpaid. Italy is the exception, where six months of parental leave can be taken before a child's first birthday and it is paid at 30 per cent of earnings. Besides, mothers can transfer part or the whole period of their leave to fathers.

The above-mentioned leave provisions have the beneficial effect of discouraging women from leaving paid employment (Gornick, Meyers and Ross 1997). Moreover, these policies are gradually recognizing the role of fathers in sharing family responsibilities. The experience of introducing parental leave in other member states has, nevertheless, proved to be rather unsuccessful because it continues to be taken overwhelmingly by women (Ditch *et al.* 1996).

Work regulations allowing for the reduction of working time for parents with dependent children is very underdeveloped in most European countries, and even more so in southern Europe. There are, however, a few good examples recorded in Italy. One is the introduction in 1994 (Finance Act) of the opportunity for men and women in the public sector to choose part-time work (Ditch *et al.* 1996). Another, again in Italy, is the municipal and regional projects on flexibilization of 'city times' in order to make paid and unpaid work more compatible, as described by Franca Bimbi.

In short, despite the fact that southern Europe is far from being gender friendly in terms of social policies and social provision, the inclusion of measures aimed at enabling women to combine paid and care work have been slowly gaining some recognition, and their legal formulation is most of the time gender neutral.


(4) *The Relaxation of Traditional Family Hierarchies.* The new economic role of women and the increasing educational level of the younger generations have changed traditional hierarchies within the family. In many families, fathers do not have the power to impose their interests on other family members, since the latter have either reached higher levels of financial independence (in the case of wives) or higher levels of cultural and symbolic power (in the case of adult children).

In southern European countries, young people tend to stay for a very long time within the parental home, many until their thirties. They do so because of the lack of (stable) employment and affordable housing, and because it is culturally accepted according to the prevalent values of intergenerational solidarity. The latter explains why, even when they have a remunerated job, they remain in the parental home until they have stabilized their income sources and have accumulated enough savings to acquire a proper dwelling. Since traditional authority structures within the family have changed, young people can use their family of origin as a fortress within which to prepare for a good start for adulthood. Thus, the path toward emancipation takes place 'within rather than from the family' as is normally the case in northern European states (Bettio and Villa 1998).

Likewise, in this new family context, young adults living with their parents enjoy greater levels of autonomy in the field of both sexual intimacy and individual freedom (Valero and Lence 1995; Mingione 1994). Sexual intercourse outside marriage has lost its traditional stigmatization, so that young people can have experience of relationships before they enter marriage (the most common form of partnership in southern Europe) at rather late ages.

Non-marital cohabitation is still rare, but it is undoubtedly an emerging form of living arrangement in southern Europe. Moreover, it is the arrangement that better guarantees 'contingent relations between partners', as argued by Montserrat Solsona, René Houle and Carles Simó in their study of Spain. They show that cohabiting couples have a higher risk of partnership breakdown compared with married couples, the reason being that the former living arrangement lasts as long as the individual interests of both partners are equally guaranteed.

Extramarital births have also gradually increased in recent years in all southern states, although at a rather slow pace in Greece (see Figure 4). In Italy and Spain, extramarital births almost doubled, and in Portugal tripled, between 1980 and the mid-1990s. These figures are statistical indicators of the increasing de-institutionalization of the traditional model of the family, as described above.

The changes described previously have advanced southern Europe toward greater equity, but there are clouds on the southern horizon.

### Legacies of the Traditional Gender Order

In southern Europe, men from older generations prefer largely to work for pay and involve themselves very rarely in unpaid work. Women, by

FIGURE 4
BIRTHS OUTSIDE MARRIAGE, SOUTHERN EUROPEAN STATES, 1960–1995

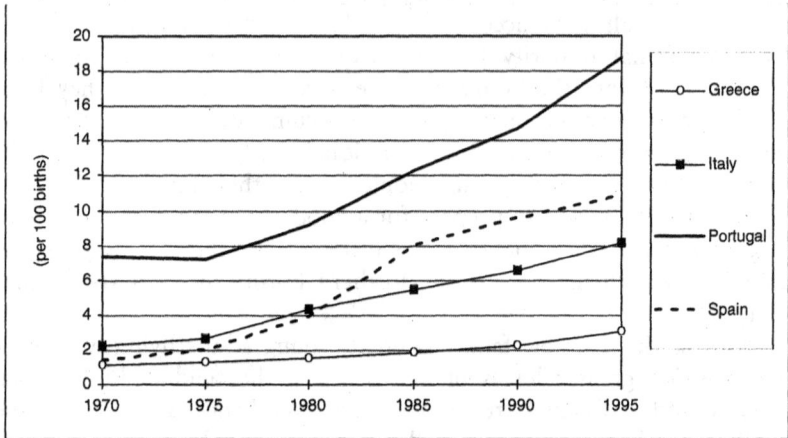

Source: Eurostat, 1997, *Demographic Statistics 1997*, Luxembourg: Council of Europe.

contrast, work many hours, involuntarily or not, without monetary reward. Young men and women are partly reproducing these work patterns of older female and male generations. In this section, the common southern European legacies of the traditional gender order in the family, the labour market and the state, and their interconnections are presented.

(1) *Inflexibility in Male Roles.* Women on average work less hours in paid employment than men, while they do more unpaid work within families than husbands and fathers do. In Spain, the amount of hours spent by women in paid and unpaid work during the whole year is double the time spent by men, since women do much more domestic work than men (Durán 1997). Moreover, the young generation of married women has mainly reproduced their mother's gender role in domestic life. Italian surveys on the use of time conducted by ISTAT show that there are few differences in the number of hours spent on family tasks by women across the age range. Young women aged 25–35 spent more time with their children than older women (35–44), but investment in other domestic tasks is very similar for both age groups (Sabbadini and Palomba

1994). Another indicator of young men's refusal to perform unpaid work is the low number of parents who take advantage of the new possibility for absence from the paid workplace under parental leave regulations.

Does increasing female employment not help to change this traditional division of domestic labour? Recent Spanish research on the division of labour within families with adult children enrolled at university in Madrid provides elements of an answer. The employment of the mother, the regular participation of the father in family tasks and the values concerning the distribution of domestic tasks of sons are the factors that most influence the participation of young people in domestic work. According to this study, the gender division of unpaid work promises to change from one generation to the next under three conditions. It might change, first, if the mother has full-time employment; second, if the father participates in domestic work; and, third, if the son has a non-traditional view of his family role (Meil-Landwerlin 1997). Thus, it is not very likely that increasing female employment alone will change the gender order in domestic life in southern Europe. Moreover, women still engage less in the paid labour force than men and if they do, they suffer from worse employment conditions than men, as discussed below.

(2) *Female Dependency on Father's and Husband's Incomes.* Young women depend for a very long period both financially and socially on their parents, since they spend a long time in education and face important entrance barriers in the labour and housing markets. Many women in southern Europe still move from financial dependency on their father to financial dependency on their spouse. Since long-lasting cohabitation with parents is the dominant pattern in most southern countries and marriage is the dominant means of family formation, few women experience living in non-family households. In addition, the considerable employment shortage in most countries (with the exception of Portugal) prevents many women from entering a financially symmetrical partnership.

In southern Europe, obstacles to gender equity on labour markets are twofold: first, there is a general problem of employment shortage that affects primarily women, as indicated by high female unemployment rates; and, second, the vertical and horizontal segregation of occupations by gender creates a high amount of female dependency on men, as shown by Kyriazis' contribution. High female unemployment rates mean that many women would like to have a paid job, but are not able to get a first job, are unable to re-enter the labour market after having cared for a child, and more frequently experience unstable jobs and recurring episodes of unemployment. Consequently, women have to a large extent to depend financially on a male family member, since few women are entitled to public income maintenance. Unemployment benefit covers a relatively small proportion of the total unemployed population in the south and women are not as well covered by unemployment benefits as men (European Commission 1993). The lower female coverage, as compared to men, results from their higher risk of having a short-term job, which does not entitle them to unemployment benefits or only entitles them to a short period of coverage. Besides, it is a consequence of the higher incidence of self-employed work, work as a family help, informal jobs and periods out of paid employment among women (Torns 1997; Jurado 1995).

Table 1 shows the main features of the labour-market situation for women in southern Europe and it also reveals the differences across countries. In Portugal, women have a relatively good chance of being in long-term employment, while in Spain many women are in the unpaid labour force, unemployed, in short-term employment or are unpaid family workers. In Greece, the situation is similar, but with a different distribution of unemployment and family help, while in Italy women are somewhat better off than in Spain and Greece considering all the

TABLE 1
WOMEN IN SOUTH EUROPEAN LABOUR MARKETS, 1994

|  | Greece | Italy | Portugal | Spain | EU-average |
|---|---|---|---|---|---|
| % of women aged 30–34 economically inactive | 40.4 | 36.7 | 19.7 | 37.7 | 30.2 |
| unemployment rate of women aged 30–34 | 12.6 | 15.3 | 8.8 | 31.1 | 13.4 |
| % of married women aged 25–49 in employment | 46.5 | 45.7 | 69.1 | 35.5 | 58.0 |
| % of female employees in temporary jobs | 10.5 | 9.3 | 10.3 | 37.9 | 12.0 |
| female family workers as % of all employed females | 25.6 | 7.8 | 2.7 | 7.7 | 4.2 |

Sources: Eurostat 1994; OECD 1996.

indicators shown in Table 1. The contributions of Francesca Bettio and Paola Villa and of Isabel Margarida André and Paulo Areosa Feio develop with more detail the Italian and the Portuguese models of women's integration in the labour force.

Furthermore, there remain significant regional differences as regards the level of female participation (see Figure 1). These differences have been related to the legacies of traditional *regional cultures of gender and work* (on this concept compare McDowell and Massey 1984; Duncan 1991). Hence, it can be hypothesized that the highest participation in the labour force of young women (aged 25–35) in the north-east coastal area of Spain (Catalonia and the Valencian Community) is related to the pre-existing tradition of female industrial employment in feminized sectors such as the clothing, food and shoemaking industries. Conversely, low opportunities for female employment in southern Spain may be related to the existence of traditional male employment in agriculture organized around *latifundios* (large agrarian holdings of more than 500 hectares) (see Baylina and Garcia-Ramon 1998). Again, Portugal constitutes an exception in its spatial homogeneity, despite an agrarian structure dominated by *latifundios* in its southern regions.

Lastly, sex differences in earnings and employment stability should be mentioned as another cause of female dependency.[2] Figures on earnings differentials reveal that in southern Europe at the beginning of the 1990s, women in manual occupations earned 17–28 per cent less than men per unit of time worked and the gap in non-manual occupations was even greater, ranging from 30 to 38 per cent (Duncan 1996). Since most couples are homogeneous with respect to their professional occupation, or the wife has an even lower occupational status than the husband, it becomes evident that in most families men have greater financial power and women have a more limited financial independence. In addition, women have a higher risk than men of losing their income without any replacement by transfer payments, as mentioned previously.

(3) *'Women-Unfriendly' Welfare States.* In southern Europe most welfare states are latecomers. The pioneer country has been Italy, followed by Greece, Spain and Portugal. However, according to some scholars, as mentioned earlier, they have their own characteristics that distinguish them from other types of welfare state (Ferrera 1996; Sarasa and Moreno 1995).

All southern European countries have a high-income-transfer model of welfare state based on occupational status and characterized by a high degree of institutional fragmentation. All have implemented a twofold system: high protection for whoever works in a stable job, that is, the adult (male) breadwinner, and very weak protection for those who do not work (Ferrera 1996; Guillén 1996). Due to the characteristics of these welfare states, to the relatively recent implementation of social rights in a time of economic and financial crisis, but also due to the strength of the family as a support network, some welfare benefits do not exist or have low levels of coverage and generosity. For instance, no national minimum income schemes exist in these countries, although in Spain since 1992 all regional governments have decided to establish a social minimum income (*Salario social*), which is a means-tested programme based on the household, with different characteristics according to the region and low levels of payment (Laparra and Aguillar 1996).

Moreover, if the level of pension benefits (measured as the percentage of the net wage) is within the European average (compare Ferrera 1996), the same cannot be said for social assistance pensions and social security minimum old-age pensions, which are very poor and mainly apply to women. As Elisabetta Addis's article shows for Italy, social assistance pensions (*pensione sociale*) grant a very low amount and are given in 80 per cent of cases to women. For Spain, the amount of non-contributive pensions in 1995 (*prestación por jubilación no contributiva*) was also very low (López 1996). In addition, these benefits are generally means-tested. Means-tested benefits have increased in past decades in southern Europe: as an illustrative example, in Spain, the number of beneficiaries of this subsystem of means-tested benefits increased tenfold from 1982 to 1992 (Laparra and Aguillar 1996). Means-tested benefits, such as social assistance benefits and non-contributive pensions, tend to reinforce women's family dependence, because their level or rights to them, or both, depend on the husband's income.

The same gender gap is found in unemployment benefits, as mentioned previously. Elisabetta Addis shows that these kinds of benefits are not only male biased, but, in addition, that the Italian reforms since 1991, which have introduced work mobility benefits, seem to have widened the gender gap even further.

Lastly, family policies, as shown for the Italian case by Franca Bimbi's contribution, are not fully developed, being mainly targeted toward families in need and dependent on family income. In particular, support for children is 'poor' in comparison with other western European countries. As a result, Greece, Portugal, Spain and Italy achieved only low rankings in terms of the generosity of child benefits for couples with children (Ditch *et al.* 1993).

Despite these social policy deficits, women in southern Europe are not more frequently without social protection than in other countries, but they are more likely to receive financial protection from other family members, in particular from men, and less likely to receive it from the state. The comparative analysis of Elisabetta Ruspini on lone mothers shows very well how the Italian configuration of the market-family-state triad, within which the family plays a crucial role, hides women's poverty risks and even protects lone mothers better against poverty than in some northern countries.

Besides, southern European welfare states display many deficits in services, such as in childcare and assistance for the elderly. State service provision has been lacking because the historical configurations of these countries have resulted in a rigid gender division of labour. Moreover, this is the result of the prevalence of the 'subsidiarity' principle in the regulation of social and caring services. According to this principle, it is first the family that has a duty to provide for a dependent family member. The state has an obligation to intervene only as a second resort and in case of the failure of the family (see, as an example, the duty of alimony between kin in art. 433 Italian civil code and art. 142 Spanish civil code) (compare, for Italy, Trifiletti 1995 and, for Spain, Valiente 1995).

The most important shortcoming of the welfare state is the lack of childcare services for the youngest children (up to three years) and the inadequacy of most childcare services in terms of quality and the times at which they are available, making it difficult for women to combine family and work. In Italy, in 1992/93, around 92 per cent of children aged three and around 100 per cent of children aged five attended public preschool programmes (Eurydice 1996), while only six per cent of children aged three and less attended public and private day-care services in 1994 (Saraceno 1998). In Spain, while the situation of children over two is not bad, in 1992/93 around eight per cent of children aged two were enrolled in a preschool, and around 100 per cent at the age of five (Eurydice 1996). In Spain, the number of children under two cared for in public centres was, in 1991–92, one of the lowest among EU countries: 0.1 per cent for those under one year of age, 0.5 per cent for one year olds and 1.4 per cent for two year olds (MEC 1994; Valiente 1995). Childcare facilities are very limited in Greece. As Nota Kyriazis' contribution illustrates, these are estimated to cover only about four per cent of children under three and 65–70 per cent of children between three and six years old. The Greek contribution illustrates that the lack of compatibility between the opening hours of childcare services and nurseries and the working hours of parents employed in the retail sector make it very difficult for parents to rely on this kind of arrangement alone, so that is estimated that around 80 per cent of Greek parents rely on relatives, and mainly grandparents, for childcare.

In addition, there are great regional variations within most southern European countries, since the poorest regions offer less childcare services (Saraceno 1997). This is the case in Spain, where the northern autonomous communities of Catalonia, Valencia and the Basque Country have higher provisions of publicly funded childcare for children under two, standing at more than ten per cent compared to less than two per cent in the other regions (data for 1993/94; European Commission 1996). Equally, Italy endures significant regional differences in both the quantity and quality of services. *Asili nido* (centres for children aged between three and 36 months) provide publicly funded care for around 30 per cent of children in the north, while they are almost non-existent in the south (data for 1991; European Commission 1996). Greece has recently decentralized responsibilities for publicly funded services to the local authorities, but, like Portugal, does not report geographical differences.

Care and services for the elderly is the other field in which states have more extensively applied the principle of 'subsidiarity' and transferred the burden of responsibility to the family, that is, to women. As a result, there are limited public service provisions for the elderly. For instance, the numbers of elderly cared for in residential homes is very low: in Spain, only approximately two per cent of the elderly were looked after in public and private residential care in 1990 (Valiente 1995). But more worrying, for those who have to provide care, is the absence of a well-developed system of social services and state provisions, which would help older people or disabled adults to be looked after in their own home (Saraceno 1998). The system of home services for the elderly seems to be available only to those who have no family members who can provide for them (Trifiletti 1995).

(4) *Women's Political Apathy.* The last important residue of a traditional gender order is the low participation of women in political life. They have increased their participation over recent years in political parties and parliaments, but a substantial gender gap persists in political participation and political involvement. In addition, general political participation is lower in southern Europe than in northern countries. Laura Morales' analysis in this book shows that the low participation and

the low political involvement of Spanish women might be understood as the result of, first, gender differences in socialization, and, second, women's educational level and employment situation. More highly educated women are more likely to participate or to be involved in political life than their less educated counterparts, and women entirely dedicated to domestic work tend to participate and to be involved less than those in employment. Thus, political involvement seems to be connected to the presence of women in spheres of public life such as educational institutions and workplaces. The presence of women in public life depends also on political and historical events, which increase the general politicization of the population.

Political participation by women, feminist movements and the impact of women's political demands were particularly high during the mid-1960s until the mid-1970s in Italy, at the moment of the revolution in Portugal (1974), during the transition into democracy (1978) and at the moment of the entry of the socialist party into government (1982) in Spain, and in the 1970s after the fall of the military dictatorship in Greece. Feminist movements had an important impact on the perception of gender roles, but probably the most long-lasting impact was achieved by legislative changes. Feminist pressures for women's rights and feminists' involvement in the parliaments of Italy, Greece and Spain, for instance, resulted in new laws on equal opportunities between men and women, in family law reforms, for the legalization of divorce and abortion, and in an increase of individual social rights for women and of family-friendly services (Kyriazis 1995; Valiente 1995). Franca Bimbi's contribution describes the role of feminism in the persistence of the 'family paradigm' in the Italian welfare state and discusses the main shortcomings of the feminist struggles in changing the Italian gender order. The diminishing strength of the feminist movement and the remaining gender gap in political participation are fundamental problems for achieving gender equity in the welfare state, the family and the labour market.

## REMOVING OBSTACLES ON THE WAY TO THE UNIVERSAL CARE-GIVER MODEL

The southern European gender order is based on a particular configuration of the state, the family and the labour market. Women's financial dependency on men is linked to highly gendered obligations with respect to unpaid work and is associated with women's difficulties in the labour market. The strength of family and kinship ties and the importance of the family as an income-pooling and service unit, combined with the highly fragmented, corporatist structure of southern welfare states and important employment shortages, make changes in gender roles difficult. The family, the labour market and the welfare state have to be changed substantially and in accordance with each other if gender equity is to be reached. Southern European women, and men in particular, have to change their preferences and behaviour with regard to their family life. Equally, women have to become more involved in public organizations (that is, in political parties, grass-roots movements and so on) in order to change institutions. Two complementary strategies seem possible to help move southern Europe toward the Universal Care-giver Model.

(1) Women living in partnerships have to refuse an asymmetric division of unpaid work. They have to negotiate symmetrical relationships with their partners that imply having similar access to leisure time and market time, as well as having time to spend together, with other family members or friends. Women's increasing educational level, men's worsening labour market conditions, the emergence of post-Fordist production forms and the increase in importance of the service sector might constitute an opportunity for the renegotiation of gender contracts. Young men in southern Europe have few chances of becoming a lifelong husband and a male breadwinner as shown by the contributions of René Houle, Carles Simó and Montserrat Solsona, and of Isabel Margarida André and Paulo Areosa Feio. Whether in the future men will still spend little time with the family, will still avoid their family obligations and women will still have to provide most caring work for children and for the other dependent family members or whether, on the contrary, a new gender contract based on the Universal Care-giver Model, a new male identity and an increase in the externalization of unpaid work away from the family will emerge depends on negotiation between men and women.

(2) Corresponding to the changes in the distribution of paid and unpaid work and in accordance with the Universal Care-giver Model as discussed previously, social policies have to change in order to support dual-earner families by partly socializing family tasks. Women and men will have to engage in collective action to achieve more care services for dependent family members. Since men and women will have to engage in unpaid work to fulfil the remaining privatized family tasks, they will also have to struggle for an employee- and family-oriented flexibilization of working

time, such as the right to leave for given phases of the family cycle and for periods of specific family need, such as the illness of dependent family members. In parallel, women will have to make every effort to encourage their partners to benefit from existing possibilities for parental leave. Another important change, not explicitly mentioned by Fraser, will have to come from the individualization of social rights. Women will have to acquire direct entitlement to current social security benefits through a universal social security system covering all citizens independently of the nature of work (paid or unpaid), working time (part-time or full-time) and type of contract (short-term or long-term).

These changes are not utopian since an increase in labour market flexibilization is occurring in most countries and two incomes are increasingly becoming an economic necessity as well as the desire of young couples. Social rights are already partly adapting to the new mosaic of employment forms: part of unpaid family work has been recognized as a contribution to the old-age pension system and maternal and parental leave have been extended and have became more generous. Probably, the most utopian transformations concern change in the perceptions and preferences of partners within families and the increase in political participation. In other words, the most difficult change seems to be the deconstruction of prevailing gender roles and, in particular, their cultural coding.

## NOTES

1. It is worth noting the fact that activity rates only indicate the proportion of women working or searching for work and, therefore, underestimate the size of the potential female labour force. Discouraged job-seekers (including many women home-makers) and atypical workers, for example, are normally not captured in the official statistics (aside from family helpers and a few regulated home-workers) (Stratigaki and Vaious 1994; Baylina and Garcia-Ramon 1998).
2. Differences in income are greater than variations in earnings, as women typically work for less time, but comparative figures are less accessible.

## REFERENCES

Baylina, M. and M. D. Garcia-Ramon (1998): 'Homeworking in rural Spain: a gender approach'. *European Urban and Regional Studies*, 5/1, pp.55–64.
Beets, G. (1997): 'European variation in education and in timing of first birth: preliminary FFS evidence'. Paper presented at the Twenty-Third General Population Conference, IUSSP. Beijing, China.
Bettio, F. and P. Villa (1998): 'A Mediterranean perspective on the break-down of the

relationships between participation and fertility'. *Cambridge Journal of Economics*, 22/2, pp.137–71.

Blossfeld, H-P. (ed.) (1996): *The New Role of Women: Family Formation in Modern Societies*, Social Inequality Series. Oxford: Westview Press.

Boh, K., M. Bak, C. Clason *et al.* (eds.) (1989): *Changing Patterns of European Family Life. A Comparative Analysis of 14 European Countries*. London: Routledge.

Bonke, J. (1995): 'Education, work and gender. An international comparison'. *IUE Working Paper EUF 95/4*. Florence: European University Institute.

Castels, F. (1994): 'Social security in southern Europe: a comparative overview'. Paper presented to the conference organized by the Subcommittee on Southern Europe of the Social Science Council. 1–2 July 1994. Istanbul, Turkey.

Daly, M. (1996): 'The gender division of welfare: the British and German welfare states compared'. Ph.D. thesis (unpublished). Department of Political and Social Sciences, European University Institute. Florence, Italy.

Ditch, J. *et al.* (1996): *Social Europe: A Synthesis of National Family Policies 1994*. Luxembourg: Office for Official Publications of the European Communities.

Duncan, S. (1991): 'The geography of gender divisions of labour in Britain'. *Transactions Institute of British Geographers*, 16, pp.420–39.

(1995): 'Theorising European gender systems'. *Journal of European Social Policy*, 5/4, pp.263–84.

(1996): 'The diverse worlds of European patriarchy'. In M. D. Garcia-Ramon and J. Monk (eds.), *Women of the European Union: the Politics of Work and Daily Life*, pp.74–110. London and New York: Routledge.

Durán, M. A. (1997): 'El papel de mujeres y hombres en la economía española'. *Revista Información Comercial Española*.

Esping Andersen, G. (1996): '¿Igualdad o empleo? La interacción de salarios, estato de bienstar y cambio familiar'. In *Dilemas del Estado de Bienstar*, pp.9–27. Fundacion Argentaria.

European Commission (1993): *Employment in Europe 1993*. Luxembourg: European Commission.

(1995): *Social Protection in Europe*. Luxembourg: European Commission.

(1996): *A Review of Services For Young Children in the European Union 1990–1995*. Luxembourg: European Commission Network on Childcare and other Measures to Reconcile Employment and Family Responsibilities.

Eurostat (1994): *Labour Force Survey. Results*. Luxembourg: Eurostat.

(1997): *Demographic Statistics 1997*. Luxembourg: Council of Europe.

Eurydice (1996): *Key Data on Education in the European Union*. Luxembourg: Commission of the European Communities.

Ferrera, M. (1996): 'Il Modello di Welfare Sud Europeo'. *Quaderni di ricerca*, 5, Università Bocconi, Poleis.

Fraser, N. (1997): *Justice Interruptus: Critical Reflections on the 'Postsocialist' Condition*. London: Routledge.

Garcia-Ramon, M. D. and J. Monk (eds.) (1996) *Women of the European Union: the Politics of Work and Daily Life*. London and New York: Routledge.

Gornick, Janet C, Marcia K. Meyers and Katerin E. Ross (1997): 'Supporting the employment of mothers: policy variation across fourteen welfare states'. *Journal of European Social Policy*, 7/1, pp.45–70.

Guillén, Ana M. (1996): 'Welfare state development in Spain: a historical and explanatory approach'. Paper presented at MIRE Conference. 21–24 February 1996. Florence, EUI.

Hernes, H. M. (1987): *Welfare State and Women Power. Essays in State Feminism*. Oslo: Norwegian University Press.

Jurado Guerrero, Teresa (1995): 'Legitimation durch Sozialpolitik? Die spanische Beschäftigungskrise und die Theorie des Wohlfahrtsstaates'. *Kölner Zeitschrift für*

*Soziologie und Sozialpsychologie*, 47/4, pp.727–52.

Koven S. and S. Michel (1993): *Mothers of a New World: Maternalist Politics and the Origins of Welfare State*. New York: Routledge.

Kyriazis, Nota (1995): 'Feminism and the status of women in Greece'. In D. Constas and T. Stavrou (eds.), *Greece Prepares for the Twenty-First Century*, pp.267–300. John Hopkins University Press.

Laparra, Miguel and Aguilar, Manuel (1996): 'Social exclusion and minimum income programmes in Spain'. *South European Society & Politics*, 1/3, winter, pp.87–109.

Leibfried, S. (1992): 'Towards a European welfare state? On integrating poverty regimes into the European Community'. In Z. Ferge and J. E. Kolberg (eds.), *Social Policy in a Changing Europe*, pp.345–79. Boulder: Westview Press.

Leilièvre, E. and A. H. Gauthier (1996): 'Women's employment patterns in Europe: inequalities, discontinuities and policies'. In *Comparing social welfare systems in Europe, Vol.I, Mire, Oxford Conference*.

Leira, A. (1992): *Welfare States and Working Mothers: The Scandinavian Experience*. Cambridge University Press.

Lewis, J. (1992): 'Equality, difference, and state welfare: labor market and family policies in Sweden'. *Feminist Studies*, 18/1, spring.

Lewis, J. and G. Amström (1992): 'Equality, difference, and state welfare: labor market and family policies in Sweden'. *Feminist Studies*, 18/1, spring.

Lewis, J. and I. Ostner (1994): 'Gender and the evolution of European social policies'. *ZeS-Arbeitpapier*, 4. Centre for Social Policy Research, University of Bremen.

López López, M. T. (1996): *La proteccion social a la familia en españa y en los demas estados miembros de la union europea*. Madrid: Fundacion BBV.

McDowell, L. and D. Massey (1984): 'A Woman's place?' In Massey, D. and J. Allen (eds.), *Geography Matters*, pp.195–215. Milton Keynes: Open University Press.

MEC (Ministerio de Educacion y Ciencia) (1994): *Estadistica de la Enseñanza en España, niveles de preescolar, infantil, General Básica y enseñanzas medias*. Madrid Centro de Publicaciones.

Meil-Landwerlin, Gerardo (1997): 'La juventud y la redefinición de las pautas de división del trabajo doméstico'. *Revista de estudios de Juventud*, 39, pp.47–66.

Mingione, E. (1994): 'Family structures and family strategies: confronting a changing division of labour in different European contexts'. *Gender and the Use of Time*. Florence: European University Institute.

OECD (1996): *Employment Outlook 1996*. Paris: OECD.

Orloff, A. S. (1996): 'Gender and welfare state'. *Working paper*, 1996/79. Instituto Juan March de Estudios e Investigaciones.

Pateman, C. (1989): 'Feminist critiques of the public/private dichotomy'. In C. Pateman (ed.), *The Disorder of Women*. Stanford: Stanford University Press.

Pedersen, S. (1993): *Family, Dependence, and the Origins of the Welfare State. Britain and France, 1914–1945*. New York: Cambridge University Press.

Perrons, D. (1995): 'Economic strategies, welfare regimes and gender equality in European employment'. *European Urban and Regional Studies*, 2/2, pp.99–120.

—— (1998): 'Gender inequality in the regions of western Europe'. *European Urban and Regional Studies*, 5/1, pp.13–25.

Pinnelli, A. (1995): 'Women's condition, low fertility, and emerging union patterns in Europe'. In K. Oppenheim-Mason and A. M. Jensen (eds.), *Gender and Family Change in Industrialized Countries*, pp.82–101. Oxford: Clarendon Press.

Sabbadini, L. L. and R. Palomba (1994): *Tempi diversi. L'uso del tempo di uomini e donne nell'Italia di oggi*. Roma: Presidenza del Consiglio dei Ministri/Istat.

Saraceno, C. (1996): 'Il costo dei figli: un diverso riconoscimento per madri e padri'. *Inchiesta*, 111, pp.23–33.

(1998): *Mutamenti della famiglia e politiche sociali in Italia, Studi e Ricerche*. Bologna: Il Mulino.

Sarasa, S. and L. Moreno (1995): *El estado del bienestar en la Europa del sur*. Madrid: Consejo Superior de Investigaciones Científicas.

Sassoon, A. (ed.) (1987): *Women and the State. The Shifting Boundaries of Public and Private*. London: Hutchinson.

Stratigaki, M. and D. Vaious (1994): 'Women's work and informal activities in southern Europe'. *Environment and Planning*, 26/8, pp.1221–34.

Torns, T. (1997): 'El paro y la tolerancia social frent a la exclusión'. Paper presented at the conference L'exlusion en question(s), organized by C. Rogerat of the Groupement de Recherche Marché de Travail et Genre del CNRS.

Trifiletti, R. (1995): 'Family obligations in Italy'. In J. Millar and A. Warman (eds.), *Defining Family Obligations in Europe, Bath Social Policy Papers 23*. University of Bath.

Valero, A. and C. Lence (1995): 'Nupcialidad, fecundidad y familia. La paradoja del comportamiento de la nupcialidad y la fecundidad en España'. *Revista Internacional de Sociología*, Tercera Epoca, 11, pp.89–114.

Valiente, C. (1995a) 'Children first: central government child care policies in post-authoritarian Spain (1975–1994)'. In J. Brannen and M. O'Brien (eds.), *Childhood and Parenthood*. Institute of Education, University of London.

Valiente, C. (1995b) 'Family obligations in Spain'. In J. Millar and A. Warman (eds.), *Defining Family Obligations in Europe, Bath Social Policy Papers 23*. University of Bath.

# Women's Flexible Work and Family Responsibilities in Greece

## NOTA KYRIAZIS

This article is based on research carried out in the retail sector in Greece regarding the reconciliation of flexible work and family responsibilities (see Kyriazis 1998b).[1] Flexible work has long been a topic of debate for the government, the trade unions and employers' associations in the context of a broader social dialogue concerning economic development, competitiveness and employment policy issues; a debate which recently culminated in the passage of legislation that includes provisions for the reorganization of working time. In view of these imminent legislative changes in Greece, it is important to consider the impact that flexibility in employment has had to date in terms of meeting its objectives.

Advocates of flexibility stress that it may provide 'solutions to a range of problems including unemployment, competitiveness, economic and social cohesion as well as equal opportunities'. By enabling people to work at varying times of the day and for varying lengths of time, it is claimed that flexible working may lead to a fairer distribution of men's and women's roles. This can be achieved through measures aimed at 'adapting the organization of work to help women as well as men reconcile family and working life and to provide more flexible employment solutions, again for both men and women' (EC 1996: 5, cited in Perrons: 4). The purpose of the research that was undertaken was to determine the extent to which flexible work does indeed contribute to equal opportunities and to a restructuring of family roles, as advocates of this form of work have claimed.

The results reported here comprise only part of a much broader study that included the views regarding flexible work of employers, trade unionists as well as employees in the retail sector. The focus of the present article, however, is on the experiences of flexibility recounted by

The author wishes to thank Dr Diane Perrons, the coordinator of the research project on which this article is based, for her collaboration and support throughout the research.

employees on the basis of in-depth interviews. Although quantitative data were also collected and will be referred to whenever necessary, what is of research interest for the purposes of this article is the *meaning* that people themselves attribute to their employment situation within the context of their family responsibilities. In other words, the objective is to gain insight into the subjective interpretations of people's employment situations, their motivations and experiences using their own conceptual systems and not those of the researcher.

In the next section, a brief overview of flexible work in Greece is presented, followed by a description of how it is practised in the retail sector. The data gathered in the context of the research undertaken are then presented and analysed.

## TYPES OF FLEXIBLE WORK

Flexible work, according to official data, is not as prevalent in Greece as in other European countries. It became institutionalized relatively recently (1990) and, except for the retail sector where a high proportion of part-timers are employed, flexible work has not been integrated on a wide scale into the Greek economy.

The most prevalent form of flexible work is *overtime work*. Firms resort to this form of work more often than part-time work to meet fluctuations in production needs.[2] A recent study of flexible work, based on data from the *1995 Greek Labour Force Survey*,[3] indicates that those who work 41 hours or more per week (40 hours per week is considered a regular full-time working week) constitute 42 per cent of the total number of persons employed – this represents the second largest category and only a slightly lower concentration of workers than in the 36–40 hour working week (43 per cent). It is noteworthy that men (48 per cent) are considerably more likely than women (34 per cent) to work extra hours. The same data indicate that *weekend work* is becoming increasingly prevalent, not only as a fourth shift, but also as an extension of the work schedule. As Table 1 on atypical forms of work in Greece indicates, 67 per cent of men and 58 per cent of women work sometimes or often on Saturday and 35 per cent of men and 28 per cent of women sometimes or often on Sunday. These levels are considerably higher than the EU average due most likely to the relatively higher proportion of persons working in the primary sector in Greece, in which weekend work is customary (Karantinos *et al.* 1997).

TABLE 1
EMPLOYED PERSONS IN ATYPICAL FORMS OF WORK IN GREECE AND THE
EUROPEAN UNION, BY GENDER, 1994 (PER CENT)

|          | Total | | Men | | Women | |
|----------|--------|-------|--------|-------|--------|-------|
|          | Greece | Eur12 | Greece | Eur12 | Greece | Eur12 |
| Total    | 100.0  | 100.0 | 100.0  | 100.0 | 100.0  | 100.0 |
| Shifts   | 10.3   | 11.6  | 11.4   | 13.2  | 8.3    | 9.5   |
| Nights   | 13.6   | 14.8  | 16.4   | 18.7  | 8.4    | 9.3   |
| Saturday | 62.9   | 49.7  | 65.5   | 52.8  | 58.3   | 45.4  |
| Sunday   | 32.2   | 26.5  | 34.0   | 29.0  | 28.7   | 22.8  |
| At home  | 4.7    | 11.8  | 3.7    | 12.0  | 6.4    | 11.5  |

Source: Karantinos et al. (1997), p.83, Table 2.3.16.

In comparison to the rest of Europe, *shift work* and *night-work* is less prevalent in Greece. This may be due to the fact that Greece has a less developed secondary sector where shift work and night-work are more often observed, while at the same time having a relatively larger agricultural sector where night-time work is not common. Within the manufacturing sector, however, the incidence of shift work has increased considerably since 1989 (52 per cent) reaching a level of 86 per cent of the total number of persons employed in manufacturing, and above the EU average of 71 per cent (Karantinos *et al.* 1997: 155). The change in the legislative framework (covered in the following section) which occurred in 1990 and which enabled firms to remain open for longer hours and to integrate greater flexibility in working time is chiefly responsible for this increase.

*Part-time work* has been rising consistently since 1991 (see Table 2),[4] although it is still at a level considerably lower (4.8 per cent of total employment) than in the rest of Europe. According to 1995 figures, 2.8 per cent of employed men work part time, whereas women part-time workers constitute 8.4 per cent of the total female workforce. While the majority of part-time workers are women (62 per cent), the gender imbalance is less than the European average (82 per cent of women work part time in the EU).

It is interesting that the proportion of part-timers who are married (69.8 per cent) is almost exactly the same as that calculated on the basis of all employed persons (70.1 per cent). Contrary to what is ordinarily assumed, the official data indicate that this form of work does not appear to be especially suited to married women with children. In fact, it is a form of work that a very small minority of people seeking work select as a matter of choice. Of those working part time in 1995, 53 per cent of

TABLE 2

CHANGES IN EMPLOYMENT BY WORK FORM AND GENDER IN 1991–95
(PER CENT)

| | 1991 | 1993 | 1995 |
|---|---|---|---|
| Total number of persons employed | 100 per cent (3,632,437)* | 100 per cent (3,720,179)* | 100 per cent (3,823,809)* |
| Employed full-time | 44.86 | 46.83 | 47.55 |
| Employed in a flexible work form | 55.14 | 53.17 | 52.45 |
| Employed full-time, temporary contract | 6.81 | 4.58 | 4.47 |
| Employed part-time, temporary contract | 1.01 | 0.99 | 1.01 |
| Employed part-time, permanent contract | 0.46 | 0.85 | 0.84 |
| Full-time, self-employed | 33.98 | 33.33 | 32.19 |
| Part-time, self-employed | 1.22 | 1.30 | 1.55 |
| Full-time, aids in family business | 10.50 | 10.90 | 10.96 |
| Part-time, aids in family business | 1.15 | 1.22 | 1.43 |

* absolute number of persons

Source: Karantinos et al. (1997: 92), Table 2.3.16.

the men and 32 per cent of the women stated that they could not find a full-time job, whereas only 19 per cent of the men and 39 per cent of the women said that they did not wish to work full time. The largest share of part-time work is in agriculture (12.5 per cent), followed by services (4.7 per cent) and manufacturing (2.5 per cent). In the service sector, there is a concentration of part-time work in retailing (more fully discussed in a following section), especially in department stores and supermarkets where the proportion of part-time workers, in some cases, runs as high as 60 per cent (Enimerosi 1997: 17).

Considering *temporary work*, 10.2 per cent of the total number of persons employed are on temporary contracts. Temporary contracts are very common in part-time work (61 per cent), representing the highest proportion in Europe. According to Rubery, Fagan and Smith (1995: 185), this is consistent with the general pattern in which countries where part-time work is not well established implement it as a less stable and more flexible work form. Women are over-represented in temporary work – while they constitute 37.4 per cent of the total employed population, they account for 41.3 per cent of those on temporary contracts. Also over-represented are young persons – the incidence of temporary contracts decreases with increasing age. With respect to the distribution of temporary work by occupation, temporary work is most prevalent among skilled technicians, unskilled workers and salespersons. It must be stressed, however, that all these data reflect forms of work in the formal economy. In the informal sector, which by some estimates amounts to 35 per cent of the gross national product (Enimerosi 1997: 17), it has been argued that 'atypical' work is so typical that the word is a misnomer (Stratigaki and Vaiou 1994). Flexible work, in general, is considerably more widespread than the official data suggest. Seasonal work, fixed-term contracts in large firms in the manufacturing sector and piecework in medium-sized firms are widely prevalent.

## RELEVANT LEGISLATION

Legislation establishing part-time work and the fourth shift was passed in 1990. With this legislation, a contract between employer and employee may be signed for a reduced number of hours than the normal, full-time schedule, calculated on a weekly or daily basis and for a fixed or indefinite term. According to this legislation, full-time workers are not obligated to accept a change of status to part-time employment, if so requested by the employer. More importantly, they may refuse to work for more hours than those agreed upon in the contract, if they have another job or family responsibilities. In addition, part-time workers are entitled to priority in hiring for full-time work in the same firm, when such positions become available. With respect to wages, part-time workers are entitled to the same wages on a pro-rata basis as those earned by full-time workers doing the same type of work. They also have the same pension and social security rights on a pro-rata basis and they are entitled to annual vacations with pay.

Greek employment legislation takes into account parental roles and incorporates regulations for the protection of the working mother (Symeonidou 1997: 107). More specifically, women are entitled to maternity leave eight weeks before and eight weeks after the birth of a child. Moreover, they are entitled to have a work schedule reduced by two hours per day for the first year after the child's birth or, alternatively, by one hour for two years. In addition, working parents can take up to six days of paid leave per year in the case of a child's (or another dependant's) illness and four days per year to visit their children's school. In companies employing 50 persons or more, either parent can take up to three and a half months unpaid leave until the child is three years old, provided that the parent requesting the leave has worked in the same firm for more than a year and their spouse is also working. As noted in Symeonidou (1997), however, few persons have made use of the parental leave provision in the legislation. This is due to the fact that firms employing more than 50 persons are relatively few in Greece, combined with the fact that the leave is unpaid and those who use it are still obliged to pay their own contributions to social insurance and, in addition, to cover the contributions of their employers. In large firms (employing 50 persons or more), parents also have the right to work for one hour less per day with a proportional reduction in pay to care for children with disabilities. All employees, regardless of size of firm, are entitled to five days wedding leave with payment for six days if they are working in the commercial sector (Kyriakoulias 1995). In the case of a birth, the father of the newborn child has a right to a day's leave with payment.

Greek legislation therefore recognizes the special problems confronting working parents and attempts to facilitate the reconciliation of work and family life. In practice, however, workers are often reluctant to exercise their rights, as the present research exemplifies, for fear of any negative repercussions on their work status that this might lead to. The paucity of work inspectors, whose job is to ensure that legislative provisions are applied in all work contexts, facilitates abuses by employers, especially in small and medium-sized firms.

## THE RETAIL SECTOR AND THE FIRMS STUDIED

Although, as has already been indicated, part-time work constitutes a very small proportion of total employment in Greece (4.8 per cent, in comparison to the EU average of 12 per cent), the proportion of part-time workers of the total number of workers in the retail sector is considerably higher (35 per cent), with the highest concentration in some of the big supermarket chains (more than 50 per cent). Other forms of flexible work (temporary work as well as Saturday work) are similarly over-represented in the retail sector (See Tables 3 and 4).[5]

TABLE 3
FLEXIBLE EMPLOYMENT IN THE WHOLESALE/RETAIL SECTOR, 1995 (PER CENT)

|  | Men | Women |
| --- | --- | --- |
| Part-time | 11.1 | 11.4 |
| Temporary work | 9.1 | 12.4 |
| Shift work | 3.8 | 6.3 |
| Night work | 5.2 | 3.4 |
| Saturday work | 78.3 | 81.7 |
| Sunday work | 14.5 | 16.2 |

*Source*: 1995 Labour Force Survey statistics presented in Mouriki (1997: 4).

TABLE 4
FLEXIBLE EMPLOYMENT IN THE PROVISION OF SERVICES AND SALES COMPARED
TO THE OVERALL ECONOMY IN 1995 (PER CENT)

| | Total All sectors | Men All sectors | Men Services and sales | Women All sectors | Women Services and sales |
|---|---|---|---|---|---|
| Part-time | 4.8 | 2.8 | 10.6 | 8.4 | 13.8 |
| Temporary work | 10.2 | 9.5 | 15.7 | 11.2 | 21.9 |
| Shift work | 10.4 | 11.6 | 31.1 | 8.2 | 16.9 |
| Night work | 13.9 | 17.0 | 38.1 | 8.5 | 16.5 |
| Saturday work | 63.8 | 66.9 | 88.9 | 58.2 | 86.2 |
| Sunday work | 32.2 | 34.6 | 55.5 | 28.0 | 35.7 |

Source: 1995 Labour Force Survey statistics presented in Mouriki (1997: 4).

Since the institutionalization of part-time work in 1990, employers in the retail sector have resorted increasingly to this work form to meet more efficiently the variability in consumer demand that occurs daily, weekly, and on a seasonal basis. The extension of store hours and the disengagement of working hours from store operating hours have greatly facilitated the use of flexible work forms in the retail sector. The impact of store operating hours on labour relations has, in fact, been a major issue of contention in recent years.

THE METHODOLOGY

The present research is based on six retail firms: two international department chains, two large supermarket chains and two traditional department stores, all of which were situated in the greater Athens area. A total of 99 employees responded to structured questionnaires, 37 of whom also took part in in-depth interviews conducted in the workplace. All employees who participated in the research were married with caring responsibilities and working either full time with a rolling day off or part time. In all cases, the store manager selected the cases according to the specified criteria (employees doing flexible work and having caring responsibilities). It is, of course, not possible to establish whether some employees were purposely passed over, that is, whether those employees that management felt would be more likely to reveal negative attitudes about their employment experience were deliberately left out. Should that be the case, then the results presented here would be even more skewed in a negative direction with respect to what the workers reveal about their work experiences as well as about the firm's practices.

Regardless, the sampling method used does not permit generalization of the quantitative results. These results constitute only a broader framework in which to analyse the qualitative data obtained from the in-depth interviews which, for reasons already indicated, comprise a more appropriate focus of analysis given the research topic.

## THE RESULTS

### Types of flexible work forms

In the retail firms examined, work is either full time (with alternate morning and afternoon schedules and a rolling day off) or part time (on a permanent or, in the overwhelming number of cases, a fixed-term contract). Those working part time vary between 24 per cent and 52 per cent of the total number of people employed. The large majority of part-time workers (70 per cent to 90 per cent) are young women with no family responsibilities or older women with grown-up children. Given that the structure of part-time work demands the ready availability of workers in the event of a required change of work schedule, women with caring responsibilities are not a highly represented category and they do not have the necessary flexibility to adapt to such requested changes. The small proportion of men employed in these positions tend also to be very young (mostly students or just entering the labour force) or, in some cases, men with heavy financial burdens who are in need of a second supplementary job.

Nearly all part-time workers are employed on a fixed-term contract, which is usually of a two-month, four-month or six-month duration. The number of hours stipulated in the contract usually varies between four and seven hours per day, three to five days a week. Nearly all work on Saturdays. Most work morning and afternoon schedules on alternate weeks, as stipulated in their contracts, but are very frequently asked by their supervisors, at very short notice (45 per cent indicated that they are given a day or less), to work a different schedule and to put in extra hours, as the need arises. Those who are employed full time work eight-hour shifts (morning and afternoon schedules on alternate weeks, five days a week, Monday to Saturday with a rolling day off). A very small proportion of women work the same schedule every week.

In almost all cases of part-time work, the women indicated that it was not a personal choice, but rather a necessity for lack of permanent full-time positions. When asked what other type of work they would prefer to do, it is interesting that most did not mention a different job but a different work schedule – they indicated that they would prefer a stable morning schedule on a permanent, full-time basis. Their sense of promotion within the firm was related to the prospect of transferring to this job category. The responses that typically came up to the question regarding the type of work they would like to do were 'any kind of job as long as it's secure', 'a morning job' and 'a job with responsibility'.

Men with family responsibilities working part time as a second job, however, were grateful to have the supplementary income and felt a personal sense of obligation to the manager who had hired them. Trying to make ends meet, the married men interviewed were simply glad to have another job. When asked if they had thought about doing something else, one of the men said: 'Let's not kid ourselves, who has the luxury to look for the ideal job?' When asked if he felt he could refuse to work if asked at short notice, he added: 'I come immediately. I drop everything. I consider it my obligation to come to work. My wife sometimes complains about this, but what can I do? I never say no.'

The late work hours, the obligation to work on Saturdays for practically all part-time employees as well as the variability of work create an employment situation that makes combining work with family obligations very difficult. Under these circumstances, therefore, employees with caring responsibilities are not likely to opt for this work form unless other employment opportunities are not easily available.

In all the firms examined most women emphatically stated that they would prefer to have a stable schedule. The alternate morning and afternoon working hours are generally viewed to be disruptive of family life. According to a divorced woman with two children (aged 12 and seven years):

> Saleswork is the most miserable occupation. I hardly see my children, especially when I work the afternoon shift. They eat alone; they study alone; they are always alone. They often say 'mum does nothing else but work; she is never here'. My oldest daughter has completely withdrawn into herself. At her grandmother's (where she is often obliged to stay when I am not home), she feels like a stranger. In reality, she is growing up alone.

Although men also complained about the afternoon schedule, they placed greater emphasis on the problems this creates in terms of meeting social rather than family obligations. A male supervisor with two children (seven and eight years old) working at one of the department stores said: 'The schedule makes it very difficult to meet social obligations, especially when you work afternoons. When you get home at 9:30 or 10:00 (if you miss the train), it's very difficult.' To this he added:

> I would prefer to work consistently mornings, but when you work in the afternoons, you can do certain things that you are not able to do otherwise, like go to a government office or to the bank – it helps. As far as the family is concerned, the morning schedule is definitely better. Personally, though, it doesn't tire me more to work in the afternoons; it just makes meeting social obligations more difficult.

The continuously re-emerging sentiment among employees, therefore, was that their work schedule was especially taxing and imposed serious constraints on their family and social life. In general, women with children felt that their absence from their homes and families in the evening presented major problems in the functioning of their households and was the most frequently cited negative aspect of their jobs.

In all cases, alternate morning and afternoon schedules are imposed by the store and only in rare cases is a stable schedule offered. It must be stressed that any changes in the work schedule are employer induced and practically all employees feel that they cannot refuse to comply. Although it was felt that under difficult family circumstances an employee could request a temporary change of schedule, it was clear that this could only be done on a rare occasion. A woman with three children (aged four, 11 and 14) working at a supermarket said:

> In general, it is the supervisor who requests a change of schedule. You can refuse one time in ten or a compromise solution can be found, depending on who your supervisor is. Only if there is a problem with the children is it taken seriously into account.

The general sentiment that emerged was a sense of powerlessness on the part of both men and women in the face of employer-generated requests for changes in the work schedule. The acute sense of employment insecurity at this time of high unemployment means that people are not willing to endanger their jobs by either not accommodating employers' requests for a change of schedule or initiating their own requests for such changes.

The recurrent feeling expressed among the women interviewed, regardless of the store, was that just having a job was important. Although the fact that they come into contact with people was cited repeatedly as a positive aspect of the job, the women had not selected this line of work as one they were particularly interested in. It was just a job that gave them a much-needed income. They worked out of economic necessity and most of them indicated that they would prefer to be at home raising their children. As a result, questions regarding promotion and career development were in a way superfluous, given that promotion opportunities, due to the structure of the firms, were very limited, as well as taking into account the low motivation of women employees as a consequence of the factors already described. Older women were even less likely than younger women to consider promotion a realistic or desirable possibility. A 47-year-old woman working in one of the supermarket stores said the following:

> There are opportunities, but I am not particularly interested because of my family responsibilities. And, there is also the fact that I am older. They now hire much younger women. Even the supervisors are young. Besides that, I want to devote more time to my family. The children need my support a lot more nowadays with all the school pressure they have.

Despite the fact that most women did not express an interest in promotion and that the work structure did not provide many promotion opportunities, the general sentiment among employees was that women had equal opportunities with men. On the other hand, practically all employees questioned felt that part-time workers were definitely disadvantaged in terms of the type of work done, the intensification of work, as well as the opportunities for training and promotion.

With respect to their salaries, all employees indicated that they are paid according to the collective agreement. As stipulated in the agreement, the pay for part-time workers is calculated on a pro-rata basis in relation to that earned by full-time workers with the same job specialization and the same number of years of work experience. Given, however, that the pay for full-time workers in retail is itself very low, part-time workers for the most part earn an income that can only constitute a small supplement to the family income (72 per cent indicated that it is less than half of the family income). However, the majority (56 per cent) considered this contribution to be vital or extremely vital and 20 per cent to be a necessary component. All women agreed that their salaries are inadequate in relation to their needs and that they would have difficulty supporting themselves, let alone their families, on what they currently earn. This is exemplified by the situation faced by divorced women who, on minimal child support and their own very inadequate income, attempt to make ends meet. All of the divorced women interviewed, however, indicated that they rely on their families for additional support. Parents, and often siblings, support them financially as well as providing childcare. In a number of cases, women who were divorced with children shared a home with their parents. In most cases, they lived in a different apartment, but in the same building. The strong family interdependencies that exist in Greece are particularly evident in these cases.

*Flexibility and Family Responsibilities*

Practically all women interviewed indicated that combining their work schedules with family and domestic responsibilities is enormously difficult. The overwhelming majority rely on their own mothers or their mothers-in-law to take care of the children when they are at work. This is due, in part, to the inadequate provision of day-care facilities both in terms of their number[6] as well as their operating hours, which do not accommodate women's evening schedules. In the three cases where a day-care centre was used for the provision of childcare in the mornings, grandmothers assumed caring responsibilities in the afternoon when the mothers were still away at work.

As a result, an overwhelmingly high proportion of parents, estimated to be as high as 80 per cent, resort to relatives, mainly grandparents, for childcare (see New Ways European Network, cited in Mouriki 1997: 3). As the present research will show, this method of childcare is often referred to as a preferred arrangement, given that extended family members tend to live in the same building or only a short distance away and also because the prevailing attitude is that children get better care in the hands of relatives. Such attitudes, however, are likely to change if more appropriate childcare facilities that cater, in a satisfactory manner, for the needs of working parents are established on a wide scale.

It is important to note, however, that although the lack of day-care facilities, in a way, forces women to leave their children in the care of relatives (since hiring a childminder would imply too big a financial cost), for some women it is a preferred option. A number of them mentioned that they were at peace while at work in the knowledge that the children were in the hands of relatives and not strangers. The fact that extended family members often occupy flats in the same building, or otherwise live in very close proximity, facilitates the use of this childcare arrangement. Typically, a woman employee in one of the department stores who has two children indicated that she has always relied on her mother and sister (also married with children of her own) to take care of the children when she was at work. All live in the same building, which makes this arrangement very convenient from a practical point of view:

> I never worried about childcare. I always had two people, my own flesh-and-blood, who took care of my children. I was always certain that they were well fed and well taken care of, that they didn't have a problem. Of course, there is always some anxiety over the children, but at least I always knew that two people who are very close to me were taking care of them.

Another woman describes the practical problems created due to the fact that she has to transport her daughter to her mother-in-law's for part of the week so as not to overburden her own mother who lives in the same building, but who also has responsibility for caring for another grandchild:

> The two grandmothers take care of my child. My mother lives in the same building, but she has to take care of my sister's child as well. So two to three times a week, I take my daughter (two years old) to my mother in law's and she sleeps there. From Tuesday to Friday I take her over to my mother-in-law's. It's difficult to wake her up in the morning and take her there before going to work. We either pick her up in the afternoon and take her back in the evening or we go and stay there until she goes to bed. I don't like to do this. Now that she is older, it's becoming more difficult. When we go there she sticks onto us like glue and doesn't want to be left there. She only wants to stay for a little while, not to sleep over.

Another male employee (29 years old, whose wife also works) working full time in the same department store, but on an alternate morning and afternoon schedule with a rolling day off, describes how important his mother, who shares their home, is to the functioning of the household:

> My mother is 70 years old. She is a pensioner. She has raised three children and five grandchildren. She is very energetic. She is in charge of our daughter (two and a half years old) as well as the housework. She is of enormous help and never complains.

Whatever the feelings that women might have about having to rely on their parents or other relatives for support in caring for their children, this is another instance of family obligations that feed into a chain of family interdependencies (Kyriazis 1998a). In the absence of a strong welfare state, the family is the main source of support. It is the family's obligation to support young people through their education and until they have managed to find a good job. Young married couples continue to seek support from their kin in caring for their children, but are also expected to provide support to their parents in return, whenever they are in need. It is worth mentioning that Greece has the lowest proportion (0.8 per cent) of people over 65 years in old people's homes and geriatric clinics in Europe – it is socially scorned to place one's parents in an institution (Symeonidou 1996).

It must be stressed that women almost exclusively bear the burden of providing care to the young and old and, in this sense, act as the link between the different generations in the extended family. The continuing importance of the extended family in Greek society is evident not only in the provision of childcare, but in the general functioning of the household as well. A male part-time worker in one of the supermarket stores said the following: 'My mother-in-law does the supermarket shopping; my father-in-law takes care of all financial errands – he likes to be outside; my wife and I share the rest of the household chores. We have perfect cooperation.'

Extended family members, primarily grandmothers, play an extremely important role in helping women cope not only with caring responsibilities, but also domestic chores. Despite this valuable assistance, however, the women indicated that they are the ones primarily responsible for household tasks as well as childcare. Although some sharing does take place, women retain a traditional role within the family. On the basis of the questionnaires administered, 44 per cent of the respondents indicated that the woman has either all of the responsibility or the main responsibility for the children and 37 per cent indicated that caring for the children is evenly divided between the husband and the wife. With respect to domestic work, more than 60 per cent indicated that it is exclusively or primarily the responsibility of the woman.

These results are corroborated by the interviews in which it became clear that women are mainly in charge of all household work and that sharing takes place primarily in relation to the children. Given that women have to work in the evenings on a regular basis, those men with work hours that enable them to be at home when their wives are at work are often in charge of the children, although in many cases with assistance from the grandparents. Interestingly enough, the interviews also indicated that financial matters are either the sole responsibility of the woman or shared by both partners. It is extremely rare for the husband to have financial control. Typically, a 32-year-old woman employed in a department store said the following:

> We are both in charge of financial matters. To be truthful, I am really the one that has control over the budget, of course always in consultation with my husband. Maybe because I'm more prudent than my husband, I keep better control. If I let my husband take charge, he will squander everything. Of course, I never act independently. Whatever I do, I ask him first. But I always manage to persuade him that what I want to do is right. So in the end, I do what I want anyway.

The feeling that women manage household finances better than men was expressed by most male employees as well. In the words of a male supervisor working in a supermarket: 'We discuss economic matters with my wife, but she is in charge. She is better at it.' Another male employee had similar views on the matter: 'My wife is responsible for the household budget. She gives me what I need and she takes care of the rest. I don't have the time to worry about it.' It seems that control over family finances in the lower social strata is viewed as an additional burden that men readily pass on to women. In other words, when money is tight, there is no power in being in a position to manage it. It is simply a task that needs to be done.

The inevitable outcome of women's difficult working schedules in combination with the heavy domestic and family responsibilities that they continue to carry despite their outside employment is that they have minimal free time. There was general agreement on this not only among the women, but among the men interviewed as well. According to the responses from the structured questionnaires, 54 per cent of the respondents felt that men had more free time, while only 17 per cent indicated that women did. This is interesting given that the overwhelming majority of male spouses (about 80 per cent), according to the questionnaires, work more than 40 hours per week (the normal full-time working week). Even with the longer working hours, men still manage to have more free time than women. This gender imbalance is evident regardless of whether men participate in household tasks, perhaps because even when they do share in domestic work, they devote less time than women. One woman characteristically said:

> My husband can sit on the veranda and drink his coffee and read the newspaper. [When I come home from work,] I have to make

sure that I get dinner ready on time, get the house organized and take care of whatever else needs to be done.

In summary, the interviews clearly indicate that most employees experience serious difficulties in combining work and family life, for reasons already described in earlier sections of this report. As far as their attitudes toward their job are concerned, almost all referred to the fatigue, the low pay and the inconvenient working schedules as very negative aspects of the job. Given agreement on these negative aspects, however, the variation in management style, the relations between supervisors and employees, and the role of the trade union made a difference to the extent to which they were simply accepted as features of the job or were magnified and a general feeling of discontent and disenchantment with their jobs and life situation was expressed.

## CONCLUDING COMMENTS

It seems that the manner in which employers in the retail sector integrate part-time work is at odds with married women's employment needs. In a time of high job insecurity, employees are not at liberty to deny employers' requests for flexibility, despite the disruption that this might mean for their family life, nor are they likely themselves to ask for changes in their work schedule when their personal life demands it. Due to the known constraints that children pose on the mother's time, employers prefer to hire young unmarried persons without family responsibilities. This preference is manifested in the low proportion of women with caring responsibilities in the firms examined. Differences in employment opportunities according to marital status and presence of children are therefore clearly evident in the hiring stage. For a fuller appreciation of this problem, data are needed on the marital status of all applicants in relation to those hired.

Once in the firm, differential treatment exists on the basis of full-time and part-time work, but not on the basis of gender (as assessed by employees). Employees on a part-time contract do the lower-level tasks that require fewer skills and less responsibility and they are less likely to be selected for training programmes. It seems that employers are not willing to invest in persons who may be with the firm only a short while (given that most part-timers have a fixed-term contract) and who may not have the necessary motivation to improve their skills and job performance. As a result, part-time workers are emerging as lower-level employees whose rights are more likely to be violated (through successive contracts of short duration with brief intervals between them during which the employee does not work for the firm) and whose opportunities for training and advancement are nil. Part-time work, given the manner in which it is applied, is therefore associated with high job insecurity and precariousness. Although flexibility in the form of part-time work may contribute to equal opportunities in the sense that it widens the scope of paid employment for women and facilitates labour entry, the low pay in combination with the short hours and the minimal promotion opportunities inevitably means that women remain economically dependent on their spouses.[7] Economic dependence, on the other hand, mitigates against any substantive changes in gender relations in the context of the family. The research indicates that, despite the difficulties that flexibility in retail creates for women in terms of combining their work and family obligations, family structures remain intact. Women retain primary responsibility for household tasks as well as the care of the children. Assistance is provided for the most part by grandmothers, who take over the care of the children as well the household tasks in general in the mother's absence. As such, traditional interdependencies are strengthened and women build up moral obligations toward the older members of their extended family that they will have to repay in the future as the need arises.

In summary, flexibility, as it is practised in the retail sector, is exclusively employer induced. As such, the reconciliation of family and work through flexibility cannot be accomplished if employers disregard the special needs of employees with family responsibilities. Mechanisms must therefore be instituted whereby such employees are given priority in the assignment of work schedules. Despite the fact that a reduced work schedule is an attractive option for women with children, the research indicates that it must be stable and predictable, given the planning required for childcare provision. On the other hand, this assumes that family structures remain unaltered and that women should ideally accommodate the requirements of their job to their traditional family obligations. In that sense, flexibility cannot be expected to have an impact on gender relations in the family, but can only serve, as the present research clearly shows, to provide a much needed supplement to the family income, while the woman's family role remains intact. Given that flexibility is associated with low-status jobs, low pay and a high level of precariousness, it does not enable women to acquire the economic independence that is a prerequisite for a change in gender relations within the family. The research clearly indicates therefore that the promotion of equal opportunities for men and women, either directly or indirectly, has not been met through the implementation of flexibility, at least in the context studied, but only in the most general sense of facilitating women's entry into paid employment.

## NOTES

1. The research formed part of a larger project, under the title 'Flexible working and the reconciliation of work and family life – or a new form of precariousness', funded by the European Commission (Directorate General for Employment, Industrial Relations and Social Affairs, Unit V/D.5) and coordinated by Dr Diane Perrons. The project was based on five case studies for Spain, Greece, the United Kingdom, Germany, France and Sweden, respectively. The results appear in the form of National Reports in a final report submitted by Perrons (1998). The views expressed in the reports do not necessarily reflect those of the Commission.
2. In 44 manufacturing firms researched in the Athens area in 1991, it was found that overtime work was the most common choice of flexible work in 80 per cent of the firms (Georgakopoulou and Kouzis 1995).
3. The 1995 data referred to in this section on flexible work are taken from Karantinos *et al.* (1997).
4. Over this period (1991–95), full-time employment for women increased by ten per cent, whereas part-time employment increased by 31.5 per cent. If statistics for a longer period are examined, however, part-time employment in 1995 was at approximately the same level that it was a decade earlier.
5. The data referred to are taken from Mouriki (1997).
6. In the country as a whole, there are 1,577 childcare centres and 5,559 nurseries run by the state. These are estimated to cover only about four per cent of children under the age of three and 65–70 per cent of children from three to six years. See Symeonidou (forthcoming; 1996: 80).
7. Perrons (1998: 39) comes to this conclusion on the basis of the results of the research conducted in all of the countries which were included in the project reported on in this paper.

## REFERENCES

*Enimerosi* (1997): 'Monthly information bulletin of the Work Institute of GSEE', 24. Athens: GSEE/INE.

Georgakopoulou, V. and Y. Kouzis (1995): *Evelixies kai Nees Ergasiakes Sheseis [Flexibility and New Labour Relations]*. Athens: GSEE/INE Labour Institute.

Karantinos, D., Ziomas, D., Ketsetzopoulou, M. and A. Mouriki (1997): *Evelikti Apasholisi kai Elastikopoiisi tou Hronou Ergasias [Flexible Work and Flexibility of Working Time]*. Athens: National Institute of Work.

Kouzis, Y. (1996–97): 'Gia to Paron kai to Mellon ton Ergasiakon Sxeseon' ['For the present and future of labour relations']. *INE Papers*, GSEE/INE Labour Institute, Double Issue 8–9, pp.9–25.

Kyriakoulias, P. (1995): 'Flexi-time in the Greek retail trade'. In the European Working Group, *Flexi-Time in the Retail Sector*. November 1995. Brussels.

Kyriazis, N. (1998a): 'Women's employment and gender relations in Greece: forces of modernization and tradition'. *European Urban and Regional Studies*, 5/1, pp.65–75.

(1998b): 'National report for Greece'. In D. Perrons, Final Report, *Flexible Working and the Reconciliation of Work and Family Life – or a New Form of Precariousness*, pp.77–117. Medium Term Community Action Programme on Equal Opportunities for Women and Men, Action Opportunities, Directorate General for Employment, Industrial Relations and Social Affairs, Unit V/D.5. Brussels: European Commission.

Mouriki, A. (1997): *Employment Development and Creation in the European Commerce Sector*. National Report for Greece for the European Project, coordinated by the Institut Arbeit und Technik.

Perrons, D. (1998): 'Comparative report/executive summary'. In D. Perrons, *Final Report, Flexible Working and the Reconciliation of Work and Family Life – or a New Form of Precariousness*, pp.3–42. Medium Term Community Action Programme on Equal Opportunities for Women and Men, Action Opportunities, Directorate General for Employment, Industrial Relations and Social Affairs, Unit V/D.5. Brussels: European Commission.

Rubery, J., Fagan, C. and M. Smith (1995): *Changing Patterns of Work and Working-time in the European Union and the Impact on Gender Divisions*. Report to the European Commission, DGV-Equal Opportunities Unit. Brussels: European Commission.

Stratigaki, M. and D. Vaiou (1994): 'Women's work and informal activities in southern Europe'. *Environment and Planning*, 26, pp.1221–34.

Symeonidou, H. (1996): 'Social protection in contemporary Greece'. *Southern European Society and Politics*, 1/3, pp.67–86.

(1997): 'Full-time and part-time employment of women in Greece: trends and relationships and life-cycle events'. In H. P. Blossfield and C. Hakim (eds.), *Between Equalization and Marginalization*, pp.90–112. London: Oxford University Press.

(forthcoming): 'Oikogeneiaki-dimografiki Politiki stin Ellada kai stis Loipes Chores tis Notias Evropis' ['Family-demographic policy in Greece and the remaining countries in southern Europe']. *Epitheorisi Koinvnikon Erevnon* [Special Demographic Issue of *The Review of the Social Sciences*].

# Development and Equality between Women and Men in the Portuguese Labour Market

ISABEL MARGARIDA ANDRÉ and
PAULO AREOSA FEIO

## THE CONTEXT: FROM THE 1960s UNTIL THE PRESENT

The rapid economic development of Portugal over the past decade was fostered, to a great extent, by the country's entry into the European Union. This economic development has been characterized by a significant modernization of the entrepreneurial sector, by improvements in qualifications, by an increase in consumption and by the upgrading of social protection, especially concerning the non-active population.

Nevertheless, this unquestionable progress has also brought with it a considerable degree of social exclusion and a deepening of social cleavages. The vulnerabilities of the female population, created by tasks and responsibilities within the family, are serious handicaps in their success and professional progress in a labour market characterized by a high degree of competitiveness and a regulatory process biased toward the availability of labour.

The current situation cannot be fully understood without setting it in the context of the past three decades. At certain points and in certain circumstances during these decades, conditions were created for an important promotion of female employment (Santos 1993; André 1994). In the 1960s, the country was fighting a war on three separate fronts (Angola, Mozambique and Guinea-Bissau) that absorbed a large part of the public budget and mobilized a large number of men of an age suitable for entry into the labour market. This deficit of male labour led to a massive drive to recruit female labour in all professional sectors. The unavailability of young males was also compensated for by waves of migration that intensified from the beginning of the 1960s and especially affected rural areas. Migration gave women a more active role in agricultural activities and in society as a whole.

The national economy was characterized by the hegemony of large economic groups enjoying recent inflows of foreign investment. The economic modernization brought about by these economic agents at the beginning of the 1970s led both to a relative political liberalization and to an increase and enlargement in scholarization. Both contributed to the greater equality of opportunities between women and men in acceding to the newly created and more demanding professional sectors. Due to these developments, by the beginning of the 1970s, female participation in the labour market was superior to that of other more developed European countries, even in some of the sectors that demand more in terms of qualifications.

With the revolution of April 1974, in a socialist revolutionary context in which intervention for the construction of effective social justice dominated, it was expected that the new political leaders, together with strong trade unions and social movements, would act to strengthen and consolidate equality between women and men. Many indicators show, however, that if ideological conviction prevented women from being sent home after the end of the colonial war (as occurred in many countries after the Second World War), the general improvement in labour conditions was much more favourable to men than to women (Walby 1986).

This difference was mainly qualitative, as the number of women entering the labour market after the revolution increased significantly. This was not only due to the new cultural values promoting social emancipation and participation, but also to the expansion of social services in education, health and social assistance, an important field of employment for women. However, a large number of these women went into professional sectors characterized by instability, while a major increase in female unemployment in the second half of the 1970s was accompanied by a stabilization of male unemployment at very low levels (André 1996; Rodrigues 1988).

At the beginning of the 1980s, Portugal began to follow liberal economic policies that led to the reprivatization of the vast public sector and to the weakening of the regulatory role of the trade unions. There was a worldwide economic crisis with high inflation, very high interest rates and a considerable public deficit. The increase in the flexibility of the labour market especially affected the male-dominated sectors organized along Fordist lines that had previously been strongly protected by the trade unions. In this period, equality between men and women in the labour market increased, although it was an equalization based on negative terms — both groups became more subject to high instability, an increasing precariousness of contracts and decreases in real wages.

## THE RESHAPING OF THE LABOUR MARKET IN A NEW REGULATORY SETTING

In the mid-1980s, the economy was already showing signs of having overcome the crisis, with a substantial development of national and foreign investment. But it was with Portugal's membership of the European Union that the growth of the national economy really took off. This acceleration of growth was mainly based on a strong process of tertiarization in which the financial, trade, tourism and enterprise support services sectors played a major role. This process was accompanied by an important increase in construction, especially in public works, in part due to the financial assistance of the European Regional Development Fund (EDRF).

These more dynamic sectors contributed quite differently to the equality between men and women. The growth of the financial services mainly favoured male employment, not because of the qualifications demanded, but largely because of the required time availability and flexible work schedules. The expansion of major commercial areas and tourism was met by a corresponding increase in the employment of women, although with inferior working conditions. Enterprise support services also generated more employment demand for women, but this was particularly for the more routine, though in some cases qualified, jobs. The expansion of public works led almost exclusively to an increase in male employment, for emigrants in the parts of the sector demanding less skills and by native labour in the more technical parts.

Overall, these developments led to a substantial reinforcement of the female presence in the labour market. However, the major qualitative transformations of the labour market have taken place through new regulatory instruments of special relevance to the equality of women and men; that is, they have been the result of professional training financed by the European Social Fund (ESF) and affirmative action in the creation of jobs or the promotion of female employment in traditionally male-dominated sectors. But we find that the most determinant factor in the promotion of female employment in recent years has been the increasing female presence in higher education, even in those areas traditionally closed to women, such as engineering and management.

## FAVOURABLE CONDITIONS FOR EQUALITY?

Notwithstanding this set of favourable conditions for the promotion of female labour activity, we want to find out to what extent the differences between men and women in the labour market have waned or been reinforced. Through employment communitary programmes, based more on a policy of subsidies than on regulatory measures, workers who are from the start more available, more informed and more aware of the opportunities presented by the different initiatives are more easily promoted. This pattern of behaviour is heavily conditioned for the majority of women, for they have constantly to combine jobs with family duties (either in execution or merely in decision making and organization), in which case, investment in a professional career is substantially limited (Perista and Lopes 1991).

Still, the reshaping of the labour market has brought growing competition. Workers' valorization, based on wage levels, mainly depends on their degree of substitution, a feature relating not only to qualifications and competence, but also to availability and mobility. In the female case, this degree of substitution is limited by the reasons already stated and by the weak development of social structures and services, especially regarding childcare and care of the elderly.

We want to show that despite an increasing equality in qualifications and numbers, disparities between women and men in the labour market reveal a considerable inertia that is particularly visible in some segments of female labour (Figure 1). The data in the *Employment Survey* (INE 1992; 1997) confirm these ideas, namely, the lack of correspondence between school qualifications and professional advancement and the worsening of labour conditions stipulated in contracts.

## EQUALITY IN SCHOOL QUALIFICATIONS

The average level of educational attainment among those of working age is still very low in Portugal, hindering the modernization of the economy. In spite of the unfavourable global situation, equality between women and men has increased considerably in recent years (Table 1). This has occurred more at the top than at the bottom of the qualification scale. The difference between women with no qualifications and men with no qualifications narrowed between 1992 and 1997, but the distance is still considerable (7.1 per cent of men and 13.3 per cent of women). In contrast, in higher education, female numbers and male numbers are very

FIGURE 1
EQUALITY AND DIFFERENCE BETWEEN MEN AND WOMEN IN THE LABOUR
MARKET – MODEL OF ANALYSIS

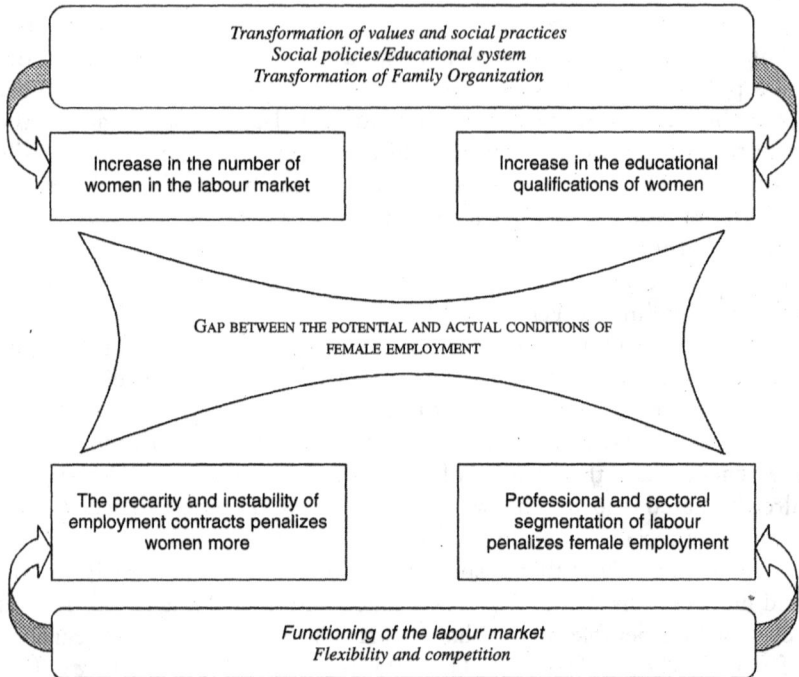

similar. This shows that women's educational patterns are more polarized than men's.

In the youth population, between 25 and 34 years old, this situation is inverted. Women's educational patterns are more favourable than men's, both at the top and bottom of the qualification scale, but mainly in the higher ranks. The number of men with more than nine years in education is 28.9 per cent and the number of women is 36.9 per cent.

The regional patterns of education in 1997 were very differentiated with the contrast being even greater in the youth population (Table 2). However, the variation sense is the same for men and for women. Overall, the levels of education are higher in the Lisbon region, average in the north and centre, and lower in the south and the islands.

TABLE 1
PROFILE OF EDUCATION (DISTRIBUTION %), PORTUGAL, 1992 AND 1997

|  | 15–64 years | | | | 25–34 years | | | |
|  | Men | | Women | | Men | | Women | |
|  | 1992 | 1997 | 1992 | 1997 | 1992 | 1997 | 1992 | 1997 |
|---|---|---|---|---|---|---|---|---|
| Pre-school | 8.5 | 7.1 | 16.6 | 13.3 | 4.2 | 3.9 | 3.5 | 3.3 |
| Primary – 1st level | 38.4 | 35.1 | 34.9 | 33.7 | 28.1 | 22.3 | 29.1 | 22.7 |
| Primary – 2nd level | 19.1 | 18.5 | 14.4 | 13.6 | 24.1 | 28.1 | 19.6 | 22.9 |
| Primary – 3rd level | 16.4 | 18.5 | 14.8 | 16.0 | 17.7 | 16.8 | 15.4 | 14.3 |
| Secondary | 10.0 | 13.0 | 10.3 | 13.3 | 15.0 | 17.2 | 15.3 | 18.1 |
| Middle and Polytechnic | 1.8 | 1.7 | 4.0 | 3.9 | 2.2 | 2.2 | 5.9 | 5.0 |
| Higher | 5.7 | 6.0 | 5.0 | 6.2 | 8.7 | 9.5 | 11.1 | 13.8 |

Source: INE, Estatísticas do Emprego, 1992 and 1997.

TABLE 2
PROFILE OF EDUCATION (DISTRIBUTION %), BY REGION, 1997

|  | Population between 15 and 64 | | | | | | | |
|  | Pre-school | | Primary | | Secondary | | Middle & Higher | |
|  | Men | Women | Men | Women | Men | Women | Men | Women |
|---|---|---|---|---|---|---|---|---|
| **Portugal** | 7.1 | 13.3 | 72.1 | 63.3 | 13.0 | 13.3 | 7.8 | 10.1 |
| Norte | 7.5 | 14.4 | 74.4 | 65.4 | 11.3 | 11.3 | 6.7 | 8.9 |
| Centro | 7.9 | 16.9 | 76.1 | 63.8 | 10.3 | 9.9 | 5.6 | 9.4 |
| LVT | 4.3 | 8.9 | 66.6 | 60.8 | 17.6 | 17.5 | 11.5 | 12.9 |
| Alentejo | 12.9 | 21.4 | 73.8 | 60.3 | 9.3 | 10.2 | 4.0 | 7.8 |
| Algarve | 11.4 | 16.9 | 75.0 | 64.9 | 9.9 | 12.2 | 3.5 | 6.2 |
| Açores | 13.1 | 14.0 | 76.0 | 68.1 | 7.7 | 11.3 | 3.0 | 6.4 |
| Madeira | 10.7 | 15.7 | 77.9 | 67.0 | 9.3 | 12.1 | 2.1 | 5.1 |
| Coefficient of regional variation | 0.31 | 0.23 | 0.05 | 0.04 | 0.27 | 0.20 | 0.57 | 0.30 |

|  | Population between 25 and 34 | | | | | | | |
|  | Pre-school | | Primary | | Secondary | | Middle & Higher | |
|  | Men | Women | Men | Women | Men | Women | Men | Women |
|---|---|---|---|---|---|---|---|---|
| **Portugal** | 3.9 | 3.3 | 67.2 | 59.8 | 17.2 | 18.1 | 11.7 | 18.8 |
| Norte | 4.8 | 3.3 | 72.4 | 67.4 | 13.6 | 13.8 | 9.2 | 15.5 |
| Centro | 4.4 | 3.6 | 71.3 | 63.6 | 13.5 | 14.2 | 10.8 | 18.4 |
| LVT | 1.4 | 2.3 | 57.5 | 47.6 | 24.2 | 25.0 | 16.9 | 25.2 |
| Alentejo | 5.5 | 5.4 | 76.6 | 64.9 | 11.3 | 15.8 | 6.6 | 13.5 |
| Algarve | 9.0 | 6.6 | 71.9 | 63.4 | 15.1 | 17.5 | 4.0 | 13.7 |
| Açores | 8.6 | 7.7 | 77.7 | 67.8 | 9.4 | 14.7 | 4.3 | 9.8 |
| Madeira | 7.5 | 4.6 | 73.5 | 64.9 | 13.6 | 20.1 | 4.8 | 9.8 |
| Coefficient of regional variation | 0.42 | 0.37 | 0.09 | 0.10 | 0.30 | 0.22 | 0.53 | 0.33 |

Source: INE, Estatísticas do Emprego, 1992 and 1997.

We need to stress, however, one significant difference between men and women. Regional contrasts are more prominent in the male population, which may mean that the degree of male investment in school education is more dependent on the specific conditions of the labour market, namely, on the requirements of employers.

Overall, education indicators suggest that men can find employment more easily even with lower levels of educational attainment, leading them to drop out of the educational system earlier. On the other hand, the higher investment of women in school education shows that that is the best way they can find to access the labour market and diversified professional opportunities. A good example of this is the presence of women in scientific fields traditionally dominated by men (Table 3).

Nevertheless, these reasons, dependent as they are on individual strategies, seem insufficient to account not only for the longer time spent by women within the education system, but also for their higher school achievement, even in secondary schools (Table 4). As a matter of fact, women's advantages in school education seem to be related to family education rules that expect them to assume a more responsible attitude and behaviour from early on. We can even say that traditional education models, confining women to the household world and men to the working world, were overthrown only to be replaced by others that were equally differentiating. In men's education, sport and interpersonal relations are more highly valued, whereas in women's education it is school performance that is more valued. This distinction provokes different sets of behaviour, with women trying to fulfil all their duties and men embracing initiative and competition (Magalhães 1998).

## THE GROWING PRESENCE OF WOMEN IN THE LABOUR MARKET

In the past few years, the rate of female labour-market activity has significantly increased, especially in the young adult age group (Figure 2). This increase is mainly due to the process of tertiary-sector development and especially to the growth in the job supply in specific parts of the tertiary sector which have distinct features that are more favourable to the recruitment of women:

- Activities demanding cheap and not very demanding labour (tourism, catering, more routine tasks in enterprise support services, and personal and domestic services), and

FIGURE 2
ACTIVITY RATES BY AGE GROUPS, PORTUGAL – 1992 AND 1997

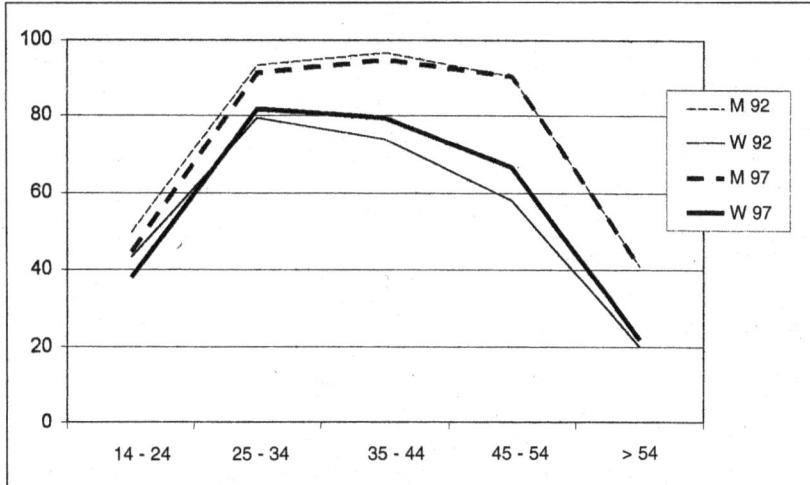

Source: INE, Estatísticas do Emprego, 1992 and 1997.

- Activities demanding particular types of school education (health and social services).

The tendency for an equalization of the number of men and women in the labour market is seen in all regions of the country, although developing at different paces (Table 5). The highest increase in the rate of female activity was observed in the two regions where the presence of women in the labour market has always been weaker, the Azores and Alentejo. These are the less-developed regions in the country where male migration, on the one hand, and the predominance of competition strategies based on the reduction of costs, on the other, leads to an expansion of the female job supply. In the Azores, despite a considerable increase in the rate of female activity in the past few years, there are still very strong hindrances to the employment of women. These obstacles exist at least in the formal market and are imposed by an economic and social development context which is to some extent pre-capitalist.

The different speeds of regional development have led to a narrowing of female activity patterns in the different regions of the country. This growing uniformity is even greater if we only consider the rates of female activity in the younger age group (25–34 year olds), which is at a very

TABLE 3
RATE OF FEMINIZATION OF VARIOUS DOMAINS OF SCIENTIFIC HIGHER
EDUCATION, PORTUGAL – 1994/1995

| | Proportion of degrees | Degrees finished |
|---|---|---|
| Educational sciences | 77.7 | 80.2 |
| Fine Arts | 59.4 | 61.8 |
| Humanities | 78.1 | 81.1 |
| Social Sciences | 63.9 | 66.8 |
| Economy and management | 52.2 | 53.1 |
| Law | 60.7 | 62.8 |
| Natural Sciences | 60.5 | 62.8 |
| Mathematics and informatics | 49.6 | 54.1 |
| Medical Sciences | 65.6 | 67.0 |
| Engenharias | 28.8 | 30.5 |
| Architecture and Urban Studies | 44.9 | 43.1 |

Source: Ministério da Educação, Estatísticas da Educação, 1994/95.

TABLE 4
PROPORTION OF MEN AND WOMEN AND SUCCESS RATES IN THE LAST YEAR OF
SECONDARY TEACHING (12TH YEAR), PORTUGAL – 1994/95

| | Gender ration of students | Pass rates | |
|---|---|---|---|
| | | Men | Women |
| Portugal Continental | 0.83 | 55.5 | 64.1 |
| Norte | 0.81 | 60.2 | 68.1 |
| Centro | 0.81 | 55.3 | 64.9 |
| LVT | 0.88 | 52.4 | 61.5 |
| Alentejo | 0.69 | 61.6 | 68.3 |
| Algarve | 0.70 | 57.0 | 56.7 |

Source: Ministério da Educação, Estatísticas da Educação, 1994/95.

high level in all regions. This means that the obstacles to the entry of women into the labour market are being quickly overcome, either in geographical contexts where economic development is faster or in those where economic difficulties persist.

As a matter of fact, marriage and motherhood seem not to limit significantly, in any region of the country, the access of women to employment. This happens because in some situations preschool education services are particularly well developed, while in others support given by intergenerational family ties allows young women a relative freedom from domestic duties. In any case, the idea of 'the woman at home' has become an outdated stereotype, even in those

TABLE 5
RATES OF ACTIVITY BY REGION, 1992 AND 1997

| | 15–64 years | | | | 25–34 years | | | |
| | Men | | Women | | Men | | Women | |
| | 1992 | 1997 | 1992 | 1997 | 1992 | 1997 | 1992 | 1997 |
|---|---|---|---|---|---|---|---|---|
| **Portugal** | 56.3 | 56.6 | 41.3 | 43.0 | 93.3 | 91.5 | 79.2 | 81.9 |
| Norte | 55.9 | 55.8 | 41.5 | 42.0 | 92.0 | 91.9 | 79.7 | 82.3 |
| Centro | 56.2 | 61.2 | 42.2 | 49.1 | 94.8 | 93.2 | 77.5 | 78.5 |
| LVT | 57.2 | 56.0 | 42.3 | 42.7 | 94.0 | 90.2 | 81.0 | 83.4 |
| Alentejo | 54.8 | 53.0 | 33.4 | 36.9 | 92.5 | 94.4 | 68.1 | 80.4 |
| Algarve | 55.1 | 53.9 | 35.2 | 35.7 | 94.9 | 90.5 | 75.9 | 80.9 |
| Açores | 54.2 | 51.9 | 25.6 | 29.0 | 93.9 | 94.1 | 57.0 | 64.4 |
| Madreira | 52.7 | 51.3 | 40.5 | 38.4 | 91.7 | 91.5 | 73.1 | 73.2 |
| *Coefficient of* | | | | | | | | |
| *regional variation* | 0.02 | 0.06 | 0.16 | 0.15 | 0.01 | 0.02 | 0.11 | 0.08 |

*Source*: INE, *Estatísticas do Emprego*, 1992 and 1997.

regions where conservative cultural values predominate. On the other hand, given the low average level of family income, the contribution made by women's wages is indispensable in many households.

## SECTORAL AND PROFESSIONAL PATTERNS

The significant increase in the presence of women in the labour market has been accompanied by an equally significant transformation in the sectoral and professional structure of female employment. The situation is distinct, depending on the dynamism of the various sectors of economic activity (Table 6). In those sectors where economic dynamism has been accompanied by a considerable increase in employment, there have been three contrasting tendencies:

- Civil construction and related activities remain a traditional domain of male employment and here male predominance has been strengthened
- In agricultural activities and in health and social services, a traditional domain of female employment, female predominance has been strengthened, and
- In a diverse set of activities which are either more male dominated (the heavy and motor industries, for instance) or more female dominated (tourism and catering, for instance), there has developed a

TABLE 6
PERCENTAGE OF UNQUALIFIED WORKERS BY REGION, 1992 AND 1997

| | 1992 | | 1997 | |
|---|---|---|---|---|
| | Men | Women | Men | Women |
| Portugal | 7.9 | 11.5 | 8.4 | 13.8 |
| Norte | 6.8 | 7.1 | 6.4 | 8.1 |
| Centro | 7.8 | 13.6 | 8.3 | 12.9 |
| LVT | 6.9 | 13.8 | 8.4 | 20.0 |
| Alentejo | 16.0 | 21.2 | 15.8 | 17.3 |
| Algarve | 9.2 | 13.6 | 11.6 | 15.9 |
| Açores | 9.1 | 9.0 | 8.0 | 9.9 |
| Madeira | 15.9 | 11.2 | 17.9 | 15.3 |
| *Coefficient of regional variation* | 0.36 | 0.33 | 0.37 | 0.27 |

Source: INE, *Estatísticas do Emprego*, 1992 and 1997.

greater balance between men and women, which is clearly due to the greater degree of equality in school education.

In those areas where there has been a decline in employment, the general trend has been toward an intensification of the male labour force in the more male-dominated activities (chemical and transport industries) and of the female labour force in the more female-dominated activities (textiles and the retail sector, for instance). This pattern seems to reflect inertia in personal recruitment strategies in those sectors more vulnerable to changes in the nature of competition.

In areas where, unrelated to the strategies of defensive restructuring, a reduction in the numbers employed has been registered, as in public administration and financial services, there is now, on the contrary, a greater balance between male and female employment. This reveals, on the one hand, the importance of school qualifications in gaining access to some professional careers and, on the other, the role played by some regulatory mechanisms in the promotion of affirmative action in the governing of access to the labour market.

We can also observe distinct differences in the male-female balance at various levels of the professional pyramid. At the bottom of the pyramid (non-qualified professions), we see a clear trend toward a significant increase in female activity, especially in the Lisbon region, where competition in the labour market and employers requirements are particularly demanding on low-skilled women.

TABLE 7
PERCENTAGE OF HIGHLY QUALIFIED WORKERS, BY REGION, 1992 AND 1997

| | Executives | | | | Technical and scientific professions | | | |
| | Men | | Women | | Men | | Women | |
| | 1992 | 1997 | 1992 | 1997 | 1992 | 1997 | 1992 | 1997 |
|---|---|---|---|---|---|---|---|---|
| **Portugal** | 12.7 | 11.2 | 9.4 | 8.9 | 5.9 | 5.7 | 7.3 | 7.1 |
| Norte | 12.4 | 11.7 | 6.8 | 6.8 | 5.5 | 5.4 | 6.9 | 6.0 |
| Centro | 19.0 | 14.7 | 21.4 | 16.1 | 4.9 | 3.1 | 7.2 | 5.7 |
| LVT | 11.0 | 9.3 | 5.9 | 6.3 | 7.9 | 8.9 | 8.7 | 10.0 |
| Alentejo | 10.7 | 10.8 | 11.7 | 10.2 | 2.4 | 2.3 | 3.6 | 6.1 |
| Algarve | 12.0 | 12.1 | 11.7 | 11.0 | 3.8 | 2.3 | 5.5 | 3.0 |
| Açores | 9.1 | 5.4 | 5.5 | 3.4 | 3.8 | 2.7 | 5.5 | 4.9 |
| Madeira | 6.1 | 6.1 | 2.9 | 2.6 | 2.3 | 3.2 | 3.7 | 3.8 |
| | | | | | | | | |
| *Coefficient of* | | | | | | | | |
| *regional variation* | 0.32 | 0.31 | 0.61 | 0.54 | 0.41 | 0.56 | 0.30 | 0.37 |

Source: INE, *Estatísticas do Emprego*, 1992 and 1997.

In the more qualified parts of the professional structure, by contrast, the conditions for female progression are relatively more favourable, especially in the Lisbon region (Table 7). This means that in the more dynamic regions of the country, the polarization of female school qualifications is clearly leading to a polarization of female employment. Overall, at the highest managerial levels, regional contrasts are greater in female employment, whereas in the technical and scientific professions, the pattern is reversed.

## QUALITY OF EMPLOYMENT

One of the major features of the recent evolution of the labour market is the trend toward flexibility in labour management, together with a rapid disaggregation of the Fordist system of regulatory norms. This process is linked to defensive strategies that lead to growing instability of employment and to the 'informalization' of contracts, a development particularly clear in periods of lower economic growth.

Between 1992 and 1997, the general pattern was one of a significant growth of unemployment and unstable employment, as a result not only of less favourable economic conjunctures, but also of intense restructuring in key sectors of the national economy, due to an increase in competition. Unemployment, in 1997, reached rates close to the European Union average. In absolute terms, women have been harder hit than men, although in this five-year period there have been greater increases in male unemployment rates (for women, an increase of 60 per cent and for men, an increase of 75 per cent). This may be explained by the fact that more intense restructuring processes have occurred in male-dominated sectors, especially in manufacturing industry. The age profile of unemployment (Table 8) reveals that this trend of narrowing male and female unemployment rates is taking place in all age groups, except the youngest. This means that now the distinction between women and men is mainly at the point of entry into the labour market and lessens over time. This seems to contradict the substantial increase in school qualifications among the younger generations of active women. In fact, these data show that, on the one hand, school education is not a sufficient condition in guaranteeing access to employment and that, on the other, the low level of training has harsher consequences for women than for men.

Concerning regional rates of unemployment, it is important to stress that geographical contrasts are much greater among the female population, with female unemployment rates reaching much higher levels in the Lisbon region and in the south. This pattern cannot be dissociated from the distinct social and economic structures of the regions, particularly the importance of small-scale peasant farming (Santos 1993). In the north and centre of the country, small-scale peasant farming plays a major role as a social cushion, absorbing a great part of the female labour liberated from the restructuring of some sectors of manufacturing and from tertiary activities with a large female workforce, such as textiles and the small-retail sector.

The growing informality and instability of contracts is clear if we look at the evolution of employment structures according to the conditions in a particular profession and the type of employee contracts. During the period under study, we see an increasing number of independent workers (Table 9), relating to an increase in informal wage relationships (in which the worker has the same kind of ties with the employer, but ceases to have a work contract). This is especially observable in many parts of the less qualified tertiary sector, in some industrial areas where home-working is relevant (as in clothes and shoemaking), and in civil construction. This professional vulnerability, often associated with an absence of public social protection, is one of the most serious forms of destabilization in the labour market. Although affecting men and women alike, this problem is of greater relevance among the female population.

As is the case for regional patterns of unemployment, in the case of isolated workers, geographical contrasts are greater among the active

TABLE 8
UNEMPLOYMENT RATES, BY REGION, 1992 AND 1997

### 1992

| | TOTAL | | 14-24 | | 25-34 | | 35-44 | | 45-54 | | >54 | |
|---|---|---|---|---|---|---|---|---|---|---|---|---|
| | Men | Women | Men | Women | Men | Women | Men | Women | Men | Women | Men | Women |
| Portugal | 3.5 | 4.9 | 8.8 | 11.5 | 3.6 | 5.7 | 2.0 | 3.5 | 1.8 | 2.1 | 2.1 | 0.8 |
| Norte | 3.1 | 4.2 | 6.4 | 8.8 | 3.7 | 4.6 | 2.0 | 3.7 | 1.4 | 0.8 | 1.4 | 0.1 |
| Centro | 2.4 | 3.2 | 6.3 | 7.6 | 2.8 | 4.9 | 1.5 | 1.6 | 1.3 | 1.3 | 0.8 | 0.8 |
| LVT | 4.2 | 6.0 | 13.8 | 15.7 | 3.5 | 6.9 | 2.2 | 3.9 | 2.2 | 2.4 | 2.9 | 1.1 |
| Alentejo | 5.6 | 11.0 | 10.7 | 23.8 | 5.7 | 12.6 | 3.5 | 6.6 | 3.2 | 8.3 | 5.3 | 3.8 |
| Algarve | 2.8 | 3.2 | 6.8 | 8.4 | 3.4 | 2.6 | 1.9 | 1.9 | 2.0 | 3.9 | 1.4 | 0.4 |
| Açores | 1.8 | 7.4 | 5.8 | 14.4 | 1.0 | 7.7 | 0.5 | 6.1 | 1.1 | 0.0 | 0.2 | 0.0 |
| Madeira | 2.9 | 3.6 | 6.4 | 13.1 | 2.4 | 3.7 | 1.9 | 2.0 | 1.4 | 0.3 | 2.2 | 0.0 |
| *Coefficient of regional variation* | *0.36* | *0.48* | *0.35* | *0.40* | *0.41* | *0.50* | *0.43* | *0.51* | *0.38* | *1.11* | *0.77* | *1.41* |

### 1997

| | TOTAL | | 14-24 | | 25-34 | | 35-44 | | 45-54 | | >54 | |
|---|---|---|---|---|---|---|---|---|---|---|---|---|
| | Men | Women | Men | Women | Men | Women | Men | Women | Men | Women | Men | Women |
| **Portugal** | **6.1** | **7.6** | **11.7** | **18.7** | **6.6** | **8.0** | **4.6** | **6.1** | **4.7** | **5.4** | **4.5** | **2.5** |
| Norte | 6.8 | 6.8 | 11.6 | 13.6 | 7.5 | 7.9 | 5.5 | 6.4 | 5.3 | 3.9 | 5.1 | 1.4 |
| Centro | 3.2 | 3.9 | 7.5 | 18.4 | 5.8 | 3.1 | 2.5 | 3.7 | 2.3 | 2.4 | 0.9 | 0.3 |
| LVT | 6.6 | 9.2 | 12.6 | 22.5 | 5.9 | 8.4 | 4.3 | 6.4 | 5.5 | 7.5 | 7.4 | 5.0 |
| Alentejo | 7.3 | 16.1 | 19.8 | 34.7 | 8.7 | 20.4 | 4.8 | 11.5 | 3.9 | 9.2 | 3.3 | 9.2 |
| Algarve | 6.8 | 9.2 | 14.3 | 23.0 | 5.0 | 11.2 | 8.3 | 5.8 | 5.4 | 5.5 | 3.8 | 5.4 |
| Açores | 2.9 | 9.3 | 9.4 | 26.5 | 1.1 | 6.7 | 1.7 | 5.7 | 1.8 | 1.9 | 0.4 | 1.7 |
| Madeira | 5.1 | 5.3 | 11.6 | 16.4 | 4.7 | 9.3 | 2.8 | 2.1 | 3.1 | 1.4 | 3.0 | 0.0 |
| *Coefficient of regional variation* | *0.31* | *0.43* | *0.29* | *0.29* | *0.40* | *0.52* | *0.48* | *0.45* | *0.37* | *0.61* | *0.65* | *0.95* |

*Source*: INE, *Estatísticas do Emprego*, 1992 and 1997.

TABLE 9
PERCENTAGE OF SELF-EMPLOYED WORKERS, BY REGION, 1992 AND 1997

|  | 1992 | | 1997 | |
|---|---|---|---|---|
|  | Men | Women | Men | Women |
| **Portugal** | 17.0 | 18.4 | 20.5 | 21.7 |
| Norte | 14.9 | 19.1 | 18.3 | 20.2 |
| Centro | 25.8 | 32.8 | 34.1 | 44.7 |
| LVT | 13.4 | 11.1 | 15.3 | 11.7 |
| Alentejo | 19.0 | 16.5 | 20.4 | 13.4 |
| Algarve | 24.2 | 16.2 | 25.2 | 18.5 |
| Açores | 19.7 | 9.3 | 18.0 | 6.5 |
| Madeira | 14.8 | 15.0 | 11.0 | 14.1 |
| *Coefficient of regional variation* | 0.24 | 0.41 | 0.34 | 0.62 |

Source: INE, *Estatísticas do Emprego*, 1992 and 1997.

female population. In the north and centre and in Madeira, the number of isolated female workers is larger than the number of isolated male workers, but in the rest of the country the reverse is true. The character of regional social and economic development, as already mentioned above, explains this pattern. As an example, it should be remembered that the externalization of female employment is particularly significant in the north and centre, mainly due to cost-reduction strategies in sectors of traditionally intensive industrial labour.

The growing instability in work relations is equally confirmed by the increase in the use of temporary contracts, which in 1997 applied to more than 14 per cent of employees (Table 10). In this respect, women have always been harshly hit, due to their greater traditional vulnerability in work relations, as well as their concentration in sectors of the labour market in which Fordist regulation has never been completely adopted.

The visible changes in demographic behaviour (a rapid decrease in birth rates, postponement of first pregnancy, and an increasing time gap between births) have to be understood as an answer to the growing demands of the labour market and to the vulnerability of working conditions (Almeida et al. 1995). In the past few years, strategies for increasing the flexibility of contracts in order to strengthen the competitiveness of companies have even hit the more developed sectors (financial activities, the more modern sectors of industry and heavily male-dominated sectors), bringing an increase in temporary contracts among the male population.

TABLE 10
PERCENTAGE OF WORKERS ON TEMPORARY CONTRACTS,
BY REGION, 1992–1997

|  | 1992 | | 1997 | |
|---|---|---|---|---|
|  | Men | Women | Men | Women |
| **Portugal** | 10.8 | 14.1 | 13.8 | 14.8 |
| Norte | 8.8 | 10.0 | 11.6 | 12.6 |
| Centro | 9.1 | 14.9 | 9.7 | 11.7 |
| LVT | 11.8 | 16.5 | 15.0 | 15.8 |
| Alentejo | 16.1 | 20.0 | 26.9 | 29.1 |
| Algarve | 13.0 | 17.3 | 19.1 | 23.9 |
| Açores | 22.6 | 20.6 | 28.0 | 23.5 |
| Madeira | 11.0 | 10.3 | 5.8 | 5.8 |
| *Coefficient of regional* *variation* | 0.34 | 0.25 | 0.47 | 0.44 |

Source: INE, *Estatísticas do Emprego*, 1992 and 1997.

There is thus a narrowing of male-female labour-market differences within an overall situation of deteriorating labour-market conditions, with particular black spots in the south and the Azores. We can therefore conclude that women's quality of employment is still inferior to men's; even though in some aspects there has been a narrowing of the gap, this has almost always been connected with a process of general deterioration. The great vulnerability of female employment is experienced in different ways in different parts of the country: through unemployment and temporary contracts in the Lisbon region and the south of the country and through an externalization of professional work in northern and central Portugal.

CONCLUSION

Although there is a lack of correspondence between progress in women's school education and the valorization of their professional situation, we cannot conclude that the gap between men and women has widened. In fact, employment-management strategies developed in the past few years, in which defensive behaviour predominates even in the more dynamic sectors, have led, in some cases, to a narrowing of the gap through a certain deterioration in male working conditions. Increasing flexibility has hit male employment as hard as female employment.

The data show, meanwhile, a new reality in the labour market: a growing cleavage between the more qualified workers, among whom equality has been strengthened, and the less-qualified group, where, on the contrary, there is a growing divergence between men and women. In the first case, the generalized access of women from higher social groups to higher education has decisively promoted their commitment to socially valued professional careers. In the second case, the high female activity rates are mainly explained by the need to strengthen family income, which leads, in many cases, to the acceptance of unstable working conditions almost always imposed by childbirth and domestic chores. This dichotomy reveals that family responsibilities weigh unevenly and are dependent on the social status of women, which still strongly penalizes the less-favoured groups. This not only means a greater sharing of domestic duties among younger and more qualified couples, but mainly the possibility of externalizing a significant part of domestic chores (André 1994). Lastly, it is important to point to the relationship between the evolution of values and cultural representations and women's participation in the Portuguese labour market. As a matter of fact, the rapid and massive entry of women into the labour market from the 1960s onward, either motivated by particular political contexts or by the pattern of specific economic specialization, has led to a slow but progressive mutation of gender roles within families and society. The cultural valorization of the professional work of women prevents childbirth and family life from keeping women away from the labour market even in situations where a dual wage is not a necessity. However, the more equal sharing of domestic chores affects only a small percentage of the population, mainly those living in large urban areas with higher levels of education (André 1994). In sum, while the dynamics of wider social change induced by changes in the labour market are extensive, there remains a significant degree of inertia in the sphere of family organization.

## REFERENCES

Almeida, A. N. et al. (1995): Os padrões recentes da fecundidade em Portugal. Lisboa: CIDM.

André, I. (1994): 'O falso neutro em Geografia Humana. Género e relação patriarcal no emprego e no trabalho doméstico'. Ph.D Dissertation in Human Geography, Lisbon University.

(1996): 'At the centre of the periphery? Women in the Portuguese labour market'. In M. D. Garcia-Ramon and J. Monk (eds.), Women of the European Union: The Politics of Work and Daily Life. London: Routledge.

Ferreira, V. (1993): 'Padrões de segregação das mulheres no emprego — uma análise do caso português no quadro europeu'. In B. Sousa Santos (ed.), Portugal: um retrato singular. Porto: Edições Afrontamento.

Magalhães, M. J. (1998): *Movimento feminista e educação. Portugal, décadas de 70 e 80.* Oeiras: Celta Editora.

Perista, H and M. Chagas Lopes (1991): 'Potencialidades e vulnerabilidades do emprego das mulheres'. *Organizações e Trabalho,* No.5/6, 1991, pp.37–46.

Rodrigues, M. J. (1988): *O sistema de emprego em portugal, crise e mutações.* Lisboa: Edições D. Quixote.

Santos, B. S. (1993): 'O estado, as relações salariais e o bem-estar social na semi-periferia: o caso português'. In B. Sousa Santos (ed.), *Portugal: um retrato singular.* Porto: Edições Afrontamento.

Walby, S. (1986): *Patriarchy at Work.* London: Polity Press.

# The Family Paradigm in the Italian Welfare State (1947–1996)

## FRANCA BIMBI

In Italy, children live with their parents until they get married, and are maintained by them so long as they stay in the family, even in families with a single breadwinner and whether they have a separate income or not (Scabini and Donati 1988; De Sandre *et al.* 1997). Nevertheless, despite the fact that the responsibility for maintaining and caring for children continues for so long and in spite of the moral and ideological emphasis on the family manifested by all political parties, there is a general lack of family policy (Gauthier 1995), something which has been a persistent feature of the postwar period (Bimbi 1997a; Bimbi and Della Sala 1998; Saraceno 1998). The causes of this lack of family policy are to be sought in three directions. First, we must remember that there still exists a profound reaction to Fascism, which, for the first and only time in Italian history, produced explicit pronatalist family policies and categorical policies for lone mothers (Saraceno 1991; De Grazia 1992). Second, the postwar Mediterranean model of welfare has featured a long period of family care for children and relatives (Bettio and Villa 1993), supported by a law on relatives' obligations in Italy, alongside residual state responsibility for family welfare (Trifiletti 1997). This means, among other things, that the state organizes its activities while constantly recognizing the legitimate priority of the family group to mediate individual rights. Third, the characteristic demographic trend (that is, the presence of profound changes but the continuing importance of traditional forms of matrimonial and intergenerational ties)[1] points to the hegemony of a shared cultural model, whose hallmark is the importance of the family group.

The family, however it is defined at various stages of the life cycle, maintains a traditional role: it continues to be seen as the primary system of social protection, regardless of the individual's relationship to the labour market and the rights of individuals recognized by the welfare state. This cultural model gives the gendered nature of the welfare regime its structure.

From the late 1960s, Italy set up a series of seemingly progressive policies that directly affected women in regard to paid work and the care of children, such as the equal-pay agreements (1962–63), the introduction of state day-schools (1968), publicly funded crèches (1971), new maternity leave (1971) and the law on parity (1977). However, these policies neither reflected nor led to changes in the representation of women's responsibility for the care of children and for the gender division of labour in the family (Bimbi 1997b).

These policies never formed a coherent framework for family policies because of ideological conflicts (and practical compromises) on the nature of the family and on the limits of women's choices as regards reproduction. The search for a compromise has characterized the conduct of the two main parties, the Christian Democrats (DC) and the Italian Communist Party (PCI), since the Second World War, just as it does the Italian Popular Party (PPI) and the Party of the Democratic Left (PDS) today.[2] Nevertheless, the ideological conflict is always resurfacing due to the influence of the Catholic Church and because the church's demands for guarantees in the political system have become greater and greater with the decline of its influence on the sexual and family behaviour of the individual.

Fear of resurgent ideological conflicts could explain the dominant paradigm regarding family policies, which is referred to as the 'family paradigm', that is, childcare is a matter for the family, and the care of the family is the responsibility of women. This went largely unchallenged in the political discourses of the major political parties until the late 1980s and 1990s. The improvement of social policies during the 1970s slowly eroded the 'family paradigm', but never supplanted its dominant position in shaping policy.

The role and nature of the family and the definition of women's 'natural' roles were a source of tension in the drafting of the constitution (1946–47) and during the discussions on the new family law (1970), divorce (1970) and abortion (1978), yet political elites avoid confrontation on family policy. Since the Second World War, Italy's consensual politics has left little room for an open political debate about family policies, the representation of women's responsibilities for the care of children and the division of household work.

The Italian enigma is why welfare policy changes took place without any major challenges to the 'family paradigm' (Saraceno 1994). The introduction of intensive family policies and new representations of women's care of children and the gender division of household work

might threaten a series of political and institutional compromises on
family and women's roles regarded as essential for the consolidation of
liberal democratic structures.

The representation of the role of women and the family, while not
occupying a prominent role, was central to the debates in the Constituent
Assembly in 1946–47. At the political-institutional level, the ideological
conflict centred on differing conceptions of women and the family. On
the one hand, Catholic ideology considered the state-family relationship
in the light of the principle of subsidiarity (Welty 1966) and defined the
family as a social unit based on natural law; on the other hand, it found
in Catholic doctrine the foundation for the moral, legal and social
regulation of the family. Within this view, the representation of women
in the paid labour market is subservient to women as mothers, as wives
and as responsible for domestic chores. The Communist position was no
less ambivalent (Togliatti 1965). On the one hand, the PCI supported
equal rights for women, especially economic rights such as equal pay and
job security. The representation of women as workers centred primarily
on women in industry. On the other hand, the PCI rarely challenged the
basic premises of the 'family paradigm' and did not attempt to place a
different representation of women and the care of children on the
political agenda for fear of jeopardizing its broader political objective of
consolidating Italian democracy and obtaining legitimacy as a party
committed to the Republic's basic principles. As a consequence, the 1947
Constitution was ambiguous on women's rights in three main areas.

The first of these is the definition of citizenship itself. Article 3 lays
down the equality of all citizens 'with no distinction of sex' and, at the
same time, obliges legislators to act in order to remove all those obstacles
that 'impede the full development of the person and the effective
participation of all workers'. Thus, the constitution implicitly follows an
equal opportunities approach, although the term 'equal opportunities'
was not introduced in Italy until the 1980s.

However, up to the 1970s, this pursuit of 'the full development of the
person' never seemed to bring the prevalent role of women as wives and
mothers into question. Nor did it seem that the 'natural' definition of a
woman's place within the walls of the home might in any way conflict
with the guaranteed 'participation of all workers' in the political and
economic management of society. Gender difference came into the
definition of a 'worker' only with respect to certain characteristic family
functions performed by women.

This becomes particularly clear when one considers the professional and economic citizenship of women. The Republic was 'founded on work', and Article 37 of its constitution lays down equal rights and equal pay 'for equal work', while at the same time offering particular protection for women workers 'to enable them to fulfil their essential family function'.

Lastly, the Italian constitution lays down an explicit limit to the recognition of family relationships: the family is defined as 'a natural social unit founded on marriage', and the 'moral and juridical' equality of 'husband and wife' is defined 'within the limits laid down by the law to guarantee the unity of the family' (Article 29).

On matters to do with the family, the Italian left was always very attentive to the requirements of the Catholic Church. So, while reformist in character and in favour of the right to work, the constitution was for a long time dominated by a view of women as wives and mothers. At the same time, the constitution sanctioned the Concordat with the Catholic Church (Article 7), and in fact offers constitutional rights only to a 'legitimate' family (with the partial exception of the protection offered to illegitimate children). So, a Catholic ideology is the basis of the social model of gender identity. The model of gender identity may have changed (both in law and the popular consciousness), but the ambiguity of the constitution still serves to explain some of the deep conflicts in Italy over the social construction of women (Bimbi 1993).

The compromise on family definitions did not change until the 1970s because, leaving their ideological differences aside, the two major Italian political parties, the PCI and DC, both agreed in attacking the consumer mentality that lay behind the new behaviour patterns of the middle and working classes. During the 1960s, the 'American way of life', according to which family income was used to satisfy individual needs and desires, was seen as the worst enemy of the traditional hierarchical relationships in the family. Catholic ideology still harked back to the peasant world as a 'golden age' of family authority (Guizzardi 1982), thrift and sacrifice, while the left tended to interpret women's demand for consumer goods and domestic appliances as a betrayal of emancipation through productive work and a retreat into the bourgeois model of the unproductive housewife. In working-class families of either a social-communist or Catholic bent, the authority of the male head of household still went unchallenged: the entry of women into factories and offices raised the problem of their emancipation as workers and not as women. This mystique of the family led to the idea of a private world that was self-sufficient in meeting the needs of everyday life. Right up until the middle of the 1960s, the Catholic Church was seen as the 'natural' agency for providing social assistance to children and the old, and so was the almost exclusive recipient of state funds (Fargion 1998). The state itself only dealt with cases of extreme poverty, offering poor relief that was available only to those with a 'poverty card', the possession of which was socially stigmatizing.

Nevertheless, in this period, economic, industrial and urban development explains the new demand for social welfare and, as a consequence, the 1968 law on state day-schools and the 1971 law on council crèches. To counter the possibility of public day-nurseries in 1971, the DC introduced a new law on compulsory maternity leave for working mothers, which covered all categories of employees for 20 weeks at 80 per cent of their salary (100 per cent in Public Administration). If mothers really had to work then at least let them enjoy good rights to maternity leave, rather than have them depend upon external social services.

With hindsight, it is possible to see that all these laws were fundamental to the expansion of women's demands for social citizenship. In particular, the laws on state nursery schools and council day-nurseries did not challenge the family paradigm on childcare as a woman's responsibility, but they made it possible for feminist collective actors to appear on the scene. The feminists' shifts in the political and conceptual approach to women's rights indicated a possible breakdown of the ambiguities and compromises regarding family matters and on the social definition of women established by the constitution.

During the 1970s, Italy's social services passed from a rather minimal, residual model of welfare state provisions to an institutional welfare regime. At the same time, the feminist debate about the identity of women and the definition of women's rights on reproductive choices turned into a parliamentary debate over civil rights. The debate on the family shifted from the emancipation of women through work to a conflict over the redefinition of both gender and generational hierarchies.

The agent that did most to bring about this change of focus was the feminist movement, which had a fundamental influence on policy between 1970 and 1978 (Calabrò and Grasso 1985). In this period, the new laws on the family, divorce and abortion challenged the previous pact on women's social stature negotiated by the existing political forces. During the 1970s, feminism greatly affected relations between the three main forces in politics: the Catholics, institutionally represented by the Christian Democrat Party and supported by the Catholic Church; the Communists, represented by the Communist Party; and the 'secular-liberals', represented by the Socialist, Republican and Liberal Parties (PSI, PRI and PLI respectively). The word 'secular' is used to refer to those political parties which are traditionally associated with firm opposition to the Catholic Church's attempts to interfere in the nation's political life. This last group of parties had been trying since the 1950s to introduce a divorce law, in the face of opposition (of different kinds) from both Catholics and Communists. The PCI, in fact, adopted a pro-family line both to satisfy its very patriarchal working-class constituency and also to avoid alienating the Catholic Church (which it considered to be a powerful popular force that would make a valuable ally). In the 1974 referendum, the Communists were forced, reluctantly, to defend divorce. During the campaign for the popular referendum they were very cautious, representing their party as a defender of family unity and an opponent of the so-called 'individualism' of which feminism was an example.

However, the law on divorce showed that Catholic opinion was not as the church and the DC had imagined it. Groups of practising Catholics, both men and women (along with Catholic feminist groups), came out in favour of the law, and even in those areas where the DC had an absolute majority (the south and in regions of the north-east), there were many more votes in favour than might have been expected (Caciagli and Spreafico 1990). The divorce vote also showed the importance of the feminist movement as an effective political voice for women. Indeed, the referendum results went well beyond what might have been expected, given the political weight of the 'secular-liberal' parties.

This was the situation in which it became possible to pass a law on abortion. In this case, however, there were practically no Catholic groups who supported the measure. Feminism had by then made itself felt within the PCI. The large demonstrations in favour of the law saw Communist women and feminists marching together, and within the party itself women were making their voices heard.

Italian feminism thus saw the fusing of two types of cultural approach: the first, a liberal-radical approach, saw the liberation of women in terms of self-determination with regard to sexuality and the family; the second approach was based on the sort of opposition to the system which was typical of Marxist thought. Looking back, the most effective achievement of the changes made during the 1970s appears to be the transformation of the traditional gift economy. The role of women in both reproduction and private life was redefined in a new scenario of social and civil rights in family life. Feminist struggles for divorce and abortion made it easier for the political parties in parliament to reach an agreement on the reform of family legislation. They saw their task as one of rendering the institution of the family formally democratic, recognizing the sovereignty of the couple within an organic vision of family rights. Conflict was much fiercer over those laws that proposed a view of family relationships in terms of individual rights. Most of the Catholic Church's pronouncements reminded Catholics, and also the Italian government, that individual rights were subordinate to the rights of the family as a group (especially where procreation and matrimony were concerned). Nevertheless, the law on abortion not only established that a woman's body was her own, but also that she had more say over the fate of the embryo than did her male partner (Ergas 1986). This was the first law to recognize a situation in which a woman's juridical status took precedence over a man's and the first measure of positive discrimination in Italian legal history.

After the new family law (1970) and abortion law (1978) were passed, the debate shifted from the definition of women and the family to the less conflictual issues of equal opportunities in the labour market (laws were passed in 1977, 1983 and 1991). Women's social citizenship (understood as a question of formal rights and equal opportunities in the field of paid work and welfare) was not central to the feminism of the 1970s, which was more interested in asserting gender difference through civil rights, seeking personal liberation through self-consciousness practices and working as a political opposition to the system. It was feminist trade unionists (who made their first appearance at the end of the 1970s) who started the discussion of equal opportunities, and women within the political parties subsequently took up these issues. The ease with which the 1977 law on 'Gender parity of employment conditions' passed through parliament was partly due to the women in the DC (at the time the Minister of Employment was Tina Anselmi, who was also chairwoman of the National Equal Opportunities Commission until 1994). The law, in fact, accepted a situation that already existed, consolidating the strength of the trade unions and legitimizing the increasing presence of educated women on the labour market (Franchi et al. 1987). The history of feminist trade unionism provides a typical example of the relationship that was gradually established between the feminist movement and the political forces representing women (Beccalli

1985). Feminism has been an important grass-roots force in the PCI since the mid-1970s, (that is, since the local elections of 1975 and the general election of 1976). This development led to a certain institutionalization of the movement (with some feminist leaders taking on an active role within political parties and trade unions) and also to a situation in which parties were willing to take up feminist issues (as in the case of the abortion law and the sexual violence law).

A crisis in both the feminist movement and the welfare state became apparent from the late 1970s onward. It was a crisis that was all part of the breakdown of the previous equilibrium that had been achieved by the Italian political system. Between the murder of Aldo Moro by a terrorist group (1979) and the breakdown of the political system ruled by parties bargaining in a non-competitive democracy (1992), the world changed. From the late 1970s, the feminist movement began to undergo an internal and external crisis as a protest movement.[3] Within feminist groups women became more interested in making a change in lifestyle and cultural involvement than in independent political action (Boccia 1987). This approach has led to the formation of hundreds of groups involved in socio-cultural activities (which can be found in the large cities and smallest towns of north and central Italy, and, to a lesser extent, in the south). Women have founded companies which are concerned with social, historical and anthropological research – companies which serve local administrations as consultants in both the area of applied social research and also in the training of staff. In central and northern Italy, the culture of social services has often resulted in the direct political involvement of feminists in local administration: women have been present as a force in the civil service unions, as part of the intellectual workforce responsible for managing social services and as local political leaders.

Overall, one could say that since 1977 Italian feminism has been in difficulty because it affects political debate at the socio-cultural level rather than at the more effective decision-making level. It has independent voices in the cultural debate, but it does not act through independent pressure groups in the political arena. An example of these difficulties is provided by the discussion of the new law on sexual violence, which has raised the question of the inviolability of a person's physical integrity (the old norms only protected women in the name of 'public morality and decency'). This issue emerged within the feminist movement at the end of the 1970s, but the new rape law, passed in 1996, was entirely discussed and negotiated in parliament and among women MPs of various parties. Even after 1996, when the first government coalition formed by the PDS (formed from part of the former Communist Party) and the PPI (formed from part of the former Catholic party) established a Minister of Equal Opportunities, feminist groups do not seem to have had an independent voice in the political arena.

Since the beginning of the 1980s (Paci 1982; Ascoli 1984), financial difficulties have introduced two new themes into the policy debate on welfare state issues: the consideration of an optimal mix between the public and private, and the redefinition of social solidarity (Ascoli 1987; Paci 1989; Ferrera 1993). As a consequence, there seems to be an increasing expectation that families (that is, women) should take on most of the work load for the care of children and old people. The debate on social solidarity led to a new emphasis on family ties and on the central importance of the gift economy to the working of the system of social reproduction. Once more, it is assumed, at least implicitly, that women are the central agents in the work of social reproduction.

In the 1980s and 1990s, discussions on the need for and possible direction of family policies were taken up again (Comitato per l'anno internazionale della famiglia 1994). The merest mention (or non-mention) of 'the family' or 'families' in the drafting of a law or type of intervention triggered off heated arguments among the various political and cultural movements involved, even before the effects of the proposed measure could possibly be assessed. There are two underlying questions. First, which definition of the family should form the basis of policy? Second, how far should women be able to exercise independence with regard to reproduction and motherhood? The definition of family welfare politics depends on the answers to these two questions.

In the 1980s and 1990s, the issue of women's independence in reproduction (the possibility that women's choices could determine the legal and social choices on reproductive matters such as contraception, abortion or *in vitro* fertilization, irrespective of whether women are married or not) has been eclipsed by this new interest in the family. The debate over the family model that should underpin welfare policies was taken up again at the beginning of the 1980s. On family welfare, the main points under discussion were as follows: how to place greater responsibility on the family and which families should receive extra financial help; whether greater importance should be given to the family group than to the individual when deciding entitlements; and, lastly, whether caring activities should be considered as having economic value and, at the same time, whether women's employment should be seen as an individual 'choice' or as a right.

In this situation, the 1989 law proposed by the PDS on 'Women's Time and City Times' was an attempt to re-establish equal opportunities in an Italian welfare state based on family responsibilities. As proposed, both men and women would have been able to take leave from work for family reasons (either as parents or as providers of health care) without suffering a loss of income, seniority or pension entitlements. The aim was to make flexible use of time something that was guaranteed to all throughout their working life.

The law was not passed. Nevertheless, the reconciliation of 'urban times' is a specific issue in feminist political debate in Italy. The debate on 'city times' has been evolving since the mid-1980s in various settings and with the participation of a variety of social actors (Balbo 1991; Tempia 1993; Bimbi 1997c). Women's groups and associations, women in trade unions and several Commissions for Equal Opportunities have proposed a gender perspective on reconciling working hours and everyday life, paid and unpaid work, the demand for more time for personal relationships and the increasing importance of one's own time. The Consumers' Association together with entrepreneurial associations that have most contact with public administration, such as those of artisans, builders and traders, have formed pressure groups to change the way in which warring time is organized.

Belloni (1997), in her survey, found that the three main aims of this public action are as follows: to rationalize the complexity of the current organization of working time in urban areas (for example, Sunday opening for shops and varying the hours for secondary schools to reduce traffic); to introduce innovations in the opening hours of public services and implement flexible hours, especially in childcare services (for example, afternoon opening for front offices); and to get a fairer deal for working women through facilities for arranging their personal time (for example, special arrangements in the organization of office hours expressly to take the needs of mothers and their children into account).

The gender use of time was given particular consideration in the measures which were adopted by city councils in the first experiments during the 1980s (for example, shifts in school timetables, flexible hours in childcare services, the negotiation of opening hours between shop owners and their clients, and so on). Some nine regions (Tuscany, Valle d'Aosta, Emilia Romagna, Veneto, Liguria, Marche, Friuli-Venezia Giulia, Lazio and Piedmont) have approved a law on the 'city times' issue.

In 1997, City Time Programmes were registered in 80 Italian cities (Belloni and Bimbi 1997), including many regional capitals, such as

Rome, Milan, Venice, Turin, Aosta, Bolzano, Trieste, Genova, Bologna, Ancona, Perugia, Naples and Bari, but also Modena (the first city to launch a City Times Project), Pistoia, Fano (with a Children's Times Project) and Catania. A number of cities have opened special offices for adjusting the organization of time, and several have adopted special projects aimed at achieving equal opportunities and increasing women's participation in public and political life. Most of these schemes were put forward by women with positions of responsibility in city administrations; some of these offices are run by women.[4]

At the national level, the proposals for new laws concerning the regulation of 'city times' (Motherhood and Fatherhood in December 1994 and Time to Work, Time to Live in March 1995) have reopened the discussion on parental leave, suggesting explicitly that childcare be shared equally between mothers and fathers. Nevertheless, at the same time, the housewife movements have proposed (from 1996) different forms of insurance and pensions for housewives, or a 'mother's salary'.

Also, the specific issues raised by the debate on family policies have met with some tangible responses at the regional level (Bimbi 1997d). Between 1989 and 1995, six regions (Emilia Romagna, Trentino-Alto Adige, Friuli-Venezia Giulia, Liguria, Marche and Abruzzo) passed laws pertaining to family policy and others are under discussion. Some limit their scope to the families of married couples, but others, going beyond the terms of the constitution (Article 29), include families not founded on marriage. We can find at least three different models. The first favours the male-breadwinner regime by giving financial incentives to extend women's responsibility for care giving. The second model is directly pronatalist, giving financial support for new marriages and childbirth. The third aims to support family solidarity by extending individual rights and encouraging measures for redressing gender imbalance.

The third model, which combines Italian familism, institutional welfare and feminism, is to be found in the earliest of the laws on family policy, passed by the Emilia-Romagna region in 1989. Starting in the 1960s, this region was the first to undertake a systematic attempt at, and partially to achieve, institutional welfare based on a comprehensive model of social citizenship. This type of experiment is of great interest because it arose in open contrast to the national model of welfare and has since become a reference point for other local experiments. There are two premises on which this law based its welfare interventions: the individual's freedom of choice in the field of sexuality and reproduction, and equal recognition of all family forms.

At the national level, the post of Minister for Social Solidarity was established in the 1990s. This minister is responsible for family policy and issues ranging from minors and young adults to the elderly and disabled, immigrants and the voluntary sector. However, the minister's department has no independent budget. In the 1996 law on the Promotion of Rights and Opportunities in Childhood and Adolescence,[5] proposed by Livia Turco, a PDS member and Minister of Social Solidarity and former President of the National Commission for Equal Opportunities, we can find the same themes as featured in the laws proposed on 'Women's Time' during 1989 and 1994–95. However, it is important to note that the Minister of Social Solidarity has been very careful to conduct a family policy by seeking the agreement of both Catholics and women's groups, especially on social assistance reform and on the issue of the sexual harassment of children.

The new Minister of Equal Opportunities, Anna Finocchiaro (a member of the PDS like Livia Turco), tried to inject into the political debate a representation of women that was more autonomous, in economic and institutional terms, of the family. A directive presented by the Minister for Equal Opportunities on 8 March 1997 contained notions, such as 'the integration of gender perspectives in government policies' and 'the promotion of a culture of gender differences', that challenged Catholic ideology. But the voice of the church is prominent in public debate as well as in private welfare provision. The search for a compromise has now shifted in the new centre-left political scenario, with different possible outcomes.

CONCLUSION

Sometimes, as in the new law on children's citizenship (1997), the family paradigm that the care of children is a woman's responsibility seems to be challenged. Sometimes, as with the proposition of a reform of social assistance and the pension system centred on family income (1993–97), the model of a familist regime or of a male-breadwinner regime (as with the 1996–97 law proposals on housewife benefits) seems to gain ground. Against this background, open political debate about the nature of the family and responsibly for the care of children becomes difficult or disruptive of the political balance, especially since church organizations are seeking to introduce a change in the abortion law. The Catholic Church claims that legislation on the family and reproduction should conform strictly to its doctrines and exerts pressure to this end

(Congregazione 1987). However, the influence of the Catholic Church on the political system seems to be stronger than its ability to affect the behaviour of the individual.

Moreover, since the end of the 1980s, on questions of abortion (Quintavalla and Raimondi 1989) and bioethics (Ventimiglia 1988; Pizzini 1992; Comitato di Nazionale Bioetica 1994; 1995), the left has taken the position of the Catholic Church more into account. The rights of the unborn child (championed at a European level by those Italian MEPs who belong to the Movement for Life) have been upheld in a 1989 document issued by the Council of Europe. In 1996, the pro-life movements presented a bill giving rights to the unborn child from the moment of conception and opening the way to a possible revision of the abortion law. At the PDS National Congress (February 1997) a motion against this proposal was approved and signed by a group of women politically close to the Minister for Equal Opportunities. Both the Leader of the PDS and the Minister of Social Solidarity criticized this motion, the former referring to 'the individual's freedom of conscience' on this issue and the latter fearing that this document could create difficulties in the political debate on family welfare policies.

The embryo statute (Comitato di Nazionale Bioetica 1996) and abortion reveal all the ambiguities and uncertainties typical of the current state of affairs of women's issues in Italy. It seems, then, that by the middle of the 1990s, nearly 50 years after the Constituent Assembly, the debate on family welfare policy was finally underway. Nevertheless, we do not know if it is possible to separate the debate on family welfare from the one on the nature of the family and on a woman's right to choose. The latter appears to pose a threat to the new political balance.

Since 1960, what constitutes family policy in Italy has been a collection of unconnected decisions reflecting a series of compromises, primarily, but not exclusively, between the PCI as the guarantor of industrial working-class interests and the DC whose Catholic base contained a number of different ideological strands. However, Italy has now begun to address questions that have been an ongoing debate elsewhere at a time of financial restraint, when there is little room to use public resources to mobilize support.

Italy is a useful case in that it illustrates that it is possible to undertake important innovations in welfare policies without any significant changes in the dominant modes of representation of the care of children and on the gender division of labour. However, it also demonstrates that there are limits to what the policies may achieve without a change in representational forms. Moreover, Italy also illustrates that political and institutional structures may present important constraints on the space or opportunities available for challenging conventional forms of representation. The irony is that just as those structures collapsed in the 1990s to allow for a debate about the new gender division of labour and the care of children, the state is limiting its sphere of intervention and its spending on social policies.

At the same time, the debate on the nature of the family and women's choices seems to be reopening deep political conflict following the discussions of the Constituent Assembly and the changes of the 1970s. The possibility of new paradigms on women's roles and the family seems to risk sparking serious conflicts in the centre-left government and within parliament, while the arguments for family policies could present an opportunity for the redrawing of the boundaries of the conflict, even if it is tempered by the constraints on social spending and the continued difficulties of challenging the familial paradigm of women's responsibility as care givers. The result may be a change in the dominant paradigms, but also a challenge to the policy gains that had been made in the previous two decades.

## NOTES

1. Italian demographic trends show that traditional behaviour coexists with dramatic change (Livi Bacci 1980; Golini 1994). The fertility rate is among the lowest in the world. In 1991, the fertility rate per woman was 1.3, giving a birth rate of 9.9 per 1,000 inhabitants. Nevertheless, abortions are decreasing. In 1991, they were 10.0 per 1.000 among never-married women and 14.0 per 1,000 for married women, while births outside wedlock are relatively few among all age groups, despite the fall in the age at which teenagers first have sexual intercourse. For the most part, in Italy, children are born within wedlock, even when they are conceived before the wedding takes place. In 1991, children born out of wedlock accounted for 6.6 per 1,000 births, almost five times less than in the UK and France, and seven times less than in Denmark. Given that the divorce rate is the lowest in the European Union and that the number of divorces and separations is rising slowly, there are relatively few lone mothers. In 1991, the divorce rate per 10,000 inhabitants was 3.0 and the separation rate was 6.0. In 1990, lone-parent families accounted for ten per cent of the total number of families, but this figure falls to 5.5 per cent if we consider only those with children under the age of 18. The only feature they have in common with lone-parent families in other countries is the great predominance of lone mothers (82.9 per cent) over lone fathers. Lone-mother families are 5.9 per cent of families with children under the age of 18. In Italy, cohabitation rarely occurs and when it does, it is very often for a limited period prior to marriage and seldom involves the birth of children. Between 1983 and 1990, the percentage of unmarried couples remained steady at about 1.3 per cent of the total number of families.

2. We have to remember that, at the end of the Fascist regime, the birth of the Italian Republican Constitution was based on the alliance between the two most important political forces: the Communist Party and Christian Democracy. Nevertheless, they have had opposite views on family definition and on women's role in the family and in the labour market, at least until 1964. The constitution represents, at the same time, a compromise on the political system and on family matters. The constitutional compromise obliges the political system to undertake a continuous bargaining on family policies and on women's issues because of the necessity to maintain constitutional principles and, at the same time, to find agreement on specific issues, which arise from different social pressures. From 1964 (Bimbi 1977), for fear of anti-authoritarian views on family relations, the PCI started to move away from the orthodox Marxist perspective of Engels on family dissolution and to open up to a catholic view concerning the nature of family values. Over this same period, the importance of social reformism has increased across a broad range of issues (in the church, unions and political parties). These changes affected political bargaining and are reflected, explicitly or implicitly, in welfare legislation.

3. This crisis has the same roots for all social movements (Melucci 1984; 1985) and is due to the difficulty of transforming the role played in the protest cycle of a new identity, that would be necessary to maintain, at the same time, a distance from the political system and the capacity for bargaining with political institutions. In Italy, the conflict between state and terrorism brought the 1970s reformist era to a close, at a time when changes in the 'family paradigm' were just beginning.

4. An outstanding example is the project in Venice, where the Women's Centre, a Council institution, has had an important role (Basaglia 1997). The centre offers various services: a library on women's studies, an Anti-Violence Centre, a Research Centre on women's work, and the National Archive for 'City Times' projects. Some 30 women's groups organize their activities there, forming pressure groups acting on the local administration. In 1994, Venice Council started a project called Women's Citizenship and Urban Life Quality, initiated by the new centre-left administration. Since then, the project has worked in two main areas involved in changes in time organization: the front offices of public services and the Women's Centre itself. The project has succeeded in changing the opening hours of front offices without either increasing employees' working hours (36 hours per week) or overall office hours (36 hours per week). All the front offices of public services in the Venice Municipality have changed their public opening times, while also gradually increasing them to a total of 15 hours out of 36. Up to 1993, front offices were almost always closed to the public in the afternoon and often shut very early for lunch (at 12.30 p.m.). Several aspects are worthy of special attention. Afternoon opening has made offices more accessible to the public; moreover, the reorganization of office hours has improved the possibility of women employees reconciling paid and unpaid work. The Women's Centre represents the core of the change: first, because the opening hours have been extended to their maximum and, second, because the women who work there have negotiated their individual hours of work on the basis of their requirements for time for themselves and for their family needs. In 1998, Venice Municipality decided to bolster this project by creating a new Deputy Major on Equal Opportunity.

5. This law, passed in 1997, recognizes the link between children's rights and equal opportunity issues for women. It is the first law on social welfare reform after the 1971 laws on maternity leave and crèches. It is also important to note the presence of an implicit federalist principle, recognizing the competency of metropolitan cities (such as Venice, Milan, Naples, Turin, Bologna and so on) for the direct management of social spending programmes.

## REFERENCES

Ascoli, U. (ed.) (1984): *Welfare State all'italiana*. Bari: Laterza.

(1987): *Azione volontaria e Welfare State*. Bologna: Il Mulino.

Balbo, L. (ed.) (1991): *Tempi di vita. Studi e proposte per cambiarli*. Milano: Feltrinelli.

Basaglia, A. (1997): 'Attenzione al genere, orari dei servizi e tempi delle donne'. In M. C. Belloni and F. Bimbi (eds.), *Microfisica della cittadinanza. Città, genere, politiche dei tempi*, pp.273–77. Milano: Angeli.

Beccalli, Bianca (1985): 'Le politiche del lavoro femminile: donne, sindacati e Stato tra il 1974 e il 1984'. *Stato e Mercato*, 15, pp.78–92.

Belloni, M. C. (1997): 'Le politiche dei tempi della città'. In M. C. Belloni and F. Bimbi (eds.), *Microfisica della cittadinanza. Città, genere, politiche dei tempi*, pp.28–138. Milano: Angeli.

Belloni, M. C. and F. Bimbi (eds.) (1997): *Microfisica della cittadinanza. Città, genere, politiche dei tempi*. Milano: Angeli.

Bettio, F. and P. Villa (1993): 'Strutture familiari e mercati del lavoro nei paesi sviluppati. L'emergere di un percorso mediterraneo per l'integrazione delle donne nel mercato del lavoro'. *Economia e lavoro*, 2, pp.3–25.

Bimbi, F. (ed.) (1977): *Dentro lo specchio*. Milano: Mazzotta.

(1993): 'Gender, "gift relationship" and the welfare state cultures in Italy'. In J. Lewis (ed.), *Women and Social Policies in Europe. Work, Family and the State*, pp.138–69. London: Edward Elgar.

(1997a): 'Lone mothers in Italy: a hidden and embarrassing issue in a familist welfare regime'. In J. Lewis (ed.), *Lone Mothers in European Welfare Regimes. Shifting Policy Logics*, pp.171–203. London: Jessica Kingsley.

(1997b): 'La cura dei bambini come bene sociale. Una prospettiva europea delle politiche familiari'. In C. Baraldi and G. Maggioni (eds.), *Cittadinanza dei bambini e costruzione sociale dell'infanzia*, pp.117–40. Urbino: Edizioni Quattro Venti.

(1997c): 'Senso civico ed interpretazioni delle città. Politiche dei tempi e cittadinanza delle donne'. In M. C. Belloni and F. Bimbi (eds.), *Microfisica della cittadinanza. Città, genere, politiche dei tempi*, pp.15–27. Milano: Angeli.

(1997d): 'La debolezza delle politiche familiari in Italia: un caso di federalismo mancato?' In F. Bimbi and A. Del Re (eds.), *Genere e democrazia. La cittadinanza delle donne a cinquant'anni dal voto*, pp.193–216. Torino: Rosemberg & Sellier.

Bimbi, F. and V. Della Sala (1998): 'L'Italie. Concertation sans représentation'. In J. Jenson and M. Sineau (eds.), *Qui doit garder le jeune enfant? Modes d'accueil et travail des mères dans l'Europe en crise*, pp.173–202. Paris: L.G.D.J.

Boccia, Maria Luisa et al. (eds.) (1987): 'Il Movimento Femminista degli anni '70'. *Memoria*, 19/20, special issue.

Caciagli, M. and A. Spreafico (eds.) (1990): *Vent'anni di elezioni in Italia. 1968–1987*. Padova: Liviana.

Calabrò, A. R. and L. Grasso (eds.) (1985): *Dal Movimento Femminista al femminismo diffuso*. Milano: Angeli.

Comitato per l'anno internazionale della famiglia (1994): *Per una politica familiare in Italia*. Roma: Dipartimento Affari sociali, Presidenza del Consiglio dei Ministri.

Comitato Nazionale per la Bioetica (1994): *Parere sulle tecniche di procreazione assistita. Sintesi e conclusioni*. Roma: Presidenza del Consiglio dei Ministri.

(1995): *La fecondazione assistita. Documenti*. Roma: Presidenza del Consiglio dei Ministri.

(1996): *Identità e statuto dell'embrione umano*. Roma: Presidenza del Consiglio dei Ministri.

Congregazione per la dottrina della fede (1987): *Il rispetto per la vita umana nascente e la dignità della procreazione*. Milano: Edizioni Paoline.

De Grazia, V. (1992): *How Fascism Ruled Women 1922–1943*. Berkeley: University of California Press.

De Sandre, P. et al. (1997): *Matrimonio e figli: tra rinvio e rinuncia*. Bologna: Il Mulino.

Ergas, Y. (1986): *Nelle maglie della politica*. Milano: Angeli.

Fargion, V. (1998): *Geografia della cittadinanza sociale in Italia*. Bologna: Il Mulino.

Ferrera, M. (1993): *Modelli di solidarietà*. Bologna: Il Mulino.

Franchi G., B. Mapelli and G. Liprando (1987): *Donne a scuola*. Milano: Angeli.

Gauthier, A. H. (1995): *The State and the Family. A Comparative Analysis of Family Policy in Industrialized Countries*. Oxford: Oxford University Press.

Golini, A. (ed.) (1994): *Tendenze demografiche e politiche per la popolazione. Terzo rapporto IRP*. Bologna: Il Mulino.

Guizzardi, Gustavo (1982): 'Famiglia e secolarizzazione. La caduta di due sacralità'. *Città e Regione*, 4, pp.72–84.

Livi Bacci, M. (1980): *Donna, fecondità e figli*. Bologna: Il Mulino.

Melucci, A. (ed.) (1984): *Altri codici*. Bologna: Il Mulino.

(1985): *L'invenzione del presente*. Bologna: Il Mulino.

Paci, M. (1982): 'Onde lunghe nello sviluppo dei sistemi di Welfare'. *Stato e Mercato*, 6, pp.152–69.

(1989): *Pubblico e privato nei moderni sistemi di Welfare*. Napoli: Liguori.

Pizzini, F. (1992): *Maternità in Laboratorio*. Torino: Rosemberg & Sellier.

Quintavalla, E. and E. Raimondi (eds.) (1989): *Aborto, perché?* Milano: Feltrinelli.

Saraceno, C. (1991): 'Redefining maternity and paternity: gender, pronatalism and social policies in Fascist Italy'. In G. Bock and P. Thone (eds.), *Maternity and Gender Policies*. London: Routledge.

(1994): 'The ambivalent familism of the Italian welfare state'. *Social Politics*, 1, pp.60–82.

(1998): *Mutamenti della famiglia e politiche sociali in Italia*. Bologna: Il Mulino.

Scabini, E. and P. Donati (eds.) (1988): *La famiglia 'lunga' del giovane adulto*. Milano: Vita e Pensiero.

Tempia, A. (1993): *Ricomporre i tempi*. Roma: Ediesse.

Togliatti, P. (1965): *L'emancipazione femminile*. Roma: Editori Riuniti.

Trifiletti, R. (1997): 'Politiche sociali in un'ottica di genere. Il caso italiano'. In F. Bimbi and A. Del Re (eds.), *Genere e democrazia. La cittadinanza delle donne a cinquant'anni dal voto*, pp.173–92. Torino: Rosemberg & Sellier.

Ventimiglia, C. (ed.) (1988): *La famiglia moltiplicata*. Milano: Angeli.

Welty, E. (1966): *Catechismo Sociale*. Torino: Edizioni Paoline.

# Social Rights of Women with Children: Lone Mothers and Poverty in Italy, Germany and Great Britain

## ELISABETTA RUSPINI

### INTRODUCTION: THE PECULIARITIES OF THE ITALIAN CASE

The aim of this article is to focus on the circumstances that explain lone mothers' poverty in Italy. In order to appreciate its peculiarities, the study of the Italian case will be developed comparatively by taking into account two other European examples, Germany and Great Britain, which are both characterized by strong diversities in their resource-distribution systems (family, labour market and welfare) and by a different form of female economic deprivation.

My basic assumption is that the structural causes of female poverty are to be found in the interaction between economic disadvantages in the labour market, welfare state institutions and domestic households. The sexual division of labour which assigns to women a primary role (largely hidden and unpaid) in the private domestic sphere and a secondary position in the labour market is reflected in the private, occupational and the public systems of welfare provision, so that the inequalities which women experience in paid work are mirrored in their different access to, and levels of, income-replacement benefits (Glendinning and Millar 1991: 32).

For the study of poverty, the Italian case is a very peculiar one. Italy shows one of the highest levels of unemployment in Europe; the peculiarity of the Italian unemployment model lies in the high incidence of unemployment among young people,[1] among women,[2] and in the concentration of unemployment in the southern regions of the country. In Italy, in fact, a deep north-south economic cleavage exists. Among southern families, the traditional male-breadwinner regime prevails, marked by the very limited presence of women in the labour market and high male unemployment (CIPE 1996). Lastly, among women, long-term unemployment is extremely high.[3]

Such labour-market characteristics interact with the Italian welfare state model, which is characterized by a strong heterogeneity of social policies (due to an ambiguous decentralization). This has led to a consolidation of 'local citizenship systems' (Negri and Saraceno 1994). Social policies are divided into three sectors: social security and pensions for insured workers (old-age, invalidity, survivors, unemployment and sickness benefits); health (on a universal basis); and welfare allowances, aimed at guaranteeing sufficient resources. High fragmentation in employment (especially in the area of pensions) coexists with universal coverage in the health sector. Social protection services overlap and intersect since they are administered by a number of different agencies, such as the Ministry of Labour, Ministry of Health and Ministry of the Interior, the National Social Welfare Institute (INPS) and regional and municipal authorities (*Regioni, Province, Comuni*) (Simoni 1996). Following Bimbi (1996), the Italian local welfare system may be seen as an attempt at a federalist administrative model with no national coordination and few certainties regarding the rights of citizens. Even provincial and local authorities within the same region have developed different criteria and means tests for the allocation of benefits and services. Moreover, the existing north-south economic dualism is mirrored in the characteristics of the Italian welfare state: concerning social assistance, if in most southern regions an 'archaic' system of poverty relief is dominant, the centre-north is characterized by a modern system of social services (Fargion 1997). Within this context, even if the effort of classifying the Italian welfare state has generated interesting results, such classifications are inadequate to an understanding of its profound heterogeneity.[4]

The third and most crucial element necessary to understand poverty in Italy is the family. Despite its weakening, the family in Italy is still a strong institution: even if the fertility rate in Italy is among the lowest in the world (1.22 in 1996) (Ditch *et al.* 1996: 4), births out of wedlock are relatively few among all age groups; the divorce rate is the lowest in the European Union and the number of divorces and separations is rising only slowly. Thus the family in Italy constitutes a safety net against poverty and social exclusion. The network of social relationships between the extended family, kin and neighbourhood represents an indispensable resource: protection against poverty is, in fact, based on personal connections, affective links, networks of exchange and a non-cash economy. Within the family, women add a great volume of non-market work that helps families to cope with the lack of resources that may come from unemployment or job instability (Laparra and Aguilar 1996).

The data used to analyse lone mothers' poverty dynamics are *household panel surveys*, the most suitable source of data for analysing movement into and out of poverty. The specific sources used were as follows:

- The *European Community Household Panel Survey* (ECHP) 1994[5]
- The *Bank of Italy Survey of Household Income and Wealth* (SHIW) 1989, 1991, 1993, and 1995
- The *British Household Panel Survey* (BHPS) 1991–95, and
- The public version of the *German Socio-Economic Panel* (GSOEP) 1991–95.[6]

The choice of countries was based both on the availability of panel data and on the estimates of the number of lone mothers. According to the 1995 *Labour Force Survey* (Eurostat 1996a), it is possible to divide European countries on the basis of the proportion of lone mothers as a percentage of all families with children under 15: in the UK, 16.2 per cent; in Finland, 11 per cent; in Germany, France, Belgium and Austria, seven to nine per cent; in The Netherlands and Ireland, six to seven per cent; and in Portugal, Italy, Greece and Spain: two to five per cent (see Table 1).

TABLE 1
LONE PARENTS AND LONE MOTHERS AS A PERCENTAGE OF HOUSEHOLDS
WITH CHILDREN UNDER 15 YEARS, 1995

|                 | Lone parents | Lone mothers |
| --------------- | ------------ | ------------ |
| Austria         | 8.3          | 8.0          |
| Belgium         | 8.5          | 7.5          |
| Denmark         | n.a.         | n.a.         |
| Finland         | 12.1         | 1.1          |
| France          | 8.9          | 7.9          |
| Germany         | 9.7          | 8.8          |
| Greece          | 3.1          | 2.7          |
| Ireland         | 6.7          | 6.3          |
| Italy           | 3.9          | 3.2          |
| Luxembourg      | 5.6          | 3.7          |
| The Netherlands | 6.8          | 6.3          |
| Portugal        | 4.4          | 4.2          |
| Spain           | 2.0          | 1.9          |
| Sweden          | n.a.         | n.a.         |
| UK              | 17.6         | 16.2         |
| EU (15)         | 8.8          | 8.0          |

*Source*: Eurostat, 1996, table 114.

The structure of the present article is as follows. In the next section, I argue for the relevance of a study on lone mothers' poverty. In the third and fourth sections, I discuss some relevant methodological issues: the definition of lone mothers and the 'measurement' of poverty. I then present some findings emerging from the cross-sectional and longitudinal analyses of ECHP, SHIW, GSOEP[7] and BHPS panel surveys. In the last section, I specifically discuss the dynamic dimension of poverty and welfare use among lone mothers for three European countries that have gathered longitudinal economic information from representative samples of their populations: Italy, Germany and Great Britain.

## WHY LONE MOTHERS?

Lone mothers represent a good analytical category for studying the relationship between the family, market and welfare state, and are a challenge to social policy. Their higher risk of poverty is heavily dependent upon the fact that they are unable to exit the condition of poverty through adequate opportunities to earn an independent income or to obtain higher social welfare and regular maintenance payments. From this standpoint, the kinds of state support lone mothers receive can be employed as a barometer of the strength or weakness of the social rights of women with families (Hobson 1994).

Lone mothers are particularly affected by the interaction of gendered processes within the family, the labour market and the welfare state. The difficulties they have to face within the labour market and the domestic sphere are multiplied if we take into account the fact that the institutional framework, originally conceived for a different kind of organization of family life, is not ready to respond to the problem of the single-parent family. Radical employment and demographic transformations are creating new tensions in the area of welfare state intervention, which is already troubled by fiscal and financial difficulties: in other words, there is, today, a growing tension between poverty and citizenship.

In the global context of European social policy, lone mothers are still an invisible subject (Bimbi 1996; Simoni 1996; Ruspini 1997d). First of all, few European policies directly target lone parents: lone mothers are usually integrated into the system of benefits and social services reserved for workers or organized on a universal basis. More specifically, lone parents may be recognized within policies targeted at broader groups: women, mothers, parents, low earners or poor people. On the one hand, they are integrated into the broader system of citizenship through paid work and, on the other, included within the categories of poor people living on the edges of the insurance system (inextricably linked and subordinated to labour-market participation). This reveals a different degree of inclusion within social policies: as proper breadwinners, as unpaid workers (mothers) or as a problematic category. They have therefore disappeared as a social group. Following Boujan (1995: 16, 17, 33), only half of the EU Member States have introduced specific allowances to meet the needs of lone-parent families[8] and the conditions for entitlement are sometimes very strict.[9] The amount of these allowances is often inadequate to cover the needs of one-parent families and payments are limited to a certain period of time.[10] In most Member States, it is still very difficult to obtain assistance in the areas of childcare, employment, vocational training and financial support.

Second, when lone mothers receive benefits directly, they are often hidden behind the rights of their children, although, in practice, the protection given to minors who live with lone mothers depends on the legal and social status of their mothers. The main reason why lone-parent families have been the focus of attention is the fact that they are mothers, that is, they are rearing children (Biuti, 1996). Nonetheless, lone mothers raise a far more complex issue: the fact that they have dependent children has to be linked to the time deficit they experience (they have to spend more time with their children, since the father is totally or partially absent), to their need to work more for the same income as two parents, and to the difficulties they face within the labour market due to caring responsibilities and the responsibility for childrearing.

Third, the existing European policies specifically addressed to lone parents are generally means-tested provisions,[11] that is, benefits reserved for the poorest. If these benefits ensure lone-mother families at least a minimum standard of living and access to various supplementary benefits and services if their income is low, it is my opinion that they have helped to maintain people living in a situation of precariousness rather than to integrate the excluded by shifting women's economic dependence from the family to the state. Their first major disadvantage is the contribution which the means-tested benefits make to the poverty trap. For example, according to Sainsbury (1996: 80), assistance benefits in the UK are characterized by both an unemployment and a poverty trap which affect the income of lone mothers. A feature of the means-tested Income Support scheme (on which lone mothers are heavily dependent) is the ineligibility of individuals in full-time employment, but not those in part-time employment. This regulation is one of several factors which may discourage women's full-time employment. Moreover, if these benefits are successfully withheld from those who do not qualify, they do not reach all those who may be entitled to them. Lastly, the third disadvantage is the impact on personal dignity: the primary fact to be proved is that the family is poor and the necessary inquiries (that have to be repeated at regular intervals) produce a much greater invasion of privacy than occurs with other forms of benefit (Brown 1988). All this implies that lone mothers are treated merely as a 'needy' category, even if they have the ability to participate fully in the labour market: the primary issue concerning lone mothers is how to improve their standard of living by reconciling work and family life. In sum, it seems social security systems have failed to take account of the reality of changes in household structures and women's work since existing measures do not recognize the complexity of women's lives and women's needs.

In the three settings chosen, the visibility of lone mothers as a social category is indeed very different. In Italy, due to the crucial role of the family, the welfare regime has no special reason to protect lone mothers, even if they may receive preferential treatment under more general provisions, such as nursery and childcare places. Although there is no national scheme of social assistance, family allowances treat lone parents slightly more generously than unmarried mothers, but only if they are workers or pensioners. As for tax benefits, only unmarried mothers and widows are considered lone parents and therefore favoured (Palomba 1992; Trifiletti, 1998). Following Bimbi (1996) and Bordin and Ruspini (1997), in Italy, there is a patchwork of local policies which are, for the most part, means-tested and aimed at minors or families in difficulty; these have developed since the second half of the 1970s and are provided by the *comune* (local council) or local health board. The *provincia* (local authority) is responsible for highly discretional and categorical policies, mainly financial assistance, to give support to unmarried mothers and children born out of wedlock – policies based on legislation to encourage population growth dating from the Fascist period. The outcomes for lone mothers in such a fragmentary welfare system are extremely varied. The amounts allocated vary to a great extent, as do the requirements for means-testing; priority categories may be different; benefits may be, to a greater or lesser extent, integrated with those of the local council or health board, or delegated to these institutions. Assistance is mainly aimed at unmarried mothers, whose children may or may not be acknowledged by the father. It is mainly the child, rather than the mother, who is considered to have the right to such benefits, although it is almost always the mother who actually receives them (Bimbi 1996).

In Germany, the protection offered to lone mothers is also weak. While German family policy is relatively generous, it is not particularly supportive of lone mothers. Following Boujan (1995), in Germany, there is no specific allowance for single parents as such, but a highly developed general income-support system instead. Lone parents on income support can get subsidies for the costs of childcare and kindergarten fees. The social assistance benefit level can be increased for a lone parent by 20 per cent for 'additional expenses' if rearing a child alone, but only if she or he has a child below the age of six or two children aged under 16 (Scheiwe 1994). The dominant approach of German public authorities to gender issues has long rested upon a conservative family policy in conjunction with social security schemes for workers and social security coverage for married or widowed housewives. The German system clearly relies on two assumptions: first, that transferring income to men is a sufficient guarantee of household well-being and, second, that household income will be distributed equally among members. Another characteristic feature is the importance of the family and voluntary support: in other words, the system presupposes that the family and, within the family, women are the greatest providers of welfare. There are a number of features that keep women with children out of the job market and favour a conservative division of family labour. For example, there is the inadequate full-time childcare facilities available to parents: most kindergartens are open only during the morning, and short school hours (lunch is not available at schools) impose heavy time constraints upon mothers (Scheiwe 1994). Parental leave legislation can also discourage mothers' employment, and, more generally, the German welfare state regime presupposes that unpaid (mainly female) care work abounds within the family (Lewis and Ostner 1994). As a consequence, the level of inequality is particularly high in the labour market, revealed by data on female labour-force participation, female-male ratios of hourly earnings and female-male ratios of unemployment rates (Norris 1987; OECD 1988).

The British welfare model is characterized by an emphasis on means-testing in the distribution of benefits. In Great Britain, lone parents are heavily dependent on Income Support. Following Millar (1998), about 1.1 million lone parents receive Income Support and 300,000 receive Family Credit (DSS 1997), both means-tested. Since 1992, Family Credit is granted to those working more than 16 hours a week, while the Income Support rules allow lone mothers to receive benefit without being required to seek paid work, until their youngest child reaches the age of 16.[12] Lone parents are entitled to a small increase in Child Benefit (that is, one-parent benefit, which is not means-tested and was worth £6.05 a week per family in 1994) and the 'lone parent premium', an additional sum paid to lone parents in receipt of Income Support. Both measures have been abolished for new lone parents by the Labour government. Benefits for lone parents cost about £10 billion in 1996/97, equivalent to about ten per cent of total benefit expenditure (Millar 1998). The British welfare system makes no formal commitment to the protection of the family as an institution (Daly 1995). Britain has institutionally refrained from developing explicit family policies, that is, policies designed to achieve specified, explicit goals regarding the family, such as day care, child-protection services, family counselling, family planning and family life education (Kamerman and Kahn 1978). Family policy has barely figured historically in public discourse or in the programme of political parties: the UK does not have a Ministry for the Family and has no Department of Family Affairs; it has never pursued a pronatalist policy or a policy designed to encourage or discourage women with children as regards employment (provisions with regard to maternity leave and childcare are kept at a very low level, the argument being that they fall outside government responsibility); and it has never made any attempt to favour one form of family over another (Chester 1994: 271–2; Gauthier 1996: 204; Bradshaw 1996: 97–8). Britain offers very poor public day-care services at high cost, a characteristic that increases the burden of unpaid caring work. As a consequence, lone mothers face with greater difficulties the double economic bind of assuming complete responsibility for children's care while attempting to make up for lost income. For this reason, Great Britain is one of the few European countries where lone mothers are less likely to be economically active or employed than mothers in general.

## LOOKING FOR LONE MOTHERS: A DIFFICULT IDENTIFICATION

Researching lone parenthood is not an easy task. Two major problems complicate research on lone mothers, especially in terms of a comparative perspective:

- The lack of a standard definition of a single-parent household and its implications for the empirical study of lone mothers' poverty, and
- The poor availability of suitable data sets for the study of lone-parent families, a crucial element for the analysis and understanding of their socio-economic situation (Bradshaw 1998).

Lone parenthood is a status that people come into in a variety of ways (Millar 1989). There are many routes of entry into lone parenthood: divorce, long-lasting separations, desertion, death of a partner and the birth of a child outside marriage. There are also different routes out: marriage, remarriage, cohabitation, placing children for adoption and children growing up and leaving home. Thus, the phenomenon of lone parents is not homogeneous across cultures and regions: lone parents can vary substantially by age, number and age of children, activity status and living arrangements. Due to the variety of transitions to lone parenthood, there is no internationally recognized definition of a lone parent and within most Member States there is no standard definition either. As a consequence, the definition of a lone-parent household can differ quite substantially between European countries. As Roll (1992) has discussed, the most ambiguous elements are related to the marital status of the parent, the family's household situation and the definition of a dependent child.

The lack of a standard definition makes it quite difficult accurately to identify lone parents and count their number, especially in a cross-national perspective. Closely connected with the lack of a standard definition, then, are the complications that emerge while trying to identify and count the number of lone parents.

In research terms, we have plenty of information about lone mothers at the national level, although this is not always fully comparative. Available estimates are usually based on a combination of heterogeneous sources: census data, data from social surveys and administrative statistics. As Millar (1989: 7) has pointed out, information based on both administrative and social survey sources has some drawbacks. Administrative statistics are strongly affected by heterogeneous definitions, while survey data, if more flexible, suffer from both non-response and small sample sizes. Moreover, surveys do not always allow a simple identification of lone-parent families, since the family composition variable needed to identify them is not always available and often varies to a great extent.

Focusing on poverty, the comparative estimates available may be out of date or only available for a small range of countries or insufficiently detailed (Bradshaw *et al.* 1996). If, broadly speaking, much previous research has been insufficiently sensitive to the range of possible factors which might explain the gender characteristics of poverty trajectories, this is particularly true for lone parents.

In my case, the identification of lone-parent families demanded a very complex methodological procedure. This is due to the complexity and diverse organization of the national panel data sets I used: different topics, levels of information, storage formats, file structures, naming conventions and time between data collections.[13]

Without harmonized databases, it is extremely difficult to perform cross-national comparative studies on panel data. To be more precise, only the ECHP, BHPS (Great Britain) and GSOEP (Germany) data sets contain a defined family-composition variable (even if with substantial differences), while SHIW (Italy) allows the identification of lone parents only through a combination of the following variables: the respondent's position within the household, links with the head of the household or reference person or respondent, and the presence of children within the household.

Moreover, as Barnes, Heady and Millar (1998) have discussed, there is the danger that the family composition variable offered (ECHP, BHPS and GSOEP data) does not pick up all multi-household lone-parent families due to the method of data collection employed. The definitions use information on personal characteristics in relation to the head of the household and therefore, by definition, to register as a lone-parent household that household must have a lone parent as the household head. However, in some cases, the lone parent may not be the head of the household. In larger households, unmarried lone mothers may live with their parents, one of whom would be regarded as the household head and the lone mother would not be picked up in the definition. Consequently, the household would not be defined as a lone-parent household.[14]

Furthermore, the definition of a 'dependent child' was highly problematic. To be more precise, I adopted the following definitions:

- For the ECHP, a dependent child was defined as a cohabiting child no older than 16 years[15]
- In the BHPS (UK), a dependent child has been defined for use in derived variable construction as one aged under 16, or aged 16–18 and in school or non-advanced further education, not married and living with a parent
- For the GSOEP (Germany), a dependent child was defined as a cohabiting child no older than 16 years, or older and in school, not married and living with a parent, and
- For the SHIW (Italy), as a cohabiting child of any age without a personal income from labour.

The reason for this methodological choice is linked to the fact that widowhood is a common marital status among Italian lone mothers

(Zanatta 1996). Children tend to stay at home until they get married and are maintained by the family so long as they stay (Bimbi 1991; De Sandre 1988; 1991). As a consequence, the number of very young lone mothers is still extremely low in Italy. It is therefore extremely difficult to identify lone mothers with dependent children by referring only to the legal age of 18 years. In order to avoid the oversampling of widows, I restricted my subsample of Italian lone mothers to those not older than 65 years.

Consequently, the definition of a lone parent I used in this study is not fully homogeneous and therefore the sample presents some diversities: a lone parent is defined as a person not living in a couple (either married or cohabiting), who may or may not be living with others (their own parents or friends, in order to take into account the phenomenon of lone-parent households) and who is living with at least one of her or his dependent children.

In order to overcome such difficulties, a greater comparability of data on social and economic conditions is required. But comparability can be achieved only through standardized design and common technical and implementation procedures. The European Community Household Panel (Europanel) represents a unique and essential source of information: it is a comparable, multidimensional panel survey between participating countries of the European Union. It was launched in response to the increasing demand in the EU for comparable and longitudinal information across the Member States on the following topics: income, work, employment, poverty and social exclusion, housing and health. Unfortunately, access to Europanel data is still quite restricted. At the moment, only micro-data files relating to three countries (Ireland, Portugal and the UK) can be transmitted centrally by Eurostat. Other countries (Germany, Spain and France) restrict access to those with a specific contract. Therefore, some parts of the data set are easily available to the user and some others can only be accessed within the Eurostat secure area. Furthermore, only the first batch of data (1994) is available for all EU countries (with the exception of Austria, Finland and Sweden) (Eurostat 1996b).

## THE DEFINITION OF POVERTY

The concept of poverty is ambiguous, and therefore difficult to define and to measure. Over the years, the concept of poverty has changed and developed in order to adapt to changing cultural and socio-economic circumstances.

Poverty is now a relative, multidimensional, dynamic phenomenon. Poverty is also a gendered phenomenon: gender is a significant differentiating factor for poverty, since the differences in the incidence and evolution of economic deprivation between the sexes are evident (Ruspini 1997a; 1997b; 1997c).

If the structural causes of female poverty are to be found in the interaction between economic disadvantages in the labour market, welfare systems and domestic household, then a new and more flexible conceptualization of the phenomenon is necessary. Women's deprivation cannot be understood and tackled using the classic instrument that belongs to the policy based upon the view that poverty is a static, permanent, gender-neutral phenomenon (that is, an 'either-or' state, with people considered to be poor or not poor). In other words, if a new operational definition of poverty is necessary, its gendered nature cannot be 'captured' in the absence of a gender-sensitive methodological approach.

It is my conviction that our insight into processes of social change can be greatly enhanced by making more extensive use of panel data. The basic feature of the panel design is the possibility of detecting and establishing the nature of individual change. Thus, I will catch the dynamic aspect between poverty and gender. The dynamic aspect of poverty is important since economic deprivation may be a persistent condition for some households, but only temporary for others. As Brueckner (1995) has pointed out, a life-course approach may serve to debunk empirically the old adage 'Once poor, always poor', since many people are only sometimes poor. The 'mobility' within poverty is, in fact, higher for women than men (Ruspini 1997a; 1997b; 1997c).

Within this context, the issue related to the identification of the poor is particularly relevant. Following Mingione's arguments (1996: 4), the poor can be identified in two ways. The first method, and the most widely used for comparative analysis, is to take the households of individuals living below the poverty line. The second method, less used due to the obvious difficulty of comparing highly diversified conditions of welfare provisions, is to consider as poor those individuals assisted by specific welfare programmes. Both methods are at the same time useful but inaccurate. The measurement of poverty on the basis of the possession of monetary resources is biased by the fact that it systematically overestimates the poor individuals and groups who can count on hidden resources or who have needs well below the average, or both. Conversely, it underestimates poverty in urban areas, where the average cost of living is higher. Identification of the poor with welfare clients also has some grave limitations, since welfare programmes are diversified and variously selective; for example, the institutional fragmentation of the Italian social security system makes such an approach difficult to apply.

What I will now try to do is to analyse the phenomenon of poverty among lone mothers using both methods. The first approach to the measurement of poverty concentrates on income levels. In other words, I use an income approach to the measurement of poverty as a proxy for economic deprivation. The heart of my measure of family and individual economic status is total disposable family income.[16] If an income approach is used, then an adjustment in needs is important, since economies of scale may arise as a household increases in size. There is a considerable range of methods which can be used to derive equivalence scales and a large number of scales are used in OECD countries. In my case, the equivalence scale used to adjust family income according to the number of people in the household has been suggested by Buhmann et al. (1988) and Burkhauser, Smeeding and Merz (1994); its elasticity lies at around 50 per cent.[17] Taking into account that low equivalence factors tend to portray poor populations as primarily composed of older people and single younger people, and higher values of the equivalent factor shift the focus to families with two or more children, I have chosen an equivalence scale that occupies a middle position.[18]

I also need to define a threshold or poverty line to distinguish households and individuals who are poor from those are not. Since the concept of poverty is ambiguous, it is not possible to draw one unique and valid poverty line, below which all individuals or households are undeniably poor. Poverty lines can indeed be set by a great variety of alternative methods, which may be divided into budget methods, subjective methods, relative methods and political methods.[19] In my case, I have chosen a relative approach that defines income as 'low' and a subpopulation as 'poor' with respect to the income level of the population as a whole. The reference point, that is, the poverty line, is defined as 50 per cent of the median[20] household equivalent income: those below the 50 per cent line may be classified as 'poor'. I use this relative measure because I want to examine differences in poverty between men and women in the two countries relative to the common standard of living.

The second approach focuses on social assistance experiences among lone mothers: Sozialhilfe for Germany, Income Support for Great Britain and social assistance benefits in Italy.[21] As already discussed, welfare programmes can be strongly diversified and variously selective; therefore, the kind of assistance lone mothers receive also varies to a great extent.

## POVERTY AND WELFARE DEPENDENCY AMONG LONE MOTHERS

Using the 50 per cent poverty line, I obtained the poverty head-count ratios, that is, the number of poor single-parent households and married mothers reported in Table 2.

TABLE 2
POVERTY HEADCOUNT RATIOS* AMONG LONE MOTHERS AND
MARRIED/COHABITING MOTHERS, HOUSEHOLD INCOME, 1993, PERCENTAGES
(ABSOLUTE FIGURES IN PARENTHESIS)

|  | Lone mothers | Lone-mother heads of household | Married/ cohabiting mothers |
|---|---|---|---|
| Italy (ECHP data) | 8.9  (62) | 8.4  (34) | 3.9 (171) |
| Germany (GSOEP data) | 27.9  (46) | 30.3  (40) | 7.0  (83) |
| UK (ECHP data) | 39.8 (186) | 45.6 (168) | 9.4 (194) |

* *Poverty headcount ratios*: percentage/number of lone mothers and married mothers below the 50 per cent poverty line.
Data weighted using cross-sectional individual weights.

*Source*: Author's calculations from ECHP and GSOEP data.

We can observe from the data that a higher percentage of lone mothers fall below the level of 50 per cent of median household income in the UK and Germany than in Italy: 39.8, 27.9 and 8.9 per cent among lone mothers and 45.6, 30.3 and 8.4 per cent among lone-mother heads of household respectively. The interpretation of these figures is twofold. First, if we consider that being a head of the household can be an indicator of the fact that a lone mother is the only one responsible for the family's well-being, it is easy to understand that lone-mother heads of household are at greater risk of poverty. This is especially true in the British case. Second, lone mothers rely on family for support. Social networks of kin and friends can be materially very significant: they may provide lone mothers with economic and childcare support in contexts where provisions are scarcely available. In Italy, the fact that lone-mother

TABLE 3
USE OF WELFARE BENEFITS§ AMONG LONE MOTHERS AND
MARRIED/COHABITING MOTHERS, 1993, PERCENTAGES
(ABSOLUTE FIGURES IN PARENTHESIS)

| | Lone mothers | Lone-mother heads of household | Married/ cohabiting mothers |
|---|---|---|---|
| Italy (ECHP data) | 1.7  (12) | 1.7  (7) | 1.5  (68) |
| Germany (GSOEP data) | 17.3  (25) | 20.4  (24) | 1.5  (19) |
| UK (ECHP data) | 67.3 (314) | 73.3 (270) | 55.7 (1146) |

§ ECHP: The variable used to analyse dependency upon welfare support refers to the following question: 'Did your household receive, at any time during 1993, social assistance payments or corresponding non-cash assistance from the welfare office?'
§ GSOEP: The variable used to analyse dependency upon welfare support refers to the following question: 'Did your household receive any social assistance benefit in 1993?'

Data weighted using cross-sectional individual weights.

Source: Author's calculations from ECHP and GSOEP data.

heads of household seem not to be at a higher risk of poverty can be linked to protection provided by the family.

Concerning social assistance experiences, Table 3 clearly shows that lone mothers, if compared to married or cohabiting mothers, are more likely to be dependent on state support. The overrepresentation of lone mothers among welfare clients is very strong in the UK: 67.3 and 73.3 per cent. By contrast, in Italy, use of social assistance among lone mothers seems rare.

The poverty trap affecting British lone mothers is fearsome. In Britain, their position within the labour market is particularly weak: strong barriers face lone mothers entering the labour force, in particular, minimal assistance with childcare and high effective marginal taxes. Childcare facilities and services are indeed very poor compared to the vast majority of EU countries. For this reason, the expansion of female labour-force participation has involved a growth in financially disadvantageous part-time work relative to full-time work; part-time work has been increasing throughout the postwar period and the majority of part-timers are women.[22] This attitude reflects the need to balance work with domestic demands in the absence of explicit welfare support for families. The expense and paucity of institutional childcare in Great Britain makes its use a major disincentive to women seeking paid employment, and for this reason the availability of part-time work has been crucial in facilitating British women's increased lifetime work experience by enabling them to combine caring for children with employment (Robinson and Wallace, 1984; Humphries and Rubery, 1988: 94). This brings to light the problematic relationship between employment and the characteristics of social security schemes: a weak labour-market position generates low or no social security contributions and thus low or no benefits. The British welfare model is characterized by an emphasis on market-based social insurance: given the gendered access to income and wealth, market provisions inevitably tend to disadvantage women and highlight their dependence on men.

In Germany, the incidence of poverty and welfare dependence among lone mothers also seems quite high. German social security programmes may have succeeded in helping families cope with the economic consequences of work-related events such as unemployment or retirement, but families also have to come to terms with family-related events such as divorce and lone parenthood. The key factor lies in the interaction between deep-seated changes in the family (such as a the decline in nuptiality, an increase in separation or divorce and in non-marital unions, and an increase in births out of wedlock) and the German 'conservative' model. In Germany, women's entitlements are largely derived from their husband's rights. Following Scheiwe (1994), marriage is the necessary condition for access to survivor's benefits and cost-free sickness insurance for a financially dependent spouse. Cohabiting mothers or lone mothers who are not obligatorily insured for sickness insurance (those employed for less than 16 hours a week) face difficulties: voluntary insurance is possible, but rather expensive. The nature of the German welfare model emphasizes, on the one hand, labour-market integration (particularly for men) and, on the other hand, the role of the family (predominantly women) as the primary provider of welfare services (Langan and Ostner 1991: 136–7). In addition, Germany continues to provide incentives to the traditional gendered division of labour, particularly via its tax system, which is heavily weighted in favour of married and one-earner couples.

Regarding Italy, the interpretation of my results is twofold. First, it seems that lower lone mothers' poverty rates are to be found where the sheltering capacity of family, kin and voluntary organizations is strong. Second, due to the fact that family solidarity is still strong and that welfare programmes are less efficient and discriminatory, the extent of economic poverty may be more 'hidden' than in other countries. Many

Italian families may integrate a stable income (in many cases brought home by a male breadwinner), a lower and much more unstable income from part-time or irregular jobs (mainly by the wife) and even an income from a grandparent's old-age pension. This means that, even if pensions, unemployment benefits or wages are low, they may add up to an acceptable level of household or family income. The family, however defined at various stages of the life cycle, continues to be the primary system of social protection (Bimbi 1996): in other words, it fills the gaps left by the welfare state. Thus, the relatively low level of economic deprivation in Italy may be due to the fact that family solidarity is strong. The incidence of social assistance among lone mothers seems also to be very low: as Mingione (1996: 6) has discussed, the more efficient, generous and non-discriminatory a programme is, the more welfare clients there are and, consequently, the more poverty it discovers. This involves not only a question of information and efficiency, but also cultural bias, discrimination and stigmatization, which can discourage potential clients for reasons of pride.

## DURATION ANALYSIS OF POVERTY AND WELFARE USE

As I have already argued (Ruspini 1997a; 1997b; 1997c), one of the most interesting elements in the analysis of poverty is the duration of the poverty experienced.[23] Taking time into consideration seems to be an appropriate way to tackle the problem of economic deprivation in a gender-sensitive manner. In other words, an analysis of the dynamic dimension of poverty allows us to answer my leading question: how do lone mothers experience poverty?

As Walker and Ashworth have suggested (1994: 11, 21), duration analysis refers both to the length of the individual spells of poverty and to the total duration of poverty experienced over a given period.[24] These are important attributes of the personal experience of poverty, since time is not simply a further dimension over which poverty can be measured: it is, instead, the medium within which poverty occurs and shapes the experience of being poor. In fact, if long spells of poverty may be assumed to be worse than short ones, the welfare implications of a single spell of poverty lasting five out of ten years are not necessarily worse than five separate spells of one year.

Again using the 50 per cent threshold, I now ask whether poverty is long term or short term, that is, what proportion of the lone-parent population was never poor and what proportion was temporarily,

TABLE 4
DURATIONS OF POVERTY, 50 PERCENTAGE POVERTY LINE,
COLUMN PERCENTAGES

| | Lone mothers | Lone-mother heads of household | Married/ cohabiting mothers |
|---|---|---|---|
| *Italy (1989, 1991, 1993, 1995)* | | | |
| Never poor | 71.5 | 63.1 | 77.8 |
| Short-term poverty | 13.8* | 20.2 | 14.7 |
| Persistent poverty | 11.2* | 12.1 | 5.2 |
| Recurrent poverty | 3.5* | 4.6* | 2.3 |
| Northern and Central Italy | | | |
| Never poor | 80.2 | 69.4 | 89.7 |
| Short-term poverty | 17.7* | 25.8 | 9.1 |
| Persistent poverty | 2.1* | 4.8* | 0.5* |
| Recurrent poverty | – | – | 0.7* |
| Southern Italy | | | |
| Never poor | 62.0 | 58.2 | 65.2 |
| Short-term poverty | 9.4* | 15.8* | 20.7 |
| Persistent poverty | 21.2* | 17.7* | 10.1 |
| Recurrent poverty | 7.4* | 8.2* | 4.0 |
| *Germany (1991–1995)* | | | |
| Never poor | 56.2 | 50.7 | 75.7 |
| Short-term poverty | 23.4 | 24.7 | 14.2 |
| Persistent poverty | 11.2 | 14.9 | 4.4 |
| Recurrent poverty | 9.2 | 9.8 | 5.7 |
| *Great Britain (1991–1995)* | | | |
| Never poor | 29.8 | 28.7 | 69.3 |
| Short-term poverty | 26.6 | 23.2 | 17.6 |
| Persistent poverty | 19.0 | 20.2 | 5.5 |
| Recurrent poverty | 24.7 | 27.9 | 7.6 |

* Less than 10 cases
Definitions:
short-term poverty: a single spell of poverty lasting 2 years or less
persistent poverty: a single spell lasting at least 3 years
recurrent poverty: more than one spell of poverty
Data weighted using longitudinal individual weights

*Source*: Author's calculations from SHIW, GSOEP and BHPS data.

persistently and intermittently poor in the periods taken into consideration. I have restricted my analysis to the 'lone-mother heads of household' subsample, since they appear to be at greater risk from poverty.

Table 4 suggests that income mobility is rather high and that poverty is a permanent situation only for a minor part of the lone-mother population. If it is true that lone mothers' spells of poverty are longer than married mothers', most poverty among lone mothers appears to be temporary. Lone mothers whose income falls below the poverty line are poor only for a fairly short time, the majority between one and two years.

It can also be seen that only a minority are locked into poverty and can be defined as 'permanently poor'. In Great Britain, 19 per cent and in Germany and Italy 11 per cent of lone mothers have been persistently poor for at least three years. For heads of household, it is 20.2, 14.9 and 12.1 per cent respectively. Not surprisingly, in Italy, the incidence of lone mothers' persistent poverty in the northern and central part of the country and the southern regions differs to a great extent: 2.1 and 21.2 per cent respectively. These figures reflect Italy's strong economic dualism.

Table 4 also shows that spells of poverty are not often regular, and that a consistent number of lone mothers who have experienced economic deprivation for two or more years find themselves below the poverty line only intermittently. If, compared to married mothers, lone mothers are more vulnerable to persistent economic deprivation (that is, they stay poor longer in a single spell), they are also more 'mobile', that is, more likely to enter and exit poverty intermittently. Lone mothers' poverty mobility rate is, once again, particularly high in the British setting: the percentage of lone mothers suffering from recurrent poverty is 24.7 per cent for non-heads and 27.9 per cent for heads of households in comparison with Germany (9.2 and 9.8 per cent) and Italy (3.5 and 4.6 per cent).

Thus, it is in Great Britain that more lone mothers are at risk of longer and recurrent spells of poverty: the UK has a low parent labour supply, with low proportions working full time and with lower proportions of lone parents working than married women. In the UK, exclusion from work (or incomplete participation) is strongly linked to poverty, which, in fact, reaches one of the highest levels in the EU. Within the liberal model, the low profile taken by the state is due to the crucial role played by the market in social reproduction. Being unable to find a place on the labour market, or even finding a marginal position, immediately results in the individual suffering from social stigma: measures for social protection are only intended for those who are not part of the market at all. Moreover, public intervention is considerably less efficient in reducing the quota of the poor in the population as compared with other

European welfare states (Ditch *et al.* 1996). This incapacity is reflected in extremely high rates of poverty, especially for certain social categories and family typologies which are typically at a disadvantage at an employment level, either because they are not able to respect the rules of the market (women as breadwinners) or because they are no longer active (the elderly).

In Germany, the welfare state prefers to provide money-transfer programmes rather than services: therefore, despite its rehabilitative ideology, it does not encourage people to support themselves (Karr and John 1989; Langan and Ostner 1991: 136–7). The orientation is toward the coverage of market-related risks: women's rights to welfare is a function of their dependence on a male breadwinner. This is why lone mothers must work in order to support their families adequately: in fact, their labour-force participation is higher than that of married women (Kamerman and Kahn 1989). As I have already argued (Ruspini 1997a; 1997b), both the (West) German and the British welfare states have operated on a strong breadwinner logic, since the idea of a 'male breadwinner' and of a 'secondary' female wage earner was built into the welfare system and welfare provisions (Lewis and Ostner 1994; Daly 1995).

In Italy, there does not seem to be a wide gap between the duration of the poverty experience for lone mothers and married or cohabiting mothers. This can be explained by the fact that Italian lone mothers are more likely to work full time than married mothers. As Bimbi (1993: 146) has pointed out, a very important factor in explaining full-time female employment in Italy is the active solidarity of women belonging to different generations: for every young working woman there is at least one older woman (mother or mother-in-law) who may not live in the same household but who plays an active part in taking care of children. As a result, the help provided by a partner and by public or private services is less crucial (Guerrero and Naldini 1996). Relatively few lone mothers depend on men's incomes for support: maintenance payments from former husbands (but not those paid for children) are subject to taxation as are the derived pensions of widows and orphans. Moreover, in the case of separation or divorce, there is no assumption of responsibility (either by way of compensation or substitution) by the state to make up for the lack of fathers' maintenance. The Italian situation is thus a mixture of rapid modernization and traditional family relationships.

I now turn to the dynamics of social assistance experiences among lone mothers. Table 5 demonstrates that they too are relatively short

TABLE 5
DURATIONS OF WELFARE USE[1], COLUMN PERCENTAGES

| | Lone mothers | Lone-mother heads of household | Married/ cohabiting mothers |
|---|---|---|---|
| *Italy (1989, 1991, 1993, 1995)* | | | |
| No use | – | – | – |
| Short-term use | – | – | – |
| Persistent use | – | – | – |
| Recurrent use | – | – | – |
| | | | |
| *Germany (1991–1995)* | | | |
| No use | 81.1 | 75.4 | 93.2 |
| Short-term use | 9.4 | 12.3 | 4.7 |
| Persistent use | 7.7 | 10.1 | 1.4 |
| Recurrent use | 1.8[2] | 2.2 | 0.7* |
| | | | |
| *Great Britain (1991–1995)* | | | |
| No use | 32.4 | 32.9 | 81.4 |
| Short-term use | 17.3 | 14.0 | 10.3 |
| Persistent use | 36.5 | 37.3 | 4.6 |
| Recurrent use | 13.8 | 15.9 | 3.7 |

1 Welfare use: social assistance benefits (Italy), Sozialhilfe (Germany); Income Support (Great Britain).
2 Less than 10 cases.
Legend:
short-term use: a single spell of use lasting 2 years or less
persistent use: a single spell lasting at least 3 years
recurrent use: more than one spell of welfare use
Data weighted using longitudinal individual weights

*Source*: Author's calculations from SHIW, GSOEP and BHPS data.

term. Nevertheless, their duration tends to be much longer in Great Britain: 37.3 per cent of lone-mother heads of households receive social assistance payments for three years or longer. As already noted, benefits are mostly means-tested: British welfare is largely oriented toward a class of the poor dependent on the welfare state. Furthermore, levels of universal transfer payments and forms of social insurance are modest and stigmatized, since the model assumes that higher levels of benefit will reduce incentives to work.

The reason for the fact that no Italian lone mothers make use of welfare benefits can be related to the small size of the subsample derived from SHIW data (113 lone mothers), but also to the fact that the stigmatization of welfare dependants is still strong. As Saraceno (1994) has discussed, in Italy, women's economic dependency on the family is not seen as a social problem. On the contrary, the dependency of the family on welfare provisions is regarded as 'bad'. The hidden assumption is that the family, through the unpaid work of women, is the 'natural' main provider of welfare. One of the characteristic features of the Italian welfare model is indeed its 'familistic' nature, that is, the importance given to family and voluntary support. The familist tendency of welfare assistance is strongly connected with the fact that the Italian welfare regime is virtually inactive as regards family policies.

My findings are consistent with earlier evidence derived from research on single-parent families' experience of social assistance by Duncan et al. (1993). Patterns of social assistance across countries appear to be very different: receipts tend to be relatively short term in Germany and the USA, somewhat longer term in Canada and much longer in the UK. The proportion of lone parents still receiving social assistance after three years was 26 per cent in Germany, 38 per cent (within the black community) and 35 per cent (within the white community) in the USA, 58 per cent in Canada and 84 per cent in the UK (Duncan et al. 1993: 8–9).

CONCLUSIONS

To summarize, my main findings are as follows.

(1) My dynamic and comparative analysis of lone parents' deprivation shows that in all three settings taken into consideration lone mothers (especially if they are heads of the household) are at greater risk of poverty in comparison with married or cohabiting mothers. Lone mothers' spells of poverty are longer than married mothers', and the risk of permanent poverty among lone-mother families seems to be exceptionally high in Great Britain. Nonetheless, most poverty among lone parents appears to be temporary, that is, short term. These results may have significant implications for both social science and public policy, since much of the debate about lone mothers has reflected the presumption of their dependency on welfare: Charles Murray's major theme (1984) was that Aid to Families with Dependent Children (AFDC) in the USA had encouraged women to become lone parents and induced dependency. As I have already pointed out (Ruspini 1997a; 1997b; 1997c), the nature of poverty has been seriously misunderstood: if lone mothers' poverty and dependency on welfare have always been conceptualized as a long-term and persistent phenomena, then a new paradigm and new policies are

needed. The gendered and dynamic nature of economic deprivation requires, on the one hand, a new analytical framework and, on the other hand, particular policies able to reduce the risk of long-term poverty and to tackle repeated, short-term spells of poverty.

(2) Poverty dynamics across countries appear very different. In Italy, lone mothers are less likely to be poor, while in Germany and particularly in the UK, lone mothers are at greater risk of economic deprivation. In Italy, the family plays a crucial role: protection against poverty is based on personal connections, affective links, networks of exchange and a non-cash economy. Following Martin's argument (1996), in Italy, there is a specific arrangement between the family, labour market and the welfare state: the crisis in the system of social welfare produces a peculiar linkage between the other elements of the triad and, within this triad, it is the family that plays the most crucial role. The crucial role played by the family is twofold. First, it constitutes a safety net against poverty and social exclusion, and, second, as Ferrera (1996: 21) has stated, the southern family largely operates as a social clearinghouse by mediating the difficult relationship between a variegated labour market and a fragmented income-maintenance system. Italian familism masks the economic weakness of women (Bimbi 1996). As a consequence, data show a paradoxical combination of a high risk of poverty for women and a relatively limited degree of economic poverty in comparison with other EU countries. Thus, tackling female poverty cannot be restricted to monetary transfers: it needs adequate support from the family and social policies, since the intersection between market and non-market activities is the key factor in allowing a suitable interpretation of the gender dimension of deprivation.

(3) Empirical evidence stresses that Mediterranean countries form a separate cluster in the universe of welfare states, an element that requires further research. Italy belongs to the so-called Mediterranean welfare states (together with Greece, Spain and Portugal), a cluster of countries that comparative welfare research has generally neglected. Mediterranean countries have, in fact, been taken into account only recently and usually been treated as less-developed, rudimentary or defective welfare states. The implicit assumption is that these countries are only latecomers and will, sooner or later, 'adapt' to one of the existing models, an assumption that denies their peculiar characteristics and makes it difficult to understand their specific functioning. This

viewpoint requires substantial revision. On the one hand, Mediterranean countries do constitute a specific group: the politico-economic context is similar, the interaction between the family, labour market and the welfare state is a peculiar one and, within this particular interaction, the family plays a very crucial role. Kinship ties are very strong; children and parents live together for a long time; economic collaboration between households is still strong; and the degree of individualization of family members is low. In Italy, the absence of explicit family policies is compensated for by strong family solidarity: family and, within the family, women are 'invisible' but necessary and irreplaceable partners of Italian social policies. But, significant differences exist and the variation among the countries is much greater than that within other groups of nations, for example, Scandinavia (Ferrera 1997).

I will close with some relevant theoretical and methodological issues concerning research on lone motherhood and lone mothers' standard of living.

(1) There is a need for a debate on the implementation of suitable policies for lone mothers. This has two main aspects. First, should we implement specific policies and regard lone mothers as a special group with distinctive needs for which provisions should be made? If it is true that support for lone parents should not be separated from policies addressed to families with children, it is, however, also important to recognize and respond to the peculiarity of lone parents' needs: single parents suffer from a time deficit in comparison with a situation in which there are two parents. As Duncan and Edwards (1997) have suggested, lone mothers need both to work more for the same income as two parents and to spend more time with their children, due to the partial or total absence of the father.

Second, what kind of policies are the most suitable for lone mothers? Empirical evidence emerging from my research suggests that a key policy goal should be the implementation of measures aimed at reconciling work and family life.[25] As Bradshaw (1998) and Millar and Ford (1998) have pointed out, more radical measures to alleviate lone mothers' poverty are called for than the cash benefits that are already on offer. Policy should be integrated across the areas of employment, childcare, housing, income support and maintenance obligations. In other words, it is necessary to support and encourage lone mothers' capacity to be economically independent by sensibly and carefully linking labour-market and family policies, and not just to answer to their needs through a general anti-poverty strategy. A lone mother should be treated as a particular kind of woman, one who is both a mother and a worker, and whose ability to participate fully in the labour market should be encouraged and not stigmatized or discouraged.

(2) It is necessary to take into account the fact that lone mothers are not a homogeneous group and to interpret this heterogeneity and explain the variability. In particular, lone-mother heads of household are more vulnerable to economic deprivation.

(3) There is a necessity for further empirical and comparative research to shed light on the different mechanisms behind lone mothers' poverty.

(4) It is necessary to design suitable data sets for the study of lone-parent families.

(5) There is a need to analyse the peculiarities of lone parenthood within the Mediterranean group of nations.

## NOTES

1. In 1995, the unemployment rate reached 32.8 per cent among young people between 15 and 24 years of age. In particular, 29 per cent of young men and 37.6 of young women were unemployed (Eurostat 1996a).
2. The activity rate of Italian women is one of the lowest in Europe: 33.9 per cent in 1995.
3. In 1994, 59.6 per cent of unemployed men and 63.3 per cent of unemployed women were long-term unemployed (that is, without a job for no less than 12 months) (Eurostat 1995).
4. Recent years have seen the growth of many different ways of comparing welfare states in terms of typologies derived from variations in structural characteristics (see, for example, Jones 1985; Esping-Andersen 1990; Taylor-Gooby 1991; Castles and Mitchell 1991, 1993; Bradshaw et al. 1993; Ferrera 1993; Leibfried 1993; Lewis and Ostner 1994; Siaroff 1994; Wennemo 1994; Gustaffson 1995; and Gauthier 1996). Using internationally available aggregate data it has become possible to develop helpful typologies as a framework for exploring particular cases. Unfortunately, the aggregate data used to build those typologies and develop comparisons across a range of indicators are quite heterogeneous and only cover some areas, and not all of the interests in the comparison of welfare states. Moreover, it is not always clear whether the data are strictly comparable, since different countries may use slightly different definitions. Lastly, the most striking absences from most of these statistical approaches are those relating to gender (even if it is clear that welfare arrangements in different countries are based on key assumptions about the different positions of men and women in society) and to the inter- and intra-specificities of the Mediterranean nations.
5. The *European Community Household Panel Survey* (ECHP) is a multidimensional and multi-purpose survey which covers income, demographic and labour-force characteristics, health, education, housing, migration and other topics. The full-scale

survey was launched in 1994, with a sample of 61,106 households (approximately 127,000 individuals) throughout the EU. European Community Household Panel data were made available during a research stay at the European Centre for Analysis in the Social Sciences (ECASS), Institute for the Social Sciences, University of Essex (June–August 1997). ECASS is a large-scale facility funded under the Training and Mobility of Researchers Programme of the European Union.

6. The *Bank of Italy Survey of Household Income and Wealth* was first conducted in 1965. There have been 23 further surveys conducted since then, yearly until 1987 (except for 1985) and every two years thereafter. The aim of the survey is to gather information concerning the economic behaviour of Italian families at the micro-economic level. The survey has a panel section, corresponding to 15 per cent of the households between 1987 and 1989, 26.7 per cent between 1989 and 1991, 42.9 per cent between 1991 and 1993, and 44.8 per cent between 1993 and 1995.

The *British Household Panel Survey*, started in 1991, comprises an initial 5,000 households and 10,000 individuals; five individual data collections are currently available. The survey has been carried out by the ESRC Research Centre on Micro-Social Change at the University of Essex. The main objective of the survey is to further understanding of social and economic change at the individual and household level in Great Britain. BHPS data used in this publication were made available through the Data Archive. Neither the original collectors of the data nor the archive bear any responsibility for the analyses presented here.

The *German Socio-Economic Panel* is a representative longitudinal study of private households in the Federal Republic of Germany. It is modelled after the Panel Study of Income Dynamics, started in 1968. Its first data collection took place in 1984, with a sample of 5,624 households and 11,610 individuals. The GSOEP is carried out and developed by the Project Group 'Socio-Economic Panel' at the German Institute for Economic Research (DIW), Berlin. The group disseminates the data to interested social scientists. In cooperation with the DIW, the Center for Policy Research at Syracuse University has prepared an English-language, public-use version of the GSOEP for the international research community. In order for the GSOEP to be used by researchers outside Germany, German law requires that the privacy of individuals and households be protected. To reduce the risk of identifying individuals or households, the public-use version of the GSOEP does not include detailed information on nationality or region and represents a 95 per cent random sample of the original data.

7. The GSOEP analysis is based upon the West German subsample.

8. These states are Austria, France, Ireland, Portugal and the UK. Outside the EU, such states include Iceland and Norway (Boujan 1995).

9. In Portugal, to receive the allowance for single parents, the parent must: be in work; be a single parent; have paid social security contributions for at least six months; be responsible for caring for a child under ten; and have an income less than 70 per cent of the minimum guaranteed salary. In Austria, the allowance for young children is granted to single parents until the child's second birthday. This allowance is subject to certain conditions: the parent must have a child under two living in the same household and must be in work or have paid contributions for 52 weeks or 24 months to the unemployment benefit office before making the application. There is also a means-tested supplementary allowance, with entitlement subject to the following conditions: the parent must have a child under three and have housing problems (Boujan 1995: 45, 87).

10. In Austria, the allowance for young children is granted to single parents until the child's second birthday; in France, API is paid until the youngest child reaches the age of three; in Portugal, the parent must be responsible for caring for a child under ten; in Norway, the Transitional Allowance is available for at least one year or until the woman's

youngest child is age ten and sometimes longer under special circumstances (Kamerman and Kahn 1989; Boujan 1995).

11. With the exceptions of Austria, Denmark and the UK (one-parent benefit), where specific benefits for lone parents are not means-tested.

12. The level of payment of Family Credit varies according to the size and type of family, according to means-tested rules similar to those used for Income Support. A 1991 survey found that lone parents were, on average, better off in work and claiming Family Credit than out of work on Income Support (Hills 1993).

13. It is important to underline that the accuracy of survey data can be affected by both non-response and small sample size. In panel studies, the sample normally diminishes selectively as time goes by: a crucial problem in most surveys on poverty is indeed the undersampling of poor people. They are hard to contact and, in a panel study, hard to retain for successive annual interviews. In my case, I made use of longitudinal weight variables to correct for undersampling. However, even if the weight variables could, as far as possible, alleviate the underrepresentation, it is difficult to assess the real efficiency of weights since this requires full knowledge of the effects of the attrition process for given variables and given types of analysis. As a consequence, analysts should be aware of the potential problems with attrition bias when analysing panel data, particularly for highly specific subgroups.

14. In ECHP, the household interview is conducted with someone defined as the 'Reference Person'. The head of household is regarded as the Reference Person if: (a) the household head is economically active (working or looking for work) or (b) there is no economically active person in the household. Otherwise, the spouse or partner of the head, if she or he is economically active, is taken as the Reference Person. If not, then the oldest economically active person in the household is the Reference Person. To qualify as the Reference Person, the person must be normally resident in the household (Eurostat 1996c).

15. The identification of lone parents within the ECHP was possible through the combination of the following variables: a 'single parent with one or more children under 16' and a 'single parent with at least one child over 16'.

16. Total household disposable income is total household income after taxes and social security transfers. Disposable income determines a household's standard of living at a given moment.

17. The equivalent factors used correspond to the square root of the number of household members (1.00 for the first adult, 1.41 for the second, 1.73 for the third, 2.00 for the fourth and so on) (Burkhauser, Smeeding and Merz 1994).

18. Equivalence scales can indeed be represented by one single parameter: equivalence elasticity, that is, the power by which needs increase as family size increases. More precisely, I assume that equivalent income (EI) can be equated to disposable income (D) and size of the household (S) in the following way: $EI = D/S^e$. This parameter expresses the variation in resources needed to maintain the level of well-being of the household as the number of components varies. It can range between the extreme elasticities of zero and one: zero implies that the economies of scale are perfect and one underlines their absence. Existing equivalence scales cover almost all of the range between zero and one. The fact that they occupy the high, middle or low position of the range constitutes an important issue, since poverty estimates, and particularly head-count ratios, are very sensitive to the choice of scale: in most countries, poverty declines as the equivalence elasticity increases. The larger the equivalence factor, the lower the poverty rate among single persons (especially if they are young women) and older married couples (Buhmann et al. 1988).

19. These statistical lines have two drawbacks. First, it is generally not known whether the derived levels of income actually support an adequate standard of living. Second, there is no a priori reason why the same fraction has to be used in all countries.

20. It would be possible to use the mean instead of the median. The median has been chosen because it is less affected by the extreme values of the income distribution.

21. The variable used to analyse dependency upon welfare support in Italy refers to the following question: 'Did your household receive, during the previous year, social assistance payments such as unemployment benefits, other forms of assistance or help from private/public offices?' (*'Lei ha personalmente ricevuto forme di assistenza come ad esempio sussidi della cassa integrazione, altri sussidi o aiuti da enti statali o privati?'*).

22. In Great Britain, part-time jobs have accounted for virtually the entire increase in women's employment in the past three decades. In Britain, roughly 25 per cent of women workers were part-timers in 1960 and by 1980 the percentage had grown to approximately 45 per cent (Sainsbury 1996: 106). This reflects the need to balance work with domestic demands in the absence of explicit welfare support for families. The expense and paucity of institutional childcare in Great Britain makes its use a major disincentive to women seeking paid employment, and for this reason the availability of part-time work has been crucial in facilitating British women's increased lifetime work experience by enabling them to combine caring for children with employment (Robinson and Wallace 1984; Humphries and Rubery 1988: 94). Part-time work is financially very disadvantageous: the hourly earnings of both manual and non-manual part-time women are less than those of full-time men and women. Furthermore, the hourly earnings of women in part-time employment are declining relative to the hourly earnings of men and women working full-time in the same industries (Lonsdale 1992: 105). In 1980, 54 per cent of part-timers earned less than £1.50 an hour, compared with 30 per cent of full-time workers, a differential largely due to the concentration of part-timers in relatively poorly paid occupational groups (Martin and Roberts 1984: 205). A major trend of the 1980s was a deterioration in the earnings of British women in part-time employment: their hourly earnings were 74 per cent of the earnings of female full-time workers and only 56 per cent of the earnings of male full-time workers (Robinson 1988: 123).

23. It is one of my aims to overcome the classic conceptualization of poverty that considers someone poor or not poor if, at a given moment, his or her resource level is below a certain line. Attention has to be paid to the duration of poverty. Deprivation can indeed be analysed as a continuous variable, composed of days, months and years (Ashworth and Walker 1992; Salonen 1993: 147).

24. A spell of poverty has been defined as beginning in the first year that income is below the poverty line after having been above it, and as ending when income is above the poverty line after having been below (Bane and Ellwood 1986).

25. Examples of measures that would enable a greater reconciliation of work and family might include good-quality and affordable childcare services, measures to encourage lone mothers to pursue training and higher education, and flexible employment patterns and more extensive provision of maternity and parental leave.

## REFERENCES

Ashworth, K. and R. Walker (1992): *The Dynamics of Family Credit*. CRSP Working Paper No.172, Centre for Research in Social Policy, Loughborough University of Technology.

Bane, M. J. and D. T. Ellwood (1986): 'Slipping into and out of poverty. the dynamics of spells'. *The Journal of Human Resources*, 21/1, pp.1-23.

Barnes, M., Heady, C. and J. Millar (1998): 'The transitions to lone parenthood in the United Kingdom'. Paper, University of Bath, March 1998.

Bimbi, F. (1991): 'Parenthood in Italy: asymmetric relationships and family affection'. In U. Bjornberg (ed.), *European Parents in the 1990s. Contradictions and Comparisons*. The State University of New Jersey, New Brunswick: Rutgers, Transaction Publishers.

(1993): 'Gender, gift relationship and the welfare state cultures in Italy'. In J. Lewis (ed.), *Women and Social Policies in Europe. Work, Family and the State.* London: Edward Elgar.

(1996): *Madri sole in Italia. Un soggetto tacitato in un regime di welfare familistico.* Working Paper, Progetto Strategico CNR 'Governance e Sviluppo Economico-Sociale', Sottoprogetto 'Distribuzione del reddito, diseguaglianze, esclusione sociale ed effetti delle politiche economiche e sociali', Unità Operativa 'Genere e disuguaglianze. Le madri sole e i nuclei monogenitoriali a capofamiglia donna', University of Padova.

Bordin, M. and E. Ruspini (1997): *Le politiche provinciali per le madri sole.* Working Paper, Progetto Strategico CNR 'Governance e Sviluppo Economico-Sociale', Sottoprogetto 'Distribuzione del reddito, diseguaglianze, esclusione sociale ed effetti delle politiche economiche e sociali', Unità Operativa 'Genere e disuguaglianze. Le madri sole e i nuclei monogenitoriali a capofamiglia donna', University of Padova.

Boujan, N. (1995): *One Parent Families in the Member States of The European Union.* Working Paper, Women's Right Series, European Parliament, Directorate General for Research.

Bradshaw, J. (1996): 'Family policy and family poverty'. *Policy Studies,* 17/2, pp.93–106.

(1998): 'International comparisons of support for lone parents'. In J. Millar and R. Ford (eds.), *Private Lives and Public Responses. Lone Parenthood and Future Policy in the UK,* pp.154–68. London: Policy Studies Institute.

Bradshaw, J., Ditch, J., Holmes, H. and P. Whiteford (1993): 'A comparative study of child support in fifteen countries'. *Journal of European Social Policy,* 3/4, pp.255–71.

Bradshaw, J., Kennedy, S., Kilkey, M., Hutton, S., Corden, A., Eardley, T., Holmes, H. and J. Neale (1996): *Policy and the Employment of Lone Parents in 20 Countries.* EU Report, European Observatory of National Family Policies, The University of York, August 1996.

Brown, J. C. (1988): *In Search of a Policy. The Rationale for Social Security Provisions for One Parent Families.* London: National Council for One Parent Families.

Brueckner, H. (1995): 'Times of poverty: lessons from the Bremen Longitudinal Social Assistance Sample'. Paper prepared for publication in D. A. Chekki (ed.), *Urban Poverty in Affluent Nations,* Vol.V of Research in Community Sociology.

Buhmann, B., Rainwater, L., Schmaus, G. and T. Smeeding (1988): 'Equivalence scales, well-being, inequality and poverty: sensitivity estimates across ten countries using the Luxembourg Income Study (LIS) Database'. *The Review of Income and Wealth,* 34/2, pp.113–42.

Burkhauser, R. V., Smeeding, T. M. and Merz, J. (1994): *Relative Inequality and Poverty in Germany and the United States Using Alternative Equivalence Scales.* Luxembourg Income Study Working Paper Series, Working Paper No.117.

Castles, F. G. and D. Mitchell (1991): *Three Worlds of Welfare Capitalism or Four?* Public Policy Discussion Paper No.21. Canberra: Australian National University.

(1993): 'Worlds of welfare and families of nations'. In F. G. Castles (ed.), *Families of Nations. Patterns of Public Policy in Western Democracies,* pp.93–128. Aldershot: Dartmouth Publishing Company.

Chester, R. (1994): 'Flying without instruments or flight plans: family policy in the United Kingdom'. In W. Dumon (ed.), *Changing Family Policies in the Member States of the European Union.* Commission of the European Communities, European Observatory on National Family Policies.

CIPE (Commissione d'indagine sulla povertà e sull'emarginazione) (1996): *La povertà in Italia 1980–1994.* Roma: Presidenza del Consiglio dei Ministri.

Daly, M. (1995): 'Sex, gender and poverty in the British and (West) German welfare states'. Paper presented at the Conference The Cost of Being a Mother, the Cost of Being a

Father, European Forum, Florence, European University Institute, 24–25 March 1995.
De Sandre, P. (1988): 'Quando i figli lasciano la famiglia'. In E. Scabini and P. Donati (eds.), *La famiglia 'lunga' del giovane adulto*. Milano: Vita e Pensiero.
(1991): 'Contributo delle generazioni ai cambiamenti recenti nei comportamenti e nelle forme familiari'. In P. Donati (ed.), *Secondo rapporto sulla famiglia in Italia*. Milano: Edizioni Paoline.
Ditch, J., Barnes, H. and J. Bradshaw (1996): *A Synthesis of National Family Policies 1995*. European Observatory on National Family Policies, University of York, Social Policy Research Unit.
DSS (1997): *Social Security Statistics 1997*. London: The Stationery Office.
Duncan, G. J., Gustaffson, B., Hauser, R., Schmaus, G., Jenkins, S., Messinger, H., Muffels, R., Nolan, B., Ray, J. C. and W. Voges (1993): *Poverty and Social-Assistance Dynamics in the United States, Canada and Europe*. Working Papers of the European Scientific Network on Household Panel Studies, Paper No.4, Colchester, University of Essex.
Duncan, S. and R. Edwards (1997): 'Single mothers in Britain: unsupported workers or mothers?' In S. Duncan and R. Edwards R. (eds.), *Single Mothers in an International Context: Mothers or Workers?*, pp.45–80. London: UCL Press.
Esping-Andersen, G. (1990): *The Three Worlds of Welfare Capitalism*. Cambridge: Polity Press.
Eurostat (1995): *Labour Force Survey. Principal Results 1994*. Statistics in Focus. Population and Social Conditions, No.6.
(1996a): *Labour Force Survey: Results 1995*. Population and Social Conditions Series, 3C.
(1996b): *The European Community Household Panel (ECHP): Survey Methodology and Implementation*, Vol.1. Luxembourg: Office for Official Publications of the European Communities.
(1996c): *European Community Household Panel (ECHP): Methods*, Vol.1, Survey Questionnaires: Waves 1–3. Luxembourg: Office for Official Publications of the European Communities.
Fargion, V. (1997): 'The effects of decentralization on the Italian welfare state. Social assistance between poverty and well-being'. In *Comparing social welfare systems in Southern Europe*, Florence Conference, Vol.3, pp.539–60. Paris: MIRE.
Ferrera, M. (1993): *Modelli di solidarietà. Politica e riforme sociali nelle democrazie*. Bologna: Il Mulino.
(1996): *Il modello di welfare sud europeo. Caratteristiche, genesi, prospettive*, Poleis, Quaderni di ricerca, 5.
(1997): 'General introduction'. In *Comparing Social Welfare Systems in Southern Europe*, Florence Conference, Vol.3. Paris: MIRE.
Gauthier, A. H. (1996): *The State and the Family. A Comparative Analysis of Family Policies in Industrialized Countries*. Oxford: Clarendon Press.
Glendinning, C. and J. Millar (1991): 'Poverty: the forgotten Englishwoman'. In M. McLean and D. Groves (eds.), *Women's issues in Social Policy*. London and New York: Routledge.
Gustaffson, S. (1995): 'Single mothers in Sweden: why is poverty less severe?' In K. McFate, R. Lawson and W. J. Wilson (eds.), *Poverty, Inequality and the Future of Social Policy. Western States in the New World Order*. New York: Russel Sage Foundation.
Hills, J. (1993): *The Future of Welfare. A Guide to Debate*. York: Joseph Rowntree Foundation.
Hobson, B. (1994): 'Solo mothers, social policy regimes and the logics of gender'. In D. Sainsbury (ed.), *Gendering Welfare States*, pp.170–87. London: Sage.

Humphries, J. and J. Rubery (1988): 'Recession and exploitation. British women in a changing workplace 1979–85'. In J. Jenson, E. Hagen and C. Reddy (eds.), *Feminization of the Labour Force. Paradox and Promises*, pp.85–105. Cambridge: Polity Press.

Jarvis, S, and S. P. Jenkins (1997): *Marital Splits and Income Changes: Evidence From Britain*. Working Paper of the ESRC Research Centre on Micro-social Change, Paper No.97–4.

Jones, C. (1985): 'Types of welfare capitalism'. *Government and Opposition*, 20/3, pp.328–42.

Jurado, T. and M. Naldini (1996): *Is the South so Different? Italian and Spanish Families in Comparative Perspective*. Working Paper No.12, International Project on Family Changes and Family Policies, MZES: Mannheim.

Kamerman, S. B. and A. K. Kahn (eds.) (1978): *Family Policy: Government and Families in Fourteen Countries*. New York: Columbia University Press.

(1989): 'Single-parent, female-headed families in western Europe: social change and response'. *International Social Security Review*, 1, pp.3–34.

Karr, W. and K. John (1989): 'Mehrfacharbeitslosigkeit und Kumulative Arbeitslosigkeit'. *MittAB*, 22/1, pp.1–16.

Langan, M. and I. Ostner (1991): 'Gender and welfare. Towards a comparative framework'. In G. Room (ed.), *Towards a European Welfare State?*, pp.127–50. Bristol: SAUS.

Laparra, M. and M. Aguilar (1996): 'Social exclusion and minimum income programmes in Spain'. *Southern European Society and Politics*, 1/ 3, pp.87–109.

Leibfried, S. (1993): 'Towards a European welfare state?' In C. Jones (ed.), *New Perspectives on the Welfare State in Europe*, pp.133–50. London: Routledge.

Lewis, J. (1993): 'Introduction: women, work, family and social policies in Europe'. In J. Lewis (ed.), *Women and Social Policies in Europe. Work, Family and the State*, pp.1–24. Aldershot: Edward Elgar.

Lewis, J. and I. Ostner (1994): *Gender and the Evolution of European Social Policies*. ZeS-Arbeitspapier No.4, Zentrum für Sozialpolitik (ZES), Centre for Social Policy Research, University of Bremen.

Lonsdale, S. (1992): 'Patterns of paid work'. In C. Glendinning and J. Millar (eds.), *Women and Poverty in Britain the 1990s.* Harvester Wheatsheaf.

Martin, C. (1996): 'Social welfare and the family in southern Europe'. *Southern European Society and Politics*, 1/3, pp.23–41.

Martin, J. and C. Roberts (1984): *Women and Employment: A Lifetime Perspective. The Report of the 1980 DE/OPCS Women and Employment Survey*. London: HMSO.

Millar, J. (1989): *Poverty and the Lone-Parent Family: the Challenge to Social Policy*. Aldershot: Avebury.

(1998) 'Policy and changing family forms: placing lone parenthood in context'. Paper presented at the Seminar Current European Research on Lone Mothers', Göteborg University, April 1998.

Millar, J. and R. Ford (eds.) (1998): *Private Lives and Public Responses. Lone Parenthood and Future Policy in the UK*. London: Policy Studies Institute.

Mingione, E. (1996): 'Urban poverty in the advanced industrial world: concepts, analysis and debates'. In E. Mingione (ed.), *Urban Poverty and the Underclass*. Oxford: Basil Blackwell.

Murray, C. (1984): *Losing Ground: American Social Policy 1950–1980*. New York: Basic Books.

Negri, N. and C. Saraceno (1994): *Le politiche contro la povertà in Italia*. Bologna: Il Mulino.

Norris, P. (1987): *Politics and Sexual Equality. The Comparative Position of Women in Western Democracies*. Boulder, CO: Rienner.

OECD (1988): 'Women's economic activity, employments and earnings. A review of recent developments'. In OECD, *Employment Outlook 1988*, pp.129–72. Paris: OECD.

Robinson, J. and J. Wallace (1984): 'Growth and utilization of part-time labour in Great Britain'. *Employment Gazette*, September 1984.

Robinson, O. (1988): 'The changing labour market: growth of part-time employment and labour market segmentation in Britain'. In S. Walby (ed.), *Gender Segregation at Work*. Milton Keynes: Open University Press.

Roll, J. (ed) (1992): *Lone Parent Families in The European Community. The 1992 Report to the European Commission*. Brussels: Commission of the European Communities Equal Opportunities Unit.

Ruggles, P. (1990): *Drawing the Line. Alternative Poverty Measures and their Implications for Public Policy*. Washington DC: The Urban Institute Press.

Ruspini, E. (1997a): 'Donne e povertà. Percorsi e caratteristiche del disagio nelle società europee occidentali: il caso della Germania e della Gran Bretagna'. Ph.D. dissertation, Department of Sociology and Social Research, University of Trento, Italy, February 1997.

(1997b): 'Gender differences in poverty and its duration: an analysis of Germany and Great Britain'. T. Dunn and J. Schwarze (eds.), *Proceedings of the 1996 Second International Conference of the German Socio-Economic Panel Study Users*. DIW-Vierteljahrshefte zur Wirtschaftsforschung, 1/97, pp.87–91. Berlin: Duncker & Humbolt.

(1997c): *Gender and Dynamics of Poverty: The Cases of (West) Germany and Great Britain*. Working Papers of the ESRC Research Centre on Micro-Social Change, Paper 97–24. Colchester: University of Essex.

(1997d): *Madri sole, povertà e politiche familiari in Europa*. Working Paper, Progetto Strategico CNR 'Governance e Sviluppo Economico-Sociale', Sottoprogetto 'Distribuzione del reddito, diseguaglianze, esclusione sociale ed effetti delle politiche economiche e sociali', Unità Operativa 'Genere e disuguaglianze. Le madri sole e i nuclei monogenitoriali a capofamiglia donna'. University of Padova.

Sainsbury, D. (1996): *Gender, Equality and Welfare States*. Cambridge: Cambridge University Press.

Salonen, T. (1993): *Margins of Welfare. A Study of Modern Functions of Social Assistance*. Torna Haellestad: Haellestad Press.

Saraceno, C. (1994): *Un familismo ambivalente: le politiche della famiglia in Italia dal dopoguerra ad oggi*. Convegno Internazionale 'Mutamenti della famiglia nei paesi occidentali', Palazzo dei Congressi, Bologna, 6–8 October 1994.

Scheiwe, K. (1994): 'Labour market, welfare state and family institutions: the links to mothers' poverty risks. A comparison between Belgium, Germany and the United Kingdom'. *Journal of European Social Policy*, 4/3, pp.201–24.

Siaroff, A. (1994): 'Work, welfare and gender equality: a new typology'. In D. Sainsbury (ed.), *Gendering Welfare States*, pp.82–100. London: Sage.

Simoni, S. (1996): *Single Mothers in Italy. A Muted Subject*. Working Paper, Progetto Strategico CNR 'Governance e Sviluppo Economico-Sociale', Sottoprogetto 'Distribuzione del reddito, diseguaglianze, esclusione sociale ed effetti delle politiche economiche e sociali', Unità Operativa 'Genere e disuguaglianze. Le madri sole e i nuclei monogenitoriali a capofamiglia donna'. University of Padova.

Taylor-Gooby, P. (1991): 'Welfare state regimes and welfare citizenship'. *Journal of European Social Policy*, 1/2, pp.93–105.

Trifiletti, R. (1998): 'Southern European Welfare regimes and the worsening position of women', *Journal of European Social Politics* (forthcoming).

Van den Brekel, C. and D. J. Van de Kaa (1994) 'The Netherlands: aspects of family policy in the setting of the second demographic transition'. In W. Dumon (ed.), *Changing Family Policies in the Member States of the European Union*, pp.225–54. Commission of the European Communities, European Observatory on National Family Policies.

Walker, R. and K. Ashworth (1994): *Poverty Dynamics: Issues and Examples*. Aldershot: Avebury.

Wennemo, I. (1994): *Sharing Costs of Children: Studies on the Development of Family Support in the OECD Countries*. Swedish Institute for Social Research Dissertation Series, No.25, Stockholm.

Zanatta, A. L. (1996): 'Famiglie con un solo genitore e rischio di povertà'. *Polis*, 10/1, April 1996, pp.63–79.

# Gender in the Reform of the Italian Welfare State

## ELISABETTA ADDIS

The welfare state is a set of institutions and policies which redistributes resources (either as money transfers or as free or subsidized services) between individuals and across different groups of people. The amount of resources moved and the specific format chosen to effect these movements deeply affect the daily lives of men and women. It is by now almost obvious to note that these practices affect power relations between men and women within and outside the family, and contribute to defining the gender roles of both sexes. The development of public services, social assistance, social insurance programmes and universal citizenship entitlements runs parallel with women's entry into the labour market, allowing participation in the labour force and providing employment. The welfare state has contributed to reshaping the role of women, to changing the traditional division of labour within and outside the family, and affected gender relations between men and women in a variety of ways. The social notions of gender itself have changed as a result of these processes.[1]

In the English-speaking world, a large body of literature has explored the many-faceted relations between gender and the welfare state (for an excellent survey of this literature, see Orloff 1996). In the debate on the reform of the Italian welfare state, many issues of redistribution (from rich to poor families, from young to old, from north to south, from employed to unemployed) were the objects of careful measurement and rich discussion. A broad consensus emerged among academics as well as among policy-makers about the sources of problems and the appropriate directions of change. The academic and policy-making community was, however, almost silent about redistribution by gender; notable exceptions were the contributions by Bimbi (1998) and Saraceno (1994) on family policies, and by Trifiletti (1996) on more general redistributive effects. The specific gender relations fostered by the present welfare state were not examined; almost no analysis was presented on the shift of resources between men and women caused by the first attempts at reform, and hence no consensus was reached about the need for and desirable direction of change in this area.

This article is a first contribution toward a more systematic analysis of gender and the Italian welfare state. I will take into consideration only cash-transfer programmes, and will not deal, here, with the provision of services. Transfers are the area where reform activity, both actual and proposed, is most pronounced. I will examine family allowances, tax exemptions, unemployment insurance, old-age pensions and the introduction, in some of these areas for the first time, of means-testing. I will review the present situation and discuss some of the proposed reforms.

## WOMEN AND WELFARE IN ITALY

I think it is useful to begin by restating how the general effects of the welfare state on gender relations are displayed in the Italian case. First, the welfare state allows women's participation in the labour market, and is itself an important source of women's employment. Italy is an extreme case, in comparison with other European countries, in that women's participation in the labour force is much lower than in countries with a similar per capita income (see Table 1), and women's unemployment, and the difference between men's and women's unemployment rates are greater than elsewhere (see Table 2).

Notwithstanding the abnormally high public debt, the Italian state does not spend more on welfare than the European average. What is above average is the ratio between cash transfers (pensions, in particular) and GDP, which is higher than in the rest of Europe (see Tables 3 and 4). Services, by contrast, are fewer and of lower quality.

The direct connection between these stylized facts is not easy to miss: participation in the labour force is low because the lack of services substituting for women's traditional care-giving work prevents women, and in particular mothers, from participating other than at a high personal and family cost. In addition, some of the direct transfers are regulated so as to give incentives for non-participation.

Unemployment and the unemployment difference between the sexes are high because the tertiary sector, private and public, which in most countries provides the main source of women's employment, is underdeveloped: Bettio and Villa (1995) compute the jobs missing in services at more than 2.5 million. In addition, there are specific labour-

TABLE 1
PARTICIPATION RATES BY SEX, SELECTED YEARS

| | 1973 | | | 1983 | | | 1993 | | | 1996 | |
|---|---|---|---|---|---|---|---|---|---|---|---|
| | F | M | Tot | F | M | Tot | F | M | Tot | F | M |
| Australia | 47.7 | 91.1 | 69.8 | 52.1 | 85.9 | 69.3 | 62.3 | 85.0 | 73.7 | 64.9 | 85.4 |
| Austria | 48.5 | 83.0 | 65.1 | 49.7 | 82.2 | 65.6 | 58.9 | 80.8 | 69.9 | 62.1 | 81.0 |
| Belgium | 41.3 | 83.2 | 62.2 | 48.7 | 76.8 | 62.8 | 54.1* | 72.6* | 63.8 | 56.1 | 72.1 |
| Canada | 47.2 | 86.1 | 66.7 | 60.0 | 84.7 | 72.3 | 65.3 | 78.3 | 71.8 | 67.9 | 81.7 |
| Denmark | 61.9 | 89.6 | 75.9 | 74.2 | 87.6 | 80.9 | 78.3 | 86.9 | 82.6 | 74.1 | 85.1 |
| Finland | 63.6 | 80.0 | 71.7 | 72.7 | 82.0 | 77.4 | 70.0 | 77.6 | 73.6 | 70.5 | 77.3 |
| France | 50.1 | 85.2 | 67.8 | 54.3 | 78.4 | 66.4 | 59.0 | 74.5 | 66.7 | 59.9 | 74.3 |
| Germany | 50.3 | 89.6 | 69.4 | 52.5 | 82.6 | 67.5 | 61.4 | 78.6 | 70.2 | 61.0 | 80.0 |
| Greece | 32.1 | 83.2 | 57.1 | 40.4 | 80.0 | 59.9 | 43.6 | 73.7 | 58.6 | 45.9 | 74.4 |
| Ireland | 34.1 | 92.3 | 63.5 | 37.8 | 87.1 | 62.7 | 39.9* | 81.9* | 61.2* | 49.4 | 78.1 |
| Italy | 33.7 | 85.1 | 58.7 | 40.3 | 80.7 | 60.1 | 43.3 | 74.8 | 58.9 | 43.2 | 75.1 |
| Japan | 54.0 | 90.1 | 71.7 | 57.2 | 89.1 | 73.0 | 61.8 | 90.2 | 76.1 | 62.2° | 90.7° |
| Luxembourg | 35.9 | 93.1 | 64.8 | 41.7 | 85.1 | 63.3 | 44.8* | 77.7* | 61.5* | – | – |
| Netherlands | 29.2 | 85.6 | 57.6 | 40.3 | 77.3 | 59.0 | 55.5* | 80.8* | 69.4* | 58.3 | 84.2 |
| New Zealand | 39.2 | 89.2 | 64.5 | 45.7 | 84.7 | 65.3 | 63.2 | 83.3 | 73.2 | 67.1 | 84.2 |
| Norway | 50.6 | 86.5 | 68.7 | 65.5 | 87.2 | 76.5 | 70.8 | 82.0 | 76.5 | 74.3 | 84.8 |
| Portugal | 57.3# | 90.9# | 64.0 | 56.7 | 86.9 | 71.4 | 61.3 | 82.5 | 71.7 | 64.1 | 81.5 |
| Spain | 33.4 | 92.9 | 62.7 | 33.2 | 80.2 | 56.6 | 42.8 | 74.5 | 58.6 | 46.2 | 74.4 |
| Sweden | 62.6 | 88.1 | 75.5 | 76.6 | 85.9 | 81.3 | 75.7 | 79.3 | 77.5 | 73.7 | 78.0 |
| Switzerland | 54.1 | 94.6# | 77.7 | 55.2 | 93.5 | 74.5 | 57.9 | 92.5 | 75.3 | 67.1° | 96.8° |
| United Kingdom | 53.2 | 93.0 | 73.0 | 57.2 | 87.5 | 72.4 | 64.7 | 83.3 | 74.1 | 66.4 | 83.1 |
| United States | 51.1 | 86.2 | 68.4 | 61.8 | 84.6 | 73.1 | 69.0 | 84.9 | 76.9 | 71.0 | 84.5 |
| North America | 50.7 | 86.2 | 68.2 | 61.1 | 84.6 | 73.0 | 68.7 | 84.2 | 76.4 | – | – |
| OECD Europe | 44.7 | 88.7 | 67.1 | 49.8 | 82.3 | 65.8 | 60.6 | 80.1 | 69.0 | – | – |
| OECD Total | 48.3 | 88.2 | 68.2 | 55.1 | 84.3 | 69.3 | 61.6 | 81.3 | 70.3 | – | – |

Fonte: OECD Employment Outlook, 1996, OECD Main Economic Indicators, July 1998.
*Last available, 1992. #First available, 1979.

market policies in place, which I refer to as 'handicap-privileges', that very effectively prevent hiring and promoting women in the private sector. These include:

- Long mandatory maternity leave (five months mandatory at 80 per cent pay at birth, plus six months elective at 20 per cent of the wage within the first two years), which prevents the hiring of young married or marriageable women
- A mandatory retirement age set at 55 for women in the private sector, which formerly prevented the employment of older women willing to re-enter the labour force after childbearing age; this provision was abolished by the Dini reforms, which I will discuss later, and
- The fact that the weekly working hours mandated by national labour contracts in the private sector are long, and other forms of shorter

TABLE 2
UNEMPLOYMENT RATES BY SEX, SELECTED YEARS

| | 1983 | | 1993 | | 1997 | |
| --- | --- | --- | --- | --- | --- | --- |
| | Women | Men | Women | Men | Women | Men |
| Belgium | 19.0 | 8.6 | 12.7 | 6.9 | 11.9 | 7.9 |
| Canada | 11.1(3) | 11.2(3) | 10.6 | 11.7 | – | – |
| Denmark | 10.5 | 8.2 | 13.7 | 11.3 | 7.8 | 7.3 |
| Finland | – | – | 15.7 | 19.5 | 14.9 | 13.2 |
| France | 10.8 | 6.3 | 13.8 | 9.9 | 14.4 | 10.7 |
| Germany (W.) | (8.0) | (8.7) | (8.4) | (8.0) | 10.6 | 9.0 |
| Greece | 11.7 | 5.8 | 14.2 | 5.4 | 14.9 | 6.2 |
| Ireland | 16.5 | 14.6 | 12.1 | 17.3 | 10.4 | 10.1 |
| Italy | 14.4 | 5.8 | 17.3 | 8.1 | 16.6 | 9.3 |
| Japan | 2.6 | 2.7 | 2.6 | 2.4 | 3.4 | 3.4 |
| Luxembourg | 5.3 | 2.6 | 1.9 | 1.5 | 5.2 | 2.7 |
| Netherlands | 14.7 | 11.1 | 10.5 | 5.7 | 6.9 | 3.9 |
| New Zealand | – | – | 8.9 | 10.0 | – | – |
| Norway | 3.8 | 3.2 | 5.2 | 6.6 | – | – |
| Portugal | 11.8 | 5.3 | 6.5 | 4.6 | 7.8 | 6.0 |
| Spain | 20.8 | 16.5 | 29.2 | 19.0 | 28.3 | 16.0 |
| Sweden | 3.6 | 3.4 | 6.6 | 9.7 | 9.7 | 10.6 |
| Switzerland | – | – | 4.7 | 3.0 | – | – |
| United Kingdom | 9.9 | 11.9 | 7.5 | 12.4 | 6.0 | 7.9 |
| USA | 7.4(2) | 7.0(2) | 6.5 | 7.0 | 5.0 | 4.9 |

*Sources*: Bonke, 1993; Eurostat Labour Force Surveys 1994, 1997.

time commitment to employment are strongly penalized, so that family life and the time available for childcare for a couple who are both employed is severely curtailed.

Let me stress that low participation and low employment are a waste of a most crucial economic resource for economic growth. The more so as Italian women are highly educated, and future economic growth in the already industrialized countries will depend more and more on an ability to take advantage of the human-capital accumulation of men and women within forms of production that have a high technological content. The Italian economy can ill afford, in the global era, to compete with other economies while keeping women trapped in an inefficient use of housekeeping time. What is at stake therefore is not just an issue of women's politics, but an issue of national economic policy.

Second, the welfare state helps determine the degree of economic dependence or independence that women enjoy. Affluence and economic independence are not the same. Given the standard of living a woman enjoys, she may have more or less control over the resources that make

TABLE 3
SOCIAL EXPENDITURE IN THE EU COUNTRIES AS A PERCENTAGE OF GNP

| Country | 1980 | 1986 | 1992 |
|---|---|---|---|
| Belgium | 28.0 | 29.4 | 27.8 |
| Denmark | 28.7 | 26.7 | 31.4 |
| Germany | 28.7 | 28.1 | 26.6 |
| France | 25.4 | 28.5 | 29.2 |
| Ireland | 21.6 | 24.1 | 21.6 |
| Luxembourg | 26.5 | 24.8 | 28.0 |
| Netherlands | 30.8 | 30.9 | 33.0 |
| United Kingdom | 21.5 | 24.3 | 27.2 |
| EU 12 | 24.4 | 26.0 | 27.1 |
| Greece | 12.2 | 19.4 | 19.3 |
| Italy | 19.4 | 22.4 | 25.6 |
| Portugal | 14.7 | 16.3 | 17.6 |
| Spain | 18.1 | 19.5 | 22.5 |

Source: Eurostat, 1993.

TABLE 4
MAIN CATEGORIES OF SOCIAL PROTECTION EXPENDITURE IN EU 12

| Country | Old age & surv. pens. | Health | Unemployment | Disability | Family |
|---|---|---|---|---|---|
| Belgium | 11.9 | 6.0 | 2.6 | 2.9 | 1.9 |
| Denmark | 11.0 | 6.0 | 4.1 | 3.0 | 3.3 |
| Germany | 12.7 | 7.7 | 2.0 | 2.2 | 2.0 |
| France | 12.1 | 8.0 | 2.0 | 3.5 | 2.2 |
| Ireland | 5.7 | 6.1 | 3.0 | 1.5 | 2.2 |
| Luxembourg | 11.2 | 5.9 | 0.2 | 3.5 | 2.7 |
| Netherlands | 11.9 | 7.1 | 2.9 | 7.2 | 1.6 |
| United Kingdom | 10.8 | 5.1 | 1.6 | 3.1 | 2.6 |
| EU 12 | 11.9 | 6.5 | 1.9 | 2.4 | 1.8 |
| Greece | 10.2 | 2.3 | 0.5 | 1.5 | 0.1 |
| Italy | 15.4 | 5.4 | 0.5 | 2.2 | 0.8 |
| Portugal | 7.0 | 5.3 | 0.8 | 2.4 | 0.8 |
| Spain | 9.4 | 5.9 | 4.8 | 2.3 | 0.2 |

Source: European Commission, 1995.

that standard possible. A person may have access to resources from four sources: from inherited or accumulated wealth belonging to that person, from earnings, from transfers from the state to that person, or from the intra-family transfer of resources. The latter, intra-family transfers, are in turn the wealth, earnings or transfers of another family member, and are therefore conditional on being a member of somebody's family and on the will of that other family member. This makes for dependency on the latter. This is the situation of children and, before the existence of the welfare state, of the disabled and elderly.[2]

It is also the situation of women who do not have inherited wealth and do not work for a wage. In Italy, these are still the majority of women of working age, and this will remain so unless the welfare state grants them direct rights, either as citizens or based on the care-giving work they do for their family, which it does not in Italy.

Direct monetary transfers in the Italian welfare state are job based to the extreme. Transfers are basically of three kinds, as follows.

(1) *Family allowances.* These may be either contribution based (*assegni familiari*) or tax based (*detrazioni*), but are paid to workers for their spouse and children.

(2) *Unemployment transfers.* These are divided into three main programmes: the *Cassa Integrazione Guadagni* (CIG) and Mobility, which may be requested for their workers by firms of more than ten employees instead of laying workers off, and the ordinary individual unemployment subsidy, which is very low. The CIG is so job based that those who in other countries would be temporarily unemployed, in Italy, are still employed, albeit in the CIG.

(3) *Pensions.* Pensions, with the exception of the 'social pension', which we will analyse later, are strictly work based. They are paid to people who cannot work (disability pensions) or who are the survivor of a worker (survivors' benefits) or who have worked and paid contributions for a number of years (seniority and retirement pensions).

The fact that the welfare state is work based, coupled with the fact that women's participation and employment are so low, implies that the main route of access for women to transfers from the welfare state is through their personal relationship to a man who is a worker, that is, through marriage. It is therefore not only familist, since services are produced in the family, but patriarchal, in that it assumes and reproduces women's dependence on men.

Third, the fact that Italian welfare state over-provides transfers and under-provides services shapes the distribution of domestic working time within the family. Italy is an extreme case of long working hours by women and short working hours for men. Italian men, providing on average nine hours of domestic work a week, are the laziest in Europe as far as domestic work is concerned (Addis 1997; ch.4). This is the mirror image of what is explained above. Lack of public services implies that there is a large amount of work to do. Low women's participation and employment imply that there are women at home ready to do it. The generosity of the pension system means that many of them are relatively young pensioners. The fact that the state provides transfers rather than services implies that in Italy it is still customary, to an extent unusual in other European countries, to hire domestic workers, mostly women, and more recently women immigrants.

Fourth and last, lack of services, lack of economic independence for women (who therefore feel that it may be risky to depend entirely on their children's fathers for their children's keep in case of divorce), lack of part-time work or jobs with flexible hours and long working hours for women who are employed, imbalances in the distribution of working time between men and women and between women who are employed and women who are not (the latter setting standards of personal care and childcare that the first cannot hope to attain), and lack of any specific programme to help mothers or single mothers, all contribute to induce a fertility rate which is the lowest in the world and in history, with 1.2 children per fertile woman. This is to me the clearest sign that in Italy there is a deep crisis not only of the 'social contract' between the elderly and the young, but also of the 'social contract' between men and women, which, together, regulate reproduction.

## MEANS-TESTING AND GENDER EQUITY IN THE WELFARE STATE

Italy is an extreme case of women's low participation, high unemployment, dependency on work or marriage for access to welfare benefits, and low fertility. All these reflect a specific problem of 'gender equity', that is, a misallocation of resources between men and women, a lack of recognition, via public intervention, both of women's autonomous right to work outside the household and of the social value of care giving, especially if devoted to reproduction.

We know that a distribution of resources among different individuals may be equitable according to one parameter, and inequitable according to another (a thorough discussion of 'equity' in income distribution can be found in Sen 1992). The welfare state attempts to achieve a distribution which is equitable according to a number of parameters, for example, need, work performed, effort, productivity, and social usefulness. Each of them defines a different dimension of equity.

These different dimensions of equity are interrelated, and they may even be in conflict. It is possible to design policies which, while improving intergenerational equity, reduce equity between rich and poor families: think of an unemployment subsidy to the young, given without reference to parental income. By the same token, it is possible to imagine policies which improve intergenerational and class equity but worsen gender equity. I will present real-life cases of the latter, for example: the ceiling on a couple's pension income, which cuts the lowest pension when the other rises above a given threshold. It is possible to imagine policies which effect redistribution between people who perform only domestic work and people who perform both domestic work and paid work. It is possible to devise policies which help family formation, and policies which deter family formation, and therefore treat differently people who choose to marry and people who choose not to marry, that is, to enter a very gendered relationship. These are matters that should be dealt with openly. If the present wave of reforms ignores the specific dimensions of gender equity, it runs the risk of worsening the unfair treatment of women, of reducing opportunities for women to enter the labour market, and of deterring family formation and fertility, while improving fairness between classes and generations.

Some of the pathologies of the Italian welfare state are linked to the unrecognised need to provide care to families. The only kind of work that was recognized as a source of independent rights was paid work. Care-givers were only acknowledged as useless dependants; not as providers of domestic goods, but as consumers lacking an adequate source of cash. As a result of this lack of recognition, job-based rights were stretched to the limits. Very early retirement (baby-pensions), false invalidity pensions, and misuse of hospitals to park frail elderly people, who do not need costly medical care but only nursing homes, are all 'creative' attempts to finance care.

In order to make public intervention equitable according to the parameters mentioned above, recognition of the fact that employment is not the only kind of work is missing. Care-giving work and reproductive work exist, are the presupposition upon which all other work and consumption are based, and the ultimate source of effective well-being for individuals. Therefore, they are relevant for social policy. Traditionally, full-time housewives provided this work. Now, it may be provided by women working in their own house, by hired help, by public services, by private services, or by men in the house. It exists, and it is productive of utility and well-being. Even if it is not easy to calculate its market value, there are ways to take it into account in fiscal and public policy.

This work exists, and somebody is doing it. It is a use of time which is different from leisure: it is work in domestic production.[3] When the person who does domestic and care-giving work for her family (usually a woman) enters the labour market, she is giving up the value of the products of her domestic work, and needs resources to replace it. Notionally, she must subtract from the value of her wages the value of the replacement costs for the services that she does not produce any more for the family. The net gain for her is smaller than for a person who does not perform such care and domestic work.

Labour supplied by women responds much more to taxation than that of men, precisely because the net hourly earnings of women, once the value of the household services that have been foregone is subtracted, are so low. Taxes are levied on the gross and are therefore proportionally higher on this net. Women's labour is, as economists say, very elastic to taxation. A subsidy is but a tax by another name. From the economic point of view, subsidizing non-participation is equal to increasing taxation on labour supplied by women. When there is a subsidy for housewives, a wife who chooses to work outside her own home must subtract from her wages the value of the services she no longer renders to her family as well as the value of the subsidy that the family loses because she works. This may happen because she loses the status of being a 'dependant' upon which family allowances and deductions are based, or because her wage increases the family income beyond the threshold for means-tested benefits. She will, moreover, pay the state taxes that will be used, among other things, to finance subsidies to women who choose to work only within the household.

The fact that women's labour supply is very elastic to taxation implies that the 'poverty trap' is even more stringent for women than it is for men. The 'poverty trap' has been an important concept, for right or for wrong, in the welfare reform debates in the UK and the USA. It is the idea that unemployed people are prevented from entering low-paid jobs by the fact that the difference between what they may earn and what they will loose in welfare benefits, if these are means-tested, is too small to compensate for the work effort. Women are therefore 'trapped' into domestic work.

Besides being inefficient, a welfare state which actively promotes the unrecognized employment of half of its citizens in domestic work and within marriage is not equitable: it biases choices against paid work and in favour of marriage. It is certainly not coherent with liberal principles. At the same time, care work that women perform in the house is a vital function for society and it contributes to its well-being. Escape from the domestic work trap, therefore, must be such that this care work does not disappear, but is distributed more fairly.

The fact that the Italian welfare system is heavy in transfers and light in services is already a form of gender bias. Public services are often provided by women and substitute for traditional women's work. Services, moreover, had until recently a rather universal character. In particular, the National Health System may have been bureaucratic and inefficient, but was so almost equally for men and for women. Through means-testing, access to services may become gender biased against women workers, a fact about which there is very little awareness. Families in which both the man and the woman work for a low wage will have an higher chance of losing access to benefits in comparison with families where only the man works for the same low wage. Therefore taxes paid by low-wage workers of both sexes will benefit only male low-wage workers and their housekeeping wives, though domestic work needs to be done in all families.

We have recently observed a creeping emergence of a variety of local means tests for access to many services, ranging from some medical procedures to nursery schools. This means-testing at the local level has often been quite crude; the unit chosen for means-testing was the nuclear family, with no consideration for possible alternatives, no allowance for the number of people who have to live on the income, its source, or the kind of service requested.

The Ministry of Finance proposed a model 'means test' to be used nationally by local administrations, with or without modifications, to regulate access to all kinds of services. This scheme has been presented in the media as the 'riccometro', (or 'wealth meter'), but it is more formally known as Indicatore della Situazione Economica (ISE), and became law in March 1998. According to ISE, a family which requires some form of social service or exemption (nursery school, exemption from co-payments for physicians' care, drugs or medical tests, and so on) should answer a questionnaire, beyond the income declaration made for tax purposes and providing information on other aspects of family composition and wealth.[4] The scheme applies an equivalency scale to the income resulting from the questionnaire, taking into account the number of people that have to live on that income, whether the parent is single, and whether there is a handicapped person in the family. A rather small allowance is made if both parents of young children work, in the form of a slight increase in the parameters of the equivalency scale.

This is probably an improvement over the crude means-testing just mentioned. In a related paper (Addis 1998), I discuss the gender effects of means-testing and the use of different techniques to address the issue of the poverty trap for women. In general, means-testing fails to take in account the number of earners, if it does not allow for a higher threshold for families with two wage earners and no 'housekeeper'. It will then punish women's work outside of the household, give an incentive to non-participation, and be inequitable toward their work.

There are various techniques which take into account the fact that women's work outside of the family, while making the household cash rich also makes it time poor. Besides the equivalency scale, one could use the exemption of a certain amount of the second earner's income from the calculation of the threshold, or a direct increase of the threshold to be excluded from the benefit. One could use a minimum-maximum method, that is, to give the subsidy to each individual earner, as long as his or her income is below a certain threshold (minimum) and as long as the spouse does not earn more than a given multiple of the minimum (maximum). One could, as a further option, use a computation of extended income. To compute extended income, we add to the monetary income the domestic work of the full-time housekeeper, or else subtract the value of the domestic work foregone if there are no full-time housekeepers in the home (Addabbo and Caiumi 1998). A fiscal deduction below a threshold of income for the household where all the adults work (rather than the present practice of applying a deduction for a household in which one of the spouses devotes all her time to domestic production, of which later) would also achieve the same aim.

In what follows, I will analyse the transfer programmes of the Italian welfare state and discuss how they may be modified in order to satisfy criteria of gender equity. I will consider equity between people who are biologically different, that is, men and women, equity between work performed in the house and outside of the house, and equity between people who choose to form a family and people who choose not to.

## Family Allowances

In Italy, there are two policies which may be classified as family-related cash transfers. The first applies to any citizen who presents an income declaration and has a 'dependant'. In addition, a second one holds for those who are employed and have a 'dependant'. One's 'dependant' may be a spouse or other family member living in the same household with an income of less than 5.5 million lire a year, or a child below 18 years of age or until 26 if they are in education.

The first is a tax credit: each person has the right to a deduction (that is, a reduction of tax otherwise due) for the dependent spouse, and one for each child or other dependant. The 1996 budget set the amount of this deduction to 336,000 lire per child or other dependant, to a maximum of 1,057,552 lire for the income bracket below 30 million lire and a minimum of 817,552 lire for the income bracket over 100 million lire. The expected cost to the public coffers is 900 billion lira. From the economic point of view, the present deduction and the increase in the parameters of the equivalency scale for the families where both parents have a job work in the opposite direction. The present deduction gives to all families where the wife does not have a job; the second, gives to families of low income where the family does have a job. Excluded are women who work in families where income is not too low.

The second are the so-called 'assegni familiari' (family allowances). They are paid out by a special fund of the National Institute for Social Provision (INPS), which is funded by contributions from all employers and all employees in prescribed amounts according to wage, except of course in the 'underground' economy. Family allowances are given to workers, paid together with their monthly paycheque, but they are means-tested, based on a family income threshold. There are 16 brackets. The threshold of the upper bracket, at 92.5 billion lira per year, is rather high. An amount is given for the dependent spouse, and an amount is given for each child. The amount given varies with the income bracket of the worker and with the number of dependants. The amount given for each dependant changes with the order number of the dependant. Table 5 shows the entire scale as of July 1998.

The first version of 'assegni familiari' was introduced in 1934, together with the 40-hour week, which implied a fall in the monthly wage that would have pushed large families deeper into poverty. Since 1978 'assegni familiari' have been tax exempt. The last major revision occurred with the law 31/3/1988 No.69. At the peak of their incidence, in 1953, the expenditure on such 'assegni' was 2.70 per cent of GDP. In 1995, it had fallen to 0.3 per cent.

The programme of the Olive Tree coalition called for an increase of the 'assegni familiari' because they are presented as a good 'family policy' to deal with the natality crisis, in particular, by one group in the coalition, the 'Social Christians'. The 'assegni' were markedly increased in 1994 and again in 1995 (20,000 lire per month per child after the first, 84,000 lire after the second). The 1996 budget increased the expenditure on the

TABLE 5
INCOME BRACKETS FOR FAMILY ALLOWANCES, JULY 1998

| People in the family | 1 | 2 | 3 | 4 | 5 | 6 | ≤7 |
|---|---|---|---|---|---|---|---|
| Annual income (m+f): | | | | | | | |
| From 0 to 20,293 | – | – | 253 | 485 | 695 | 953 | 1,200 |
| 20,294 to 25,111 | – | – | 222 | 427 | 658 | 932 | 1,163 |
| 25,112 to 29,929 | – | – | 179 | 369 | 606 | 916 | 1,131 |
| 29,930 to 34,744 | – | – | 127 | 306 | 548 | 879 | 1,094 |
| 34,745 to 39,563 | – | – | 85 | 216 | 468 | 789 | 983 |
| 39,564 to 44,381 | – | – | 50 | 158 | 421 | 757 | 946 |
| 44,382 to 49,199 | – | – | 30 | 111 | 342 | 705 | 904 |
| 49,200 to 54,015 | – | – | 30 | 75 | 263 | 657 | 851 |
| 54,016 to 58,832 | – | – | 25 | 50 | 199 | 615 | 825 |
| 58,833 to 63,649 | – | – | 25 | 50 | 178 | 436 | 772 |
| 63,650 to 68,468 | – | – | 25 | 45 | 178 | 299 | 567 |
| 68,469 to 73,286 | – | – | – | 45 | 152 | 299 | 424 |
| 73,286 to 78,104 | – | – | – | 45 | 152 | 256 | 424 |
| 78,105 to 82,922 | – | – | – | – | 152 | 256 | 366 |
| 82,923 to 87,740 | – | – | – | – | – | 256 | 366 |
| 87,741 to 92,559 | – | – | – | – | – | – | 366 |

'assegni' by 1,900 billion lira. In the presence of a disabled person, the income brackets have been shifted so that the thresholds are higher, but they are still calculated on the basis of joint income. Most of this increase is due to a 25 per cent rise in the cheques given to single parents. Given that most single parents are mothers, this is a step in favour of single working mothers, which goes toward the recognition of women's work. With the exception of a recent increase in benefits to single parents who are workers, the 'assegni' system mirrors gender relations in the family and society in the 1950s and 1960s. They would work, as a means to achieve a more equitable distribution of income between rich and poor people, if most families were 'bi-parental', with a continuously employed man and a housekeeping woman, and if the male worker was willing to redistribute his earnings fairly to wife and children. An increasing number of families do not meet these conditions, because of youth unemployment, women's employment, delayed family formation and internal conflict within families.

Unemployment is high, especially among men and women in the childbearing years. Thus, linking provision for poor children to the job of the head of the family is not an ideal solution, as the children of the unemployed receive nothing. Unemployment and a lack of independent rights in the welfare state delay family formation and therefore autonomous access to this benefit as long as the benefit is granted to young people who remain in the original household of a worker. As a result, a record number of young men in Italy live with their parents through their twenties and well into their thirties. The 'assegni', in addition, cannot manage labour-market transitions from one job to the next, with short spells of unemployment in between, which characterize the youth labour market and the labour market of an economy experiencing continuous technological change.

Besides being job centred, the 'assegni' are patriarchal in that they assume that whatever is given to the head of the family will be fairly redistributed to the wife and to the other members of the family. Such is often not the case. Because of this patriarchal bias, they are inadequate for managing a situation of family instability, separation and divorce. If the couple splits, the unemployed spouse of a worker has no independent right to them. In the event of family breakdown, they may accrue to the parent (the father) who has a job, even if in more than 90 per cent of cases, courts give custody of the children to the mother.

The job-centred and patriarchal character of the Italian welfare state is most clearly marked not by the programmes which do exist, but by the programmes which do not exist. There are no programmes designed to help the children of people who divorce or enter single parenthood and do not have a job.

In addition to all this, being means-tested on the joint income of the family, the 'assegni' are lost if the wife's earnings take the family income above the thresholds. The considerations of an earlier paragraph therefore apply. They discourage women from seeking paid employment, and may constitute for them a form of 'poverty trap'.

In my opinion, a general reform of the Italian welfare state should remove the 'assegni' in favour of provisions which are both universal in coverage, to cover young unemployed men and women, and targeted toward need using a correct selection mechanism. Failing that, it is urgent that at least the latter aspect of the gender bias of the 'assegni familiari' is overcome. The one I personally favour would be the minimum-maximum option mentioned above. 'Assegni' for every child may be awarded to any worker who earns less than a small amount X (for example, 20 million lire), as long as the spouse does not earn more than a large amount Y (for example, 80 million lire). This is a solution that does not strictly respect equity in the distribution of income between families, but it is certainly more equitable toward the work of women, and it does not provide incentives for non-participation.

*Unemployment Benefits*

There is widespread consensus among economists,[5] sociologists and policy-makers that the Italian way of dealing with social insurance against the risk of unemployment is very inadequate to the task. The system is based on a host of programmes. In the past, the centrepiece was Cassa Integrazione Guadagni (CIG), divided into Ordinary and Special CIG funds, and it is still the largest programme. Introduced in 1968, CIG Ordinaria (CIGO) is a mandatory contribution fund, opened at the INPS, to finance labour hoarding by firms facing temporary falls in demand. The request for CIGO must be made by the company, and must be accepted by the local Inspectors for Work. CIGO pays 80 per cent of a wage, for three to 24 months. The employment relationship between the firm and the worker is never broken: at the end of the period in CIGO, supposedly when the temporary problems of the company are solved, the worker goes back to work at the same firm.

CIG Speciale (CIGS) was meant for firms with more than 200 employees, purportedly to cover those cases when the problems were long term, such as restructuring plants, but still resolvable. It should last up to 48 months, but it has been known to last, with legal and bureaucratic trickery, for up to ten years. Since 1988, it has been financed directly by the Treasury. In fact, it was and still is a very generous programme for collectively dismissed workers, who are, however, still formally employed and therefore prevented from looking for a new job. In 1991, Law No.233 introduced some changes, reducing the time of the benefit, and introducing the '*indennita di mobilita*' (mobility benefit), and a programme of **early retirement** for people at the end of CIG. Mobility benefit is similar to CIG, except it officially applies to firms with more than 15 employees, lasts 12 months, and is paid in cases where it is acknowledged that the firm will not reopen. It is also paid after the end of CIG benefits for firms with more than 200 employees.

Other forms of collective benefits recently introduced are the special benefits for the construction workers, who used to be heavy users of CIG for the winter months and are now under a separate programme. The ordinary benefit for individual lay-offs, applied to people who therefore do not belong to the collective, firm-managed programmes, pays only 30 per cent of the last wage for six months; the worker must have worked legally and paid contributions for two years before qualifying.

By subsidizing labour hoarding, CIG boosts Italian firms' productivity and biases competition with other European firms, and is therefore under attack by the European Union. CIG is a job-based, age- and gender-biased programme: it favours those who have a job against those who have never held a stable job; the old against the young; people who work in large firms against people who work in small firms or individually like domestic helpers. Since women are on average younger, may never have landed a stable job, and are on average employed in smaller firms, it is biased against women. A study by Trifiletti (1996) shows that the changes introduced in 1991 further decreased women's access to CIG benefits — a clear example of a reform that, while improving the overall quality of public intervention in the labour market, worsened its bias against women.

Proposals to eliminate the CIG system and its 'mobility' component altogether, in favour of an individually based, rather than collectively based, unemployment subsidy or in favour of some form of minimum guaranteed income are opposed by both employers and trade unions. The case of unemployment subsidies is an example of the fact that the lot of women is, in general, improved by measures, based on citizenship, which have universal coverage. Such measures acknowledge the citizen's right to a security net independent of their performance in paid employment, and therefore implicitly acknowledge domestic and care-giving work.

Conversely, the kind of fragmented career, with shorter hours, periods of withdrawal from participation due to care-giving work and re-entry into the labour market in a different job that was once characteristically feminine is now more and more common to both sexes, as retraining is a constant need in a time of fast technological change. Therefore, overcoming the job-centred model, today, is not only equitable toward women, but it would adjust public intervention to the needs of a changing labour market.

### Pensions

Until the early 1990s, this familist, patriarchal welfare state was stingy with regard to family assistance and unemployment benefits, but quite generous in its pension system. The ratio between contributions and benefits was very low with respect to the European average. It was very generous to workers and as a consequence also to their dependent wives. Survivors' benefits were high with respect to the European average. The work performed by women in the household was never explicitly recognized as a source of citizen's rights. But the benefits devised for workers have been stretched, sometimes beyond legality, to subsidize women's work in the household, by providing them with 'semi-fake' disability pensions, very early retirement, voluntary contributions to pension schemes after work interruptions and such like. Early retirement was the improper way in which the Italian state coped with men's unemployment problems and with the need to provide for (women's) care work within the family.

Before the recent wave of reforms, the Italian system provided for the end of the working life by means of two programmes: voluntary seniority pensions (*anzianità*), linked to the number of years for which the employed had paid contributions, and mandatory old-age pensions (*vecchiaia*) for all at a prescribed age. The system is a pay-as-you-go system; current pensions are paid out of the contributions that today's workers pay. When these have not been large enough, the Treasury has made up the difference. The system was acknowledged to be financially unsustainable in the medium run before the reforms, and there are still arguments about its sustainability today.

Before the reforms, the seniority pension allowed retirement on request after having paid contributions for 15 years, six month and one day in the public sector, although 25 years of contributions were needed in the private sector. The amount of benefits ceased to increase after 40 years of contributions, even if the worker kept working beyond 40 years until the mandatory retirement age. Those who took seniority benefits could get a second job before the mandatory retirement age. Early retirement was in fact the security net which enabled many elderly women to provide free services to their family and many elderly men to provide cheap labour working for small firms within the black economy or in self-employment without contributions being paid.

In the private sector, the mandatory retirement age was set at 55 for women and 60 for men, and in the public sector at 60 for both ages, though in some careers it was possible to obtain an extension to 65. To obtain the maximum benefit in the private sector a woman would have to have been working since the age of 15. This obvious bias was partially compensated for by the fact that women, and not men, could pay voluntary contributions in addition to the normal amount to cover the equivalent of one year for each child, and thus get slightly larger benefits. The labour-market effects of a mandatory retirement age of 55 were never compensated for, but were significant. In the few instances when a woman could access the high echelons of a career in the private sector, she would be passed over because she was about to retire. Since the cost of hiring and training a woman of 45 coming back to work after childbearing age was not recoverable in the period of ten years before retirement, women were not hired in middle age. However, revealing a typical insider-outsider effect, the trade unions traditionally opposed raising the mandatory retirement age for women, even voluntarily, and notwithstanding the fact that, if women wanted to retire before the mandatory age, they could of course get seniority benefits.[6]

The reforms were enacted in several waves by the governments of Amato (1992–93), Ciampi (1993–94) and Dini (1995–96). The most recent reform is gradually phasing in a new system, which will be fully operational only for those who are newly hired. Under the new system, benefits will not be earnings related but contributions related. Rules defining retirement age have been changed to make the system financially viable: the age of retirement may vary, but the mandatory character of retirement at age 65 has been retained. This is common practice in Europe, as opposed to the USA. I spot a peculiarity here. For the worker, if receiving a pension is a right, retiring at a prescribed age is a duty. Even if he or she would still like to work and the employer agrees, he or she still has to retire. Italy is living in a cultural climate in which most politicians praise flexibility in the labour market, liberalism toward individual choice, and labour-market institutions more similar to those in the USA in order to reap the same employment levels. Nonetheless, no proposals have been put forward to abolish the obligation to stop working and make retirement a voluntary choice jointly exercised by the worker and the employer. My guess is that this peculiarity is related to the fact that it would then be necessary to introduce, after a certain age, a degree of discretion by the employer in firing an older worker. This would go against the grain in a system of industrial relations where no discretionary firing is allowed.

In the new system, approved under the Dini government, the mandatory retirement age is set at 65 for both sexes, although retirement after the age of 57 is permitted with a penalty of 3 per cent of the pension for each year in advance of retirement age. The years of contribution required for seniority benefits have been increased to 35. Early retirement in one form or another is therefore eliminated. People who have more than 18 years of contributions can retire according to the old rules. People who have been hired for the first time after the enactment of the reform are subject to the new rules. People who have been working and contributing for less than 18 years will see their pension calculated partly according to the old and partly according to the new rules. In order not to penalize people who are about to retire and make plans and choices based on that expectation, the recent reforms created a creeping system, in which the age of mandatory retirement and the number of years of contribution required are moved forward one year at a time.

For that part that is presently earnings related, benefits have been reduced: they are now calculated over the entire working lifetime, rather than on the last five years of working life. They will be reduced progressively from 80 per cent to a lower percentage. The possibility of most voluntary contributions has been cancelled.

In addition, survivors' benefits have been curtailed subject to means-testing. It used to be that widows and widowers received 80 per cent of the benefits that would have accrued to the worker. Now, if their income from any source, including a widow's work or her retirement pension, exceeds 26,755,950 lire, the benefit is cut by 25 per cent; if the income is more than 35,674,600 lire it is cut by 40 per cent; and if it is more than 44,593,250 lire it is cut by 50 per cent. As an exception to the general rule that for those people who have already begun to enjoy their benefits there has been no change, benefits for survivors who are already receiving them and whose income was above the level of 26,755,950 lire, mentioned above, have been frozen at the present level.

From the gender point of view, equalization of the mandatory age of retirement for the two sexes, while a positive labour-market measure, creates a problem. Who will now provide the childcare that elderly women have been providing until now, and who will deal with the typical bureaucratic quagmire of public services in Italy? Nowadays, minding grandchildren and queuing in various offices is typically grandmother's task. The lack of availability on the part of retired grandmothers, in addition to the lack of affordable good-quality nursery schools, may further squeeze young working mothers' already tight time resources, and therefore further hamper young women's fertility or their participation rate.

The lengthening of the period for which contributions are required for seniority pensions is gender biased because women tend to have shorter contributive histories with gaps in their working careers due to family-related events. This should be balanced by the fact that the system will become entirely contributory, providing old-age pensions to people with as few as five years of contribution.

Cuts in survivors' benefits are of course particularly adverse to women, since, as women have a longer life expectancy than men and marry men who are older, women are the beneficiaries of most survivors' pensions. It is, in addition, a blatant violation of equity between women who work for a wage and women who are full-time housekeepers. A woman who still works, or who has a substantial pension from her own job will be penalized, and will see her survivors' benefits cut. A working widow with children should notionally subtract from her wage the cost of whatever services she uses to replace her own domestic work, the benefits she loses because of means-testing, and, in addition, the amount of survivors' pension that she loses by going to work. It may very well be that she is better off choosing to stay at home, because her extra-domestic work adds very little to the wealth of her family. The fruits of her work will be literally taken back by the state.

Means-testing survivors' benefits may be construed as equitable between people with different incomes because it cuts benefits to elderly widows or widowers who are already sufficiently well off, but it may also be construed as inequitable in failing to distinguish between women who worked only inside the home and women who have worked inside the home and have earned a wage. Women's earned income is treated as if it were unearned rent from property; no allowance is made of the fact that in order to earn it, women have to make an alternative use of their time, subtracting from other socially productive activity in their home.

There is a clear case of a double standard at work. In the case of survivors' pensions, the consensus is that the duty of the welfare state is to provide only a decent minimum. Women who work and earn are already sufficiently well off, therefore, it is fair and legitimate to cut survivors' benefits, even if this reduces the equity between work effort and **social retribution,** and between contributions made to pension funds and receipts accruing from those contributions. In the case of high seniority pensions already accruing to not so elderly men, the same reasoning did not apply, and the argument that the welfare state should provide only a decent minimum was rejected. Proposals to apply a cap on higher pensions, in the form of a proportional cut to be applied after means-testing never gained any support, on the grounds that they would upset the relationship between contributive history and **levels of repayment,** which the system aimed to preserve. Yet these are pensions that accrue to elderly men who are already well off. Contributions by a man whose wife does not hold a job are thus worth more than those of a man whose wife does.

It is particularly noteworthy that these provisions concerning survivors, so blatantly unfair to women workers, went almost unnoticed in the public debate over the pension system. Elderly women and women who work have very little public voice, or women are the only ones who may be persuaded to accept sacrifices for the common good, or both.

*'Minimum Pensions' and 'Social Benefits'*

In the past, people who, at the mandatory retirement age, did not have a long enough history of contributions had the right to a minimum pension. The same minimum pension accrued to people who worked for 15 years (*minimo*) or less (*integrata al minimo*). After the fifteenth year, the pension increased with job seniority. In 1996, the minimum benefit was equal to 659,000 lire per month. This was means-tested: if there was no other income, the INPS paid the full amount; if there was an income from any source of twice this minimum, excluding the home, severance pay and the minimum pension itself, the right to this benefit was lost.

The first wave of reform under the Amato government introduced some changes: the number of years before benefits increased was moved from 15 to 20 years and the means test was moved from personal income to family income. The rule was that a single person should not have an income double the benefit and a couple three times the benefit in order to maintain the right to the benefit.

These moves were again clearly gender biased: it is women who tend to have a short history of contribution and therefore to be claimants of these pensions. Means-testing of the couple's income eliminated the pensions of those women who had worked for a short period of time and whose husbands were still working or had a modestly high pension.

The second wave of reforms, under the Dini Government in 1995, cancelled the right to a minimum pension for those with fewer than 18 years of contributions. They will have the right only to 'social benefit' (*assegno sociale*), which for the year 1998 was equal to 6,593,000 lire per year. This is not a pension, but is legally classified as 'assistance'.

Dini adjusted backward, at least in part, the threshold for those already receiving the 'minimum pension'. The government kept the reference to joint, rather than single, incomes, but the threshold for a couple receiving minimum benefit was set at four times the minimum benefit, that is, double the threshold for single pensioners, an improvement from the point of view of women.

In the past, people who, at age 65, had no history of contributions whatsoever because they did not ever pay any contribution (whether because they did not work or because they were always hired illegally) had the right to the so-called 'social pension'. It was the only form of guaranteed minimum income existing in Italy. The amount was lower than that of the 'minimum pension'. In 1995, it was set at 357,000 lire per month. In the past 20 years, the number of recipients of these benefits has decreased from 840,000 in 1974 to 718,000 in 1995, as women began to have enough contributions to get the 'minimum'. Some 78 out of 1,000 elderly citizens receive the 'minimum pension', 80 per cent of them women. Of these, 41 per cent are in the south, 22.3 per cent in central Italy and 36.2 per cent in the north. As shown by Monacelli (1996), the threshold for this 'social pension' was set in a rather peculiar way. The target set for a couple was more than three times the target set for a single person. Couples or families with many people received enough to live near the poverty line, while single, divorced and widowed people were heavily penalized. For a couple who both have a social pension, the death of one of the spouses could mean sudden further impoverishment for the other. It appeared as if the state preserved the family as long as two elderly people were living together. Once an elderly person finds herself alone (in most cases, an elderly person over 65 with a right to social pension is a woman), she has no option but to join another family, typically her children's.

In 1996, the 'social pension' was replaced by the 'social benefit', which became, therefore, the single measure through which the Italian state deals with the poorest part of the elderly population. For the year 1998, the yearly amount of the 'social benefit' was 6,593,600 lire (507,200 lire a month for 13 months) for single people with no income. If their income is between zero and 6,593,000 lire, people have the right to integration benefit of up to 6,593,000 lire. Above that level they have no right to the benefit. If people are married, then a joint income threshold exactly double that amount applies. If person X earns nothing and their spouse less than 6,593,000 lire, person X receives the benefit. If the spouse earns between 6,593,000 lire and 13,187,200 lire, person X gets a reduced cheque to integrate an income of 13,187,000 lire for the couple. If the spouse earns more than 13,187,200 lire, person X gets nothing.

The effects of this measure are not easily evaluated, and probably they are not particularly important from the point of view of increased efficiency of the system. Yet fairness is still a value regarded as important in society, even when the consequences of unfairness will be borne only by those who suffer it. Because of the difference in the average age of marriage between men and women, husbands reach 65 before wives do. At that age, a small wage income for the wife may make the husband loose the benefit. When both spouses are over 65, then the fact that one of the two (usually the husband) qualifies for a low pension, implies that he has lost benefits for the spouse, and is now as well off as the person who did not work at all. He must be willing to share his already low income equally with his spouse, and she cannot in any way make sure that this happens. Moreover, a couple that never worked is made as well off as a couple where each worked for a low wage for as many as 19 years before reaching retirement. One may argue that if we want to raise the extreme low end of the income distribution to a given minimum level, we will always be unfair to those who had reached that level by themselves. Yet, in my opinion this is one of the clearest cases in which it would not have been at all unfair to let some couples be slightly richer than others. Here, at the poorest end of the income distribution, treating each individual, married or not, as single is the only way to avoid leaving elderly married women in a position of total dependency on their husbands.

The last item in the pension reform was the institution in the INPS in 1997 of a voluntary fund for home-makers, or 'casalinghe'. People who have no other job and are therefore full-time home-makers, or anybody else, now have the opportunity to insure themselves against accidents and to earn the right to a pension by paying voluntary contributions into this fund. While the symbolic value of this act is certainly very positive, because it affirms the citizenship of women who are full-time housekeepers, the financial value of starting such insurance may be questionable for women who are married, given the fact that survivors' benefits are then means-tested.

## CONCLUSIONS

What can we say then about the model of gender relations that the Italian welfare state assumes and reproduces? Is the present wave of reform going to change it, and if so, in what direction?

Before the recent waves of reforms, the Italian welfare state was with respect to the European average heavy in transfers and poor in services. The transfer programmes were, in turn, mostly job based. Therefore, they were too generous with pensions and too stingy with assistance, and unable to cope with some situations of need. They were also patriarchal, in the sense that the right of women to welfare was based on their personal relationship to a worker, on whom she was assumed to be 'dependent'. No autonomous right of women as citizens or as providers of care-giving work was recognized. Instead, the Italian welfare state stretched to the limits job-based benefits, which were then used for women to provide care. Some of the pathologies of the Italian welfare state (early retirement, misuse of disability benefits and abuse of health facilities for assistance purposes) are related to this unwillingness to provide explicitly for care work.

The model of gender relations that was upheld was the traditional one of male breadwinner and female housekeeper. In this view, women's work is in the home, and she will be independently helped only if the male provider ceases to function as such. Women's work outside of the home in this view was considered a quirk, an exception, a private choice for women who had a very high earning capability, and could indulge in both the traditional feminine role and the traditionally masculine one, with higher social status attached to the latter. It was assumed that the state had no duty to support such trespassing.

Nonetheless, because the entry of women into the labour market is a powerful trend in economic development, the female employment rate has grown over the years, notwithstanding the lack of a proper system of services and transfers and albeit at a slower rate than in other European countries. Women should therefore have begun as workers to enjoy the benefits that the job-based welfare system had denied them as citizens and care providers. But as soon as they arrived, as Trifiletti (1996) describes, the mat was pulled from under their feet, so to speak. Benefits had to be cut because of the financial crisis.

This model of gender relations is still the underlying pattern of the Italian welfare state. It has not been replaced by a new system designed along different lines. The upholding of the breadwinner-housekeeper model well beyond its sell-by date was and is a source of problems for the system, and not only for women. By creating distortions, it was as much a factor in the crisis of the welfare state as the simple demographics between the elderly and the young, even if not as often and as explicitly recognized. It was a factor in the financial crisis because, by preventing women's entry into the labour market, it deprived the system of contributions. If women's employment could grow quickly to European levels, the problem of a lack of contributors to the pay-as-you-go scheme would improve. It was a factor in the consensus crisis because benefits, which were meant for one worker to keep a family, were perceived as too generous when two workers were married and had no dependent adults. The fact that this was never recognized means that, in the most recent wave of reforms, the Italian welfare state was merely adjusted, rather than being explicitly revised to remove its principal gendered features.

Cutting benefits to those workers who are married to another worker, through means-testing joint income, was chosen as one of the main reform options. It is an option that reinforces, rather than changes, the old model of gender relations. It may dissuade the second worker in a couple from ever seeking a job, because the benefits that are foregone become too large. This starts a vicious circle in which no service sector develops because no services are needed, and therefore women's employment does not grow. It has very clear redistributive implications: women workers outside of the house have helped a great deal to foot the bill for the financial health of the country and for entry to post-Maastricht Europe.

The size of the cuts was almost mandatory once the Maastricht treaty was in place, but most scholars would agree that how to cut and where to cut are, at least partially, discretionary choices. They were made according to the political consensus about what it is 'fair' to cut or where there is less opposition to the cuts. Cutting benefits for workers married to other workers (in fact, cutting benefits to women who work outside the household, which is the main effect of means-testing by joint income of the couple) was only one possible option, and by no means the only one available. Cutting benefits to the richest workers was another, as was freezing everybody's rights to benefits and thereby leaving people's relative positions unchanged.

The choice of penalizing working couples undermines the internal coherence of the system. It is still heavily centred on the worker, but the worker is central, if he is a man, and no longer central, if she is a woman. The patriarchal character of the system, therefore, increased rather than decreased, in that it was moved into the public sphere. Men are worth more not only among family members, but also among workers, a view of gender which was until now acknowledged only by employers who practised wage discrimination. Women are given many incentives to remain in a position of dependency. If they choose to become workers, they are not treated like men, but less well. Women's rights in the welfare system are completely different according to whether they choose to work for pay or not to work for pay, to marry or not to marry. The final set of activities, through which most commodities become of use to people in their homes, is therefore the main source of well-being and is still almost completely off the agenda, a private act beyond public recognition. The source of the pathological distortions is still there, and the conditions for realigning women's participation and employment rates with European standards have not been improved: if anything, means-testing may worsen the problem.

The reform of the welfare state could have been the occasion for introducing a new social contract for women. Facing the need to cut expenditure because of financial crisis, reform could have been oriented differently. Transfers could have been cut overall, but redistributed on the basis of independent rights to those who provide care. Assistance for severe need could have been improved by targeting, without creating new poverty traps. The quality of services could have improved if labour-market policies had given women, who staff these services, the opportunity to enter the labour force in larger numbers and to work without neglecting family care.[7] In other words, policies could have been oriented by a different view of gender relations: one in which women's agency and women's autonomous rights were recognized and women's freedom to choose respected. Where people of different sexes are together engaged in raising families, sharing domestic work and providing the financial resources needed for the task. This is a view of gender relations which is rather widespread, but which seems not to have made inroads, yet, into the policy-making community in charge of the Italian welfare state reforms.

There is still time. The process of reform of the Italian welfare state is far from over. After the recent change in government, from Prodi to D'Alema, some of the issues I have been discussing are slowly coming to the fore. We may still hope that the final product of the leftist intervention in welfare will finally make Italy 'a normal country' in terms of its gender relations.

## NOTES

1. I use 'gender' to indicate a set of physical and mental characteristics, and the proper, normal, behaviour that each culture attributes to people on the basis of their biological sex. Gender, therefore, changes widely in time and space, through history and in different cultures and civilizations. For a thorough discussion of the concept of 'gender', see Nelson (1996).
2. It is interesting to note that in the present political debate, in Italy, young people's dependence on their original family is considered a problem, while women's dependence on their husbands is not. It is true that youth unemployment rates in Italy are very high. But young people are not therefore poor: they share in their original family resources, and their standard of consumption may be as high, if not higher, than in those countries where they earn their own living. Yet we hear a lot of the problem of generational equity, and very little about the problem of gender equity.
3. Conventional economic models use leisure as the only alternative variable to waged labour, assuming that since leisure has a positive value, as do goods produced in the household, the two are equivalent. But from the point of view of social policy this cannot work: reproduction and the welfare of children, sick people and the aged may depend on the amount of 'leisure' that women can afford. The answer of the Italian welfare state is to finance this 'leisure' through men. Clearly, many women are saying that this arrangement is just not good enough.
4. One may wonder why the declaration for income tax purposes is not, by itself, a proper way to measure income. The official reason given by those who accept the 'riccometro'

is that the '*riccometro*' asks questions about consumption, rather than income, and then 'assumes' an income from a given level of consumption. The unofficial reason is that income tax cheating in Italy is notoriously high, in particular in the commercial sector, which is characterized by many small firms. The hope is that, while lying to the tax authority in order to save taxes is socially acceptable, voluntarily filing for social assistance on false pretences would be frowned upon socially. Or, maybe, those who cheat on their taxes will not do it if they are told that those who file for assistance will be more severely audited.

5. For a thorough description of the unemployment benefit system and its history, see Dell'Aringa and Samek Ludovici (1996).
6. The only possible explanation of this fact is that the mandatory age forced a choice that otherwise would have not been accepted in the family. This may have been a husband's choice to have a full-time housekeeper, imposed on their wife, or a wife's choice not to carry a double burden, imposed on their husbands, or the desire by employers and workers not to have to deal with elder women on the job.
7. In the political discourse, we hear that the job-centred character of the welfare system should change to become family centred. Even liberal forces seem to share in the consensus about this aim. There are exceptions, especially within the left: most notably Francesca Izzo, the MP in charge of women's policies in the Party of the Democratic Left (PDS). But, overall, neither the right nor the left had the clarity of view to see the superiority, in the long run, of a new social pact with women in terms of efficiency and increased productivity of the entire economic system, and to assert it forcefully. Equity toward women was sacrificed to the needs of political alliance, and to spare more organized constituencies from the cuts.

## REFERENCES

Addabbo, T. and A. Caiumi (1998): 'Extended income and inequality by gender in Italy'. Paper presented to the twenty-fifth conference of the IARW, Cambridge, August 1998, and CNEL, research project directed by A. Picchio.

Addis, E. (1997): *Economia e Differenze di Genere*. Bologna: CLUEB.
(1998): 'Gender effects of means testing: the Italian case'. Paper presented to the Conference Reforming Social Assistance and Social Services, Forum 'Recasting the European Welfare states', European University Institute, 11–12 December 1998, mimeo.

Atkinson, A. B. (1995): *Public Economics In Action*. Oxford University Press.

Bettio, F. and P. Villa (1996): 'Un modello al bivio'. In *DWF*, 4.

Bettio, F. and P. Villa (1995): 'A Mediterranean perspective on the breakdown of the relationship between participation and fidelity', *Cambridge Journal of Economics*.

Bimbi, F. (1998): 'Cittadinanza delle donne e politiche familiari'. Paper presented to the seminar Genere e Cittadinanza in Europa, Roma, 25–26 June 1998, mimeo.

Bonke, J. (1993): 'The distribution of time and money in the family'. In S. Carlsen and J. L. Lansen (eds.), *The Equality Dilemma*. Copenhagen: The Danish Equal Status Council.

De Leonardis, O. (1998): *In un diverso Welfare*. Milano: Feltrinelli.

Dell'Aringa, C. and L. Samek Ludovici (1996): 'Gli ammortizzatori della disoccupazione: l'esperienza italiana'. *Qualita Equita*, 3.

Esping-Andersen, G. (1996): *Welfare States in Transition*. London: Sage.

Equal Opportunity Unit, Div.V, (1997): *Individualizing Social Rights*. Report, January 1997.

Ferber, M. A. and J. A. Nelson (eds.) (1993): *Beyond Economic Man: Feminist Theory and Economics*. Chicago: University of Chicago Press.

Ferrera, M. (1998): *Le trappole del Welfare*. Bologna: Il Mulino.

Gershuny, J. (1995): 'Gender convergence and public regulation'. Paper presented at the Forum on Gender and The Use of Time, Florence, European University Institute.

Gustavsson S. and F. Stafford (1994): 'Three regimes of childcare: the US, The Netherlands and Sweden'. In R. Blank (ed.), *Social Protection versus Economic Flexibility*, pp.333–62. Chicago: Chicago University Press.

Monacelli, D. (1996): 'Assessing public action in Italy: elderly assistance and the social pension scheme'. Mimeo, Bank of Italy.

Nelson, J. (1996): *Feminism, Objectivity, and Economics*. London: Routledge.

Orloff, A. S. (1996): 'Gender in the welfare state'. *Annual Review of Sociology*, 22.

Pennacchi, L. (1997): *Lo Stato Sociale del futuro*. Roma: Donzelli.

Rossi, N. (1997): *Meno ai padri e piu' ai figli*. Bologna: Il Mulino.

Saraceno, C. (1994): 'The ambivalent familism of the Italian welfare state', *Social Politics*.

Sen, A. (1992): *Inequality Re-examined*. Oxford: Oxford University Press.

Trifiletti, R. (1996): 'Mediterranean welfare regimes and the worsening position of women'. Paper presented at the Interdisciplinary Women's Studies Seminar, European University Institute, Florence.

# To What Extent does it Pay to be Better Educated? Education and the Work Market for Women in Italy

FRANCESCA BETTIO and PAOLA VILLA

Recent evidence in Italian news articles and academic journals draws attention to the fact that women appear to perform systematically better than men at all levels of education. Parallel to this, empirical studies of the female labour supply suggest that women's participation in the labour market in Italy may be particularly responsive to education. Some econometric studies have estimated that female participation is more responsive to a given wage increase in Italy than in other industrialized countries, education being one of the key variables driving this increase (Colombino and Di Tommaso 1996; Di Tommaso 1998). Comparative analyses of participation patterns in Europe have found that Italy records one of the highest gaps in participation between poorly and highly educated women (Rubery *et al.* 1996).

These findings are not obvious, particularly in view of the fact that it does not pay as much in terms of salary to acquire more education in Italy as it does, say, in the USA, the UK or other industrialized countries. This article is a preliminary attempt to make sense of these findings.

Our first point is that education fulfils important roles in addition to that of increasing one's human capital and wage prospects, the character and importance of these roles being conditional on given institutional environments. In the specific context of Italy, the drive to acquire educational credentials disproportionately biases female participation in favour of the most educated women. Yet, because of the poor job-creation capacity of the Italian economy, education affords a competitive edge at the individual level, but may have perverse effects at the aggregate level. This is our second point in this article.

In all countries, education is changing women's tastes toward waged work over and above the economic returns it may afford. In the Italian context, education also acts as an 'access card' to many occupations or as the next step in the career ladder (Borzaga 1994), partly because school and college certificates are given full legal status. Moreover, due to high structural unemployment and the relatively low cost of education, the latter has often served to postpone entry into an exceedingly crowded job queue, thus offering a sheltered 'parking lot' to young Italian women and men waiting for a job. Partly because of its role as a 'parking lot', education performs badly as a signal to firms of the intrinsic abilities of job applicants, contrary to what economic theory suggests (Spence 1973). This is reinforced by the fact that school selectivity is often perceived as excessively random.

Even in its role of human-capital investment, education is affected by the way the Italian labour market operates. By ensuring high protection for incumbent employees, the Italian labour market tends to impose a stark choice between the alternative of not investing in education and exiting the labour market early (or not entering at all) and that of acquiring good educational qualifications with the idea of clinging to employment for life. In Italy, not only is labour-market discontinuity penalized by the loss of seniority rights, which still count significantly toward pay increases and promotions, but also the prospects of re-entering are poor because of the low turnover in employment among adult workers. In particular, the strategy of exiting and entering the market in concomitance with motherhood, which prevails in other European countries, is still unpopular among Italian women partly because of the penalties involved.[1]

For all these reasons, poorly educated women account for a lower share of the working female population in Italy than elsewhere. Indeed, the evidence presented below suggests that female participation is more responsive to education than to motherhood status.

Precisely because (formal) education is more than just a means to acquire competence, its relationship with unemployment is contradictory, especially in the case of women. At the individual level, it makes sense to invest in education in order to gain a competitive edge, or simply to stay on in the labour market without acquiring the stigma of being unemployable. At the aggregate level, however, more education does not help to clear the job queue and may even lengthen it, for example, by increasing the number of women within the labour supply who are determined to stay on in the labour market despite poor prospects of employment.

Section two will briefly review recent trends in educational attainment by gender from a comparative perspective. Section three will discuss how education has influenced female participation in Italy, while section four will concentrate on the relationship with unemployment.

## WOMEN ARE OVERTAKING MEN IN FORMAL QUALIFICATIONS

### Formal Education

Italy still has some way to go in closing the educational gap with the most developed nations. But women are rapidly closing the gender gap in education within the country.

International comparisons of levels of education are fraught with difficulty. The specific problem with Italy is that, if the indicator chosen is the share of students attending a course in the relevant age group, Italy comes close to the OECD average (see Table 1). If the indicator is the attainment of school certificates, the country falls behind the OECD average, especially with regard to college and university education (ISTAT 1995). This inconsistency between indicators is due to a very high drop-out rate in Italy, particularly at university level. The Italian university system used to offer only relatively long BA degree courses until shorter and lighter diploma courses were (slowly) introduced in the 1990s. With a few exceptions, moreover, enrolment was not conditional on an entry test, and low selectivity increased the drop-out rate.

TABLE 1
ENROLMENT RATES IN ITALY AND THE OECD COUNTRIES (1991)

| Age (years) | Students/Population by Age (%) | | | | | | | |
|---|---|---|---|---|---|---|---|---|
| | 17 | 18 | 19 | 20 | 21 | 22 | 23 | 24 |
| Italy | 62.8 | 52.4 | 39.1 | 30.2 | 24.4 | 20.5 | 17.7 | 14.8 |
| OECD Average | 73.0 | 56.7 | 41.5 | 31.9 | 24.0 | 19.5 | 14.5 | 11.1 |

Source: ISTAT (1995)

However the Italian system of education may rank vis-à-vis other developed countries, it has manifestly benefited women, who have practically closed the gender gap in quantitative terms and are making significant gains in the desegregation of curricula.[2] By the early 1990s, a larger share of 18-year-old women than men had completed higher secondary education.[3] Moreover, by 1992–93, young women entering university education overtook young men in quantitative terms. As more and more women entered university, they also began to study traditionally non-female subjects. As a result, women's share of university students (enrolled) was more than 50 per cent in 1995–96, their share of new graduates being 53.1 per cent; moreover, women are distributed among subjects in such a way that few remain segregated (Table 3).

The number of countries in which more young women than men hold graduate degrees is large and increasing (OECD 1995; Rubery *et al.* 1996: 69–71), but in all of them the segregation of curricula persists and feeds into employment patterns. Italy is making better progress than most on this score. In 1992, Italy recorded the second lowest concentration of female graduates in the human sciences in a group of 11 European countries (Table 2); in 1995, nine out of 14 graduate subjects recorded a fairly balanced share of women among students, ranging from 40 per cent to 60 per cent (Table 3).

TABLE 2
CONCENTRATION BY SUBJECT OF WOMEN GRADUATING (1992)

|  | Human Sciences | All Other Subjects* |
|---|---|---|
| Finland | 60.0 | 40.0 |
| Ireland | 57.8 | 40.2 |
| Greece | 53.9 | 46.1 |
| Denmark | 53.4 | 46.6 |
| The Netherlands | 52.4 | 47.6 |
| Spain | 50.9 | 49.1 |
| United Kingdom | 47.2 | 52.8 |
| Sweden | 40.7 | 59.3 |
| Germany (old Länder) | 39.8 | 60.2 |
| Italy | 35.0 | 65.0 |
| Belgium | 32.4 | 67.6 |

* Engineering, Natural Sciences, Medicine, Law, Business and Economics.

*Source*: OECD (1995, Table R14).

Not only are certified educational attainments for women now higher than they are for men, but female educational performance is systematically better, whatever indicator is chosen to assess it (Table 4). Thus, higher percentages of women successfully complete primary school, secondary school, and university courses; on average, women complete their educational courses in a shorter time, and they also earn higher marks.

The determination with which Italian women pursue good standards of performance in education warrants some explanation. This is unlikely to be found in wage differentials alone. According to recent evidence

TABLE 3
SHARE OF WOMEN AMONG UNIVERSITY STUDENTS
BY SUBJECT (1981–96)

|  | Academic Year 1981–82 Students Enrolled | Academic Year 1992–93 Students Enrolled | Academic Year 1995–96 Students Enrolled | Academic Year 1995–96 Graduates |
|---|---|---|---|---|
| Sciences and maths | 53.8* | 51.4* | 37.8 | 45.7 |
| Chemistry and pharmacology | – | – | 59.3 | 59.5 |
| Biology | – | – | 59.1 | 62.7 |
| Medicine | 35.8 | 53.3 | 52.1 | 46.9 |
| Engineering | 15.1** | 23.4** | 14.0 | 11.4 |
| Architecture | – | – | 46.9 | 46.9 |
| Agronomy | 22.2 | 36.2 | 41.3 | 36.4 |
| Economics | 31.5 | 43.6 | 44.7 | 44.0 |
| Political Science | 39.1 | 49.8 | 52.4 | 53.2 |
| Law | 42.5 | 54.9 | 56.2 | 54.4 |
| Literature | 76.2*** | 80.1*** | 72.9 | 76.5 |
| Languages | – | – | 87.7 | 90.1 |
| Education | – | – | 89.1 | 87.2 |
| Psychology | – | – | 79.8 | 81.7 |
| TOTAL | 43.6 | 50.8 | 52.8 | 53.1 |

Note:     * also includes chemistry, pharmacology and biology.
         ** also includes architecture.
         *** also includes languages, education and psychology.

Source: ISTAT, Annuario di Statistiche dell'Istruzione (various issues), Annuario Statistico
Italiano (1997a, Table 7.14: 185).

based on the European Household Panel and the structure of Earnings
Surveys – the two main Community sources on wages – returns to
education are high in Italy compared with the rest of Europe; however
the male–female earnings differentials among graduates is the highest in
the Community, and, like elsewhere, Italian women tend to be
overqualified for the position they occupy (Bettio and Villa 1992; Rubery
and Fagan 1993; Boje 1996). It has been noted in other countries that
women use qualification leverage to gain access to professions
(Crompton and Sanderson 1990). In Italy, this 'access card' role played
by education is amplified by the fact that certificates are given full legal
status. In the professions, in the public sector, and in the still large sector
of semi-public firms (utilities, banks and some manufacturing areas),
entry or promotion to a position is often conditional on having obtained
a given certificate. Moreover, the grades of final-level examinations, or

TABLE 4
PERFORMANCE IN EDUCATION BY SEX IN ITALY, VARIOUS INDICATORS
(1992–96)

|  | Male | Female |
|---|---|---|
| Share of 18 year olds completing higher secondary education (1992–93) | 48.5 | 55.2 |
| Share of 15–19 year olds not completing lower secondary education in 1995 | 5.0 | 4.3 |
| Share of 20–24 year olds not completing lower secondary education in 1995 | 3.9 | 3.7 |
| Pass rate for upper secondary education | 87.3 | 92.9 |
| Share of year repeaters, upper secondary education 1994–95 | 9.3 | 4.9 |
| Drop-out rate, upper secondary education 1994–95 | 7.9 | 5.3 |
| Rate of completion of upper secondary diplomas in 1994–95 over 100 registered 5 years before | 70.7 | 78.8 |
| Students completing the '*Maturità*' (per cent) per 100 19 year olds in 1995 | 55.8 | 63.0 |
| Graduate students completing BA courses per 100 registered 6 years before | 33.1 | 38.2 |

*Source*: ISTAT (1997b).

age on graduation, are sometimes explicitly given a score in the selection process. Rules of this kind not only enhance the certainty that good performance in education gives a competitive edge, but also dilute the potential discrimination inherent in more discretionary selection procedures. Thus they are of special value to women.

*Vocational and Continuous Training*

The overall picture is bleaker for training, although even in formal training courses women are doing better than men. Female as well as male workers receive relatively little formal training in Italy compared with other European countries. The share of employees attending formal courses in 1990 (ranging from general education to specific training) was the third lowest in Italy, after Belgium and Greece (Eurostat data).

Renewed efforts to set up a more efficient system nationwide were made in the 1990s under pressure from the European Community. In 1990, formal training was finally regulated (Law No.492/1990) and received appropriate funding. Some three years later, the national agency in charge of the coordination and monitoring of training, ISFOL, admitted that the regional authorities charged with organizing training at the local level had largely failed (ISFOL 1993).

TABLE 5
TOTAL NUMBER OF STUDENTS ATTENDING FORMAL TRAINING BY GENDER (1992–96)

| | Basic training courses Corsi post-obbligo | | | Advanced training courses Corsi post-diploma | | | Other courses | | | Total | | |
|---|---|---|---|---|---|---|---|---|---|---|---|---|
| | MF | F | %F | MF | F | % F | MF | F | %F | MF | F | %F |
| 1992–93 | 165,717 | 77,924 | 47.02 | 63,626 | 40,725 | 64.01 | 94,294 | 32,297 | 34.25 | 323,637 | 150,946 | 46.64 |
| 1993–94 | 162,430 | 74,807 | 46.05 | 88,228 | 55,311 | 62.69 | 107,784 | 40,642 | 37.71 | 358,442 | 170,760 | 47.64 |
| 1994–95 | 151,634 | 68,340 | 45.07 | 80,327 | 50,737 | 63.16 | 115,488 | 43,150 | 37.36 | 347,449 | 162,227 | 46.69 |
| 1995–96 | 148,991 | 71,049 | 47.69 | 44,202 | 27,083 | 61.27 | 185,767 | 71,085 | 38.27 | 378,960 | 169,217 | 44.65 |
| (%) | (39.3) | (42.0) | | (11.7) | (16.0) | | (49.0) | (42.0) | | (100) | (100) | |
| Var. per cent 1992–95 | −10.09 | −8.82 | | −30.53 | −33.50 | | 97.01 | 120.10 | | 17.09 | 12.10 | |

Source: ISTAT (1997a, Table 7.8: 181).

However, there is some evidence that proportionally more women than men attend training courses (see Table 5). Overall, 378,960 people attended formal training courses organized at the regional level in 1995–96, and almost 45 per cent of them were women (compared with a female share of the labour force of only 37 per cent). About 40 per cent of all students enrolled attended basic training courses, that is, courses for students who had received only compulsory schooling (*corsi post-obbligo*): the rate of feminization for these courses was high (47.7 per cent), and much higher than the proportion of women in the labour force with low educational attainments. About 12 per cent of all students attended advanced training courses, that is, courses organized for students with higher educational degrees (*corsi post-diploma*): the rate of feminization was even higher in this case (61.3 per cent). The remaining 49 per cent of those receiving formal training consisted of adults (employed, unemployed and redundant workers) attending further training, retraining, specific training courses and the like (other courses): in this case, the rate of feminization was lower (38.3 per cent), albeit increasing and slightly higher than the feminization rate of the labour force.

It is not that Italian firms offer a great deal of training.[4] It was estimated that barely five per cent of wage agreements negotiated at the firm level in 1990 provided for on-the-job training. The introduction of youth-training contracts in 1984 ought to have ensured training for young entrants, yet it is generally agreed that the actual training content of these schemes was modest, sometimes nil. Firms made heavy use of these contracts because they offered the double advantage of sizeable reductions in social contributions and temporary contracts. It is therefore of little consequence that the initial bias toward men in the allocation of these contracts gradually lessened.

The effects on employability of attending training courses are unclear or marginal: it has recently been estimated that formal training significantly improves the chances of finding a job, conditional on the strength of the local economy, that is, only in some areas of the centre-north, where unemployment is in any case low (Bulgarelli and Ranieri 1994). It is therefore plausible that participation in formal vocational training courses offers unemployed job-seekers (women and men) yet another 'parking lot' to fall back on in addition to, or as an alternative to, extra years of schooling.

EDUCATION IS DRIVING FEMALE LABOUR-MARKET PARTICIPATION

Education, if not training, is shaping the identity of Italian women around waged work. The success recorded in education has brought with it not only increased investment in human capital, but also emancipation from traditional cultural values and higher aspirations with regard to work and lifestyles. In short, the Italian experience strongly suggests that education is a powerful, independent factor driving participation and attachment to waged work.

In strictly quantitative terms, the postwar growth in female participation in Italy was not exceptional, for it proved insufficient to close the gap with other European countries. Between 1975 and 1990, the rate of growth of the female activity rate in Italy was roughly in line with that recorded for the EU 15. However, because the figure for Italy was ten percentage points below the average European rate to begin with (in 1975), the gap did not close. Indeed, it has widened since the early 1990s on account of strong discouraging factors during the recession. Thus, in 1996, Italy still ranked third from bottom within the European Union (the female activity rate being 57.4 per cent for the EU 15 and 43.7 per cent in Italy).

From a comparative perspective, however, two features of this process of growing participation stand out clearly, namely a pattern of non-interruption and responsiveness to education. Figure 1 documents the age-participation profile for successive cohorts of Italian women, with the oldest and the youngest cohorts aged 45–49 and 25–29 years in 1992, respectively. All the cohorts exhibit an uninterrupted profile over the childbearing interval, with the probable exception of the oldest cohort for which a slight dip is observable between 20 and 34 years of age. In other words, continuity is the hallmark of Italian participants who have entered the labour market since at least the mid-1960s.[5]

However, even the youngest cohorts reach a plateau by age 25 at rates no higher than 65 per cent. This indicates that (i) a non-marginal group of women still does not enter the labour market at all and (ii) past age 25 some of the best educated women enter and replace other women who exit early in connection with childbearing (in Italy, the average age of completion of a college degree is around 25 years).

The next Figure (Figure 2) suggests, in fact, that education may be a crucial divide in both respects. In 1991, not only did the gap between the most poorly educated women (level 2.1 or lower secondary education) and the best educated (college degree or above) range from 14 to 57

FIGURE 1
PARTICIPATION OF SUCCESSIVE COHORTS ON ITALIAN WOMAN OVER
THEIR LIFECYCLE

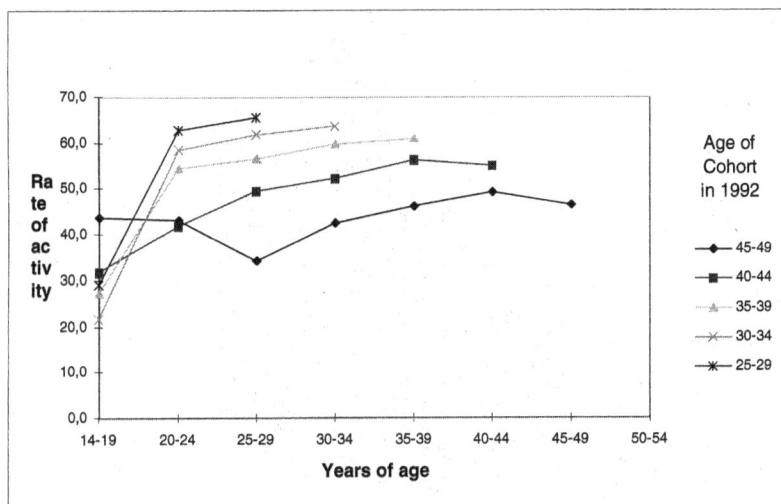

*Note*: Because the exact age interval for the first age group (14–19) changed over the years the activity rates in this age range are our own estimates based on the original data.

*Source*: ISTAT, Labour Force Sample Survey, various years. Data refer to synthetic cohorts.

points, depending on the age group, but also very few women older than 30 and with poor education were found in paid employment. Of course, the age-participation profiles in Figure 2 do not warrant inferences about behaviour over the life cycle because they may simply reflect differences between old and young cohorts of women. Nevertheless, the profiles for well-educated and poorly educated women are sufficiently consistent with a priori expectations to justify the conclusion that they do reflect the tendency for the former to exhibit continuity of participation over the life cycle while participation over the life cycle for the latter is 'curtailed'.

Also, if we further break down the data by motherhood status in order to control for the effect on participation of having young children, the distinctively different participation pattern of poorly educated women is even more clear and participation turns out to respond to education even more than motherhood. Consider, first, the participation rates for young women only (20–39 years old) by educational attainment and by the presence of small children (see Table 6). With a participation rate of 94.6

FIGURE 2
FEMALE PARTICIPATION BY AGE AND LEVEL OF EDUCATION, 1991

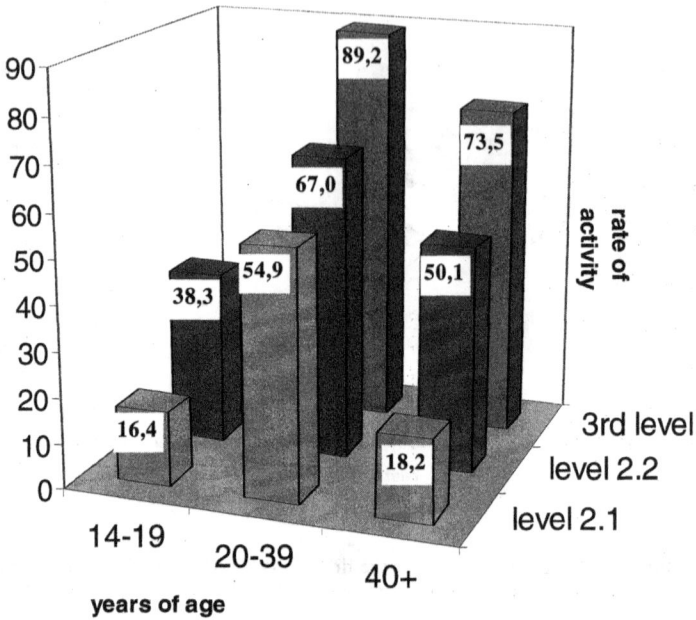

per cent, a childless, highly educated woman in the 20–39 age bracket is almost certain to be in the labour market. For the least educated but equally childless woman in the same age group, the chances of participation diminish by as much as a third (–30 percentage points).

Consider next mothers of young children (zero to 14) aged 20–39 years and 50–59 years respectively (see Table 7): mothers of comparable educational levels show surprisingly little differences in activity rates, whether they belong to the old or to the young generation. Conversely, within each age group the rate of activity more than doubles for highly educated women compared with the less educated.

In comparison to (lack of) education, motherhood thus appears to reduce participation by a smaller amount. On average, each child following the first reduces the participation rate by 14.8 points, and the first child takes the biggest toll. How big this toll is, however, depends very much on the mother's level of education. The best-educated mothers of young children (at least one child aged zero to 14 years), in

TABLE 6
PARTICIPATION RATES OF ITALIAN WOMEN* AGED 20–39 YEARS OLD BY
SELECTED CHARACTERISTICS (1991)

| | All levels of education | Level 3 | Level 2.2 | Level 2.1 |
|---|---|---|---|---|
| No children | 73.9 | 94.6 | 83.5 | 64.9 |
| 1 child | 57.9 | – | – | – |
| 2 children | 47.0 | – | – | – |
| 3 children or more | 35.0 | – | – | – |
| Child aged 7–14 yrs | 54.1 | – | – | – |
| Child 3–6 aged yrs | 50.6 | – | – | – |
| Child < 2 yrs old | 50.2 | – | – | – |
| Child < 14 yrs old | 51.6 | 88.6 | 67.4 | 42.4 |

* Women who are household heads or the spouses of household heads.
*Source*: Eurostat, Labour Force Survey (our calculations on unpublished data).

TABLE 7
PARTICIPATION RATE OF MOTHERS OF YOUNG CHILDREN (0–14 YEARS) BY
EDUCATIONAL LEVEL AND COHORT (1991)

| | Women aged 20–39 | Women aged 40–59 |
|---|---|---|
| Level 3 | 88.57 | 89.13 |
| Level 2 | 67.41 | 67.66 |
| Level 1 | 42.37 | 35.11 |
| All levels | 51.58 | 46.07 |

*Source*: Eurostat, Labour Force Survey (our calculations on unpublished data).

fact, boast a rate of 88.6 per cent, which is only six percentage points lower than their childless counterparts. The least-educated mothers record a rate of 42.4 per cent, which is 22.5 percentage points lower than their childless counterparts.

Comparative evidence suggests, in fact, that underrepresentation of poorly educated women may largely account for the noted participation gap that Italy still records *vis-à-vis* most other European countries. In all the European countries, education has been found to encourage participation, controlling for motherhood and age. However, in two European countries, Italy and Greece, its impact is significantly higher. As a recent comparative analysis shows (Rubery *et al.* 1996: 72–4, Chart 1.3.2), the difference in the probabilities of being part of the labour force between a mother with a graduate degree and aged 20–39 and a mother of the same age but with a basic education exceeds 40 percentage points only in these two countries and falls to between 20 and 30 points in most other European countries.[6] The participation gap is again widest in Greece and Italy[7] when comparison is made between highly educated and poorly educated non-mothers in the same age group.

An interesting question arising from this apparent commonality between Italy and Greece is whether the factors identified in the introduction as accounting for the greater responsiveness of female participation to education in Italy are also found in Greece, namely, a high degree of protection for incumbent employees, high structural unemployment and the legal entitlements attached to educational certificates. While this is not implausible, we must leave the issue for future research.

A second question that cannot be fully addressed here is whether in Italy (or in Greece) at least part of the 'missing' segment of poorly educated participants are hidden in the folds of the black economy. Even if this were the case, the divide between the educated and poorly educated female segments would still be stark, although it would concern employment conditions rather than employment opportunities.

## BETTER PERFORMANCE IN EDUCATION, YET HIGHER UNEMPLOYMENT

In Italian sociological literature, it is often argued that education is fuelling aspirations more than securing opportunities for work. In fact, female unemployment has been a major component of the rise in participation, during the past two decades. The rate of female employment grew by 3.6 percentage points in the period considered (1975–96), as against an 8.0 point increase in the rate of activity, and rising unemployment accounts for the difference. On the one hand, increased educational attainment by young women has encouraged entry to and discouraged exit from the labour market. On the other hand, the expansion in labour demand for women has not grown at the same rate as the female labour supply, so that an increasing number of young women have experienced unemployment, especially long-term unemployment.

Notwithstanding the closing of the gender gap in education and the relatively high level of formal training attained, women continue to encounter difficulties in finding employment, much more so than men. They are more likely to be employed in atypical work (in particular, fixed-term contracts) and they are at greater risk of losing their jobs. Thus, the gains achieved by women in education have not been matched by equivalent gains in terms of employment. The question therefore naturally arises of whether education really pays for Italian women. Our answer is a qualified 'yes' at the individual level and a paradoxical 'no' at the aggregate level.

Starting with the aggregate level, the female unemployment rate in Italy was 16.6 per cent in 1996, almost double the value for men (9.3 per cent), and was the result of an increase dating back to the 1970s. There are two main components in female unemployment, which may be labelled 'structural' and 'own' components, for convenience.

The 'structural' component affects female and male participants and stems from the very low capacity of the Italian economy to create additional employment in recent decades. Between 1980 and 1996 total employment (accounted for in terms of standard labour units) exhibited a pronounced cyclical pattern. In particular, the marked increase in total employment during the 1980s (+1.456 million) was almost nullified by the dramatic decrease that accompanied the recession of the 1990s (–1.243 million). The latter practically destroyed the entire net creation of jobs brought by the expansion of the 1980s.[8]

The 'own' component of female unemployment stems from the fact that a vast, latent reserve of female labour still exists, so that any increase in demand is likely to draw additional female supplies out into the market in a spiralling 'generation' of unemployment. Indeed, jobs for women have increased since the 1980s, despite the overall stagnation of employment. The highly cyclical behaviour of total employment conceals, in fact, diverging trends in male and female employment. Data from the national Labour Force Survey (Figure 3) show that female employment recorded a significant increase during economic upturns, with male employment remaining almost constant; conversely, over recessionary periods, male employment fell dramatically, while female employment remained stationary.

Occupational segregation in service-type jobs for women and in manufacturing employment for men accounts for these diverging trends. Industrial employment, which had been relatively stable throughout the 1970s, began to decline in the early 1980s, with a net loss between 1981 and 1991 amounting to some 817,000 labour units, entirely due to the contraction recorded in waged employment. This loss was more than offset by an overall expansion in self-employment, as well as by a certain amount of growth in waged employment in private services and the public sector. As a result, male employment stagnated in the 1980s, while female employment expanded at a moderate rate, absorbing all of the net

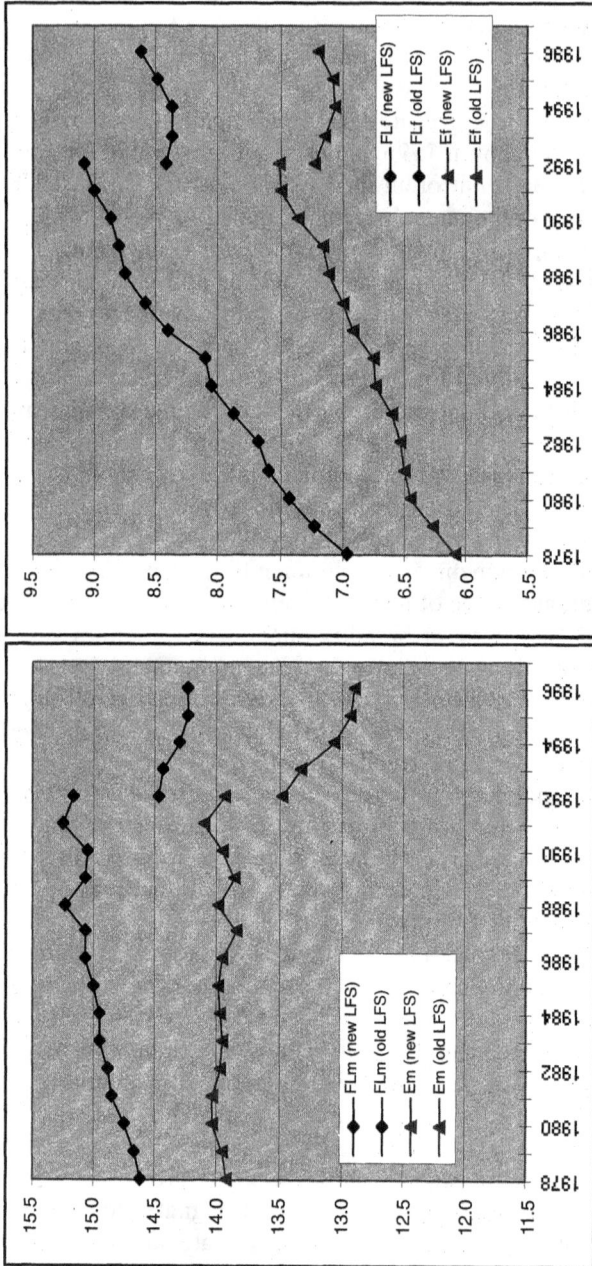

FIGURE 3
TOTAL EMPLOYMENT BY GENDER 1992–97 (THOUSANDS)

Legend: LF = labour force; E = employment; f = female; m = male

*Note*: The discontinuity in the series is due to the changes introduced by ISTAT in the statistical definition of labour market variables.

increase. This gender imbalance in net labour demand was compounded by the recession of the 1990s, when both industrial and service employment declined, but losses were much higher in industry.[9]

In a context in which any increase in demand draws out yet more women into the labour market and in which the economy is capable of attaining only modest overall expansion, the effects of discouragement (that is, the choice of opting out of the labour force because employment prospects are too poor) help keep female unemployment down. Hard evidence on the effects of discouragement is not easily available, but flow data on transitions in and out of unemployment provide some indirect evidence that these effects are not negligible for women, as we discuss elsewhere (Bettio and Mazzotta 1995; see also Borzaga 1994).

Here, we are not so much interested in the size of these effects of discouragement as in the possibility that more education for women weakens them, thus indirectly boosting female unemployment. This may happen in two mutually reinforcing ways. In so far as the cost of schooling is low and mainly borne by the family of origin, extra years of schooling may be chosen in order to postpone joining an exceedingly long job queue (education as a 'parking lot' for the unemployed). At the same time, the greater the investment in education, the more lasting the resilience to discouragement once the job queue has been entered.

This naturally leads to the question of whether education pays at the individual level. Our answer is that for individual participants, especially women, it still makes some sense to invest in education in order to minimize the risk of unemployment.

Let us start by noting that differences in unemployment rates across age groups and educational levels are reasonable proxies of differences in the (expected) length of unemployment. Table 8 shows that, for whatever educational level is selected, unemployment rates (for both men and women) are very high for young cohorts leaving school and entering the labour market, and decrease slowly thereafter. Thus a young job seeker entering the labour market is faced by a long queue (longer for women than for men) independent of the school qualification acquired; that is, the risk of unemployment is high for both poorly educated and highly educated women and has been increasing over time.

Nevertheless differences across educational levels remain significant within each age group. In particular, if we take the age group 30–34, the unemployment rate systematically diminishes as we move from poorly educated women (having completed primary school, or less) to the highly educated ones (with university degrees). The former face an

TABLE 8
UNEMPLOYMENT RATE BY AGE, EDUCATIONAL ATTAINMENT AND GENDER (1997)

| | Male | | | | | | Female | | | | | |
|---|---|---|---|---|---|---|---|---|---|---|---|---|
| | University degree | Upper secondary school | Vocational school | Junior secondary school | Primary school (or less) | Total | University degree | Upper secondary school | Vocational school | Junior secondary school | Primary school (or less) | Total |
| 15–19 | – | 42.00 | 18.92 | 30.49 | 31.43 | 30.91 | – | 55.71 | 34.38 | 40.93 | 29.41 | 42.95 |
| 20–24 | 23.08 | 35.29 | 18.46 | 24.53 | 38.18 | 28.36 | 28.76 | 43.74 | 26.02 | 33.33 | 50.00 | 38.10 |
| 25–29 | 25.78 | 16.94 | 10.81 | 14.47 | 24.71 | 16.18 | 16.54 | 22.66 | 15.13 | 22.98 | 42.42 | 23.69 |
| Total 15–29 | 25.53 | 25.30 | 14.92 | 20.53 | 29.89 | 22.20 | 22.55 | 34.02 | 21.43 | 29.88 | 41.67 | 31.28 |
| 30–34 | 10.85 | 7.01 | 5.67 | 8.74 | 19.83 | 8.84 | 9.41 | 13.60 | 12.50 | 18.88 | 34.88 | 16.27 |
| 35–39 | 2.78 | 3.57 | 3.45 | 6.03 | 13.87 | 5.31 | 5.88 | 9.43 | 10.16 | 16.03 | 26.39 | 12.30 |
| 40–44 | 0.88 | 1.95 | 2.94 | 4.24 | 8.93 | 3.67 | 4.26 | 5.33 | 5.94 | 10.43 | 16.90 | 8.09 |
| 45–49 | 0.48 | 1.68 | 2.38 | 3.60 | 6.81 | 3.49 | 4.14 | 3.24 | 5.71 | 7.89 | 11.43 | 6.49 |
| 50–54 | 0.64 | 2.44 | 2.00 | 3.57 | 6.29 | 3.94 | 4.54 | 2.38 | 5.71 | 7.14 | 8.47 | 5.92 |
| 55–59 | 0.95 | 1.88 | 4.76 | 3.60 | 7.39 | 4.60 | 5.46 | 1.43 | – | 3.75 | 6.04 | 4.43 |
| 60–64 | 0.00 | – | – | 3.16 | 5.41 | 3.78 | 4.35 | – | – | 3.85 | 3.90 | 2.72 |
| 65–69 | – | – | – | 4.00 | – | 0.73 | 0.49 | – | – | 10.00 | 3.85 | 4.08 |
| Total 15–69 | 5.30 | 10.13 | 7.86 | 10.40 | 9.51 | 9.54 | 11.15 | 18.65 | 13.60 | 19.16 | 13.74 | 16.84 |

Note: Unemployment rates refer to the labour force by type of degree obtained.

Source: ISTAT (1998).

unemployment rate of 34.9 per cent, the latter of 9.4 per cent. Similar conclusions can be drawn by comparing participants with different educational attainments within each remaining age group. Thus, investment in education is still a tool enabling one to compete in the individual race against unemployment.

## CONCLUSION

Italian women have entered the educational system in increasing numbers, closing the gender gap. The progress achieved is important not only because the qualifications of the young generations of women entering the labour market have improved, but also because new cultural values have been disseminated, in particular the desire for economic independence and for personal fulfilment through paid work.

The most direct and obvious implication of the progress in education concerns the prevailing pattern as well as the growth in female participation. Motherhood (as well as marriage) continues to restrain participation, given that some women still exit the labour market at the time of childbirth and do not return. However, because education weakens the impact of motherhood on participation on several counts, and because the share of well-educated participants is higher in Italy than elsewhere in Europe, strong labour-force attachment has been the hallmark of participation for the largest segment of Italian women from the early postwar period and has become more pronounced over time.

At the same time, (open) female participation remains low and the association of rising educational standards with both a low rate of employment and high unemployment for women raises a puzzle. One answer to the puzzle is that advances in education have not unambiguously lowered female unemployment. Even though, at the individual level, any increase in education reduces the risk of unemployment, at the aggregate level the same increase is likely to expand the queue of new job seekers having invested sufficiently in education to be less easily discouraged by the lack of job opportunities.

These are somewhat disturbing findings. First, insofar as the low participation of Italian women is in part involuntary, the lack of adequate job opportunities is not evenly distributed but mainly affects the least educated. Second, because the capacity of the Italian economy to create additional employment is low, for reasons other than the skill composition of the labour supply, education may not unambiguously improve women's (and men's) chances of finding jobs. Indeed, the Italian experience in this respect provides a good example of why it may be advisable to shift the focus from merely supply-side to demand-side policies in order to address effectively the problem of low female employment and participation.

On a more optimistic note, the refreshing findings are that segregation in school curricula is being significantly eroded and that women's educational attainments are such that they are now outperfoming men. This was hardly predictable on the basis of human-capital theory, and it emphasizes that economists should conceptualize education as consisting of more than human-capital investment alone.

## NOTES

1. This point is discussed at some length in Bettio and Villa (1996a: 48–53).
2. On the desegregation of curricula, see Spanò (1995).
3. The proportion of 18-year-old women having completed higher secondary education increased by 20 percentage points in ten years (from 35.2 per cent in 1981–82 to 55.2 per cent in 1992–93); the corresponding increase for men was much smaller (from 38.4 per cent to 48.5 per cent).
4. Good comparative data on continuing vocational training (CVT) within firms have been recently made available by Eurostat (1996). According to the first survey on CVT (carried out by Eurostat in 1994) within the European Union (EU 12), nearly 60 per cent of firms with ten or more employees implemented various CVT schemes. In Italy, the percentage of firms providing CVT was only one per cent.
5. The data in Figure 1 refer to 'synthetic' cohorts. For example, the level of participation for the youngest cohort at the age of 25–29 and 20–24, respectively, is equated with the rate of participation for the age group 25–29 in 1992 (the reference year) and for the age group 20–24 five years previously, that is, in 1987. Synthetic cohorts are a reasonably good approximation of longitudinal data when the latter are not available.
6. Rubery's analysis is based on unpublished data from the Eurostat Labour Force Survey for 1993 (non-mothers) and 1994 (mothers). Unpublished data from the same survey have also been used for Figure 2 and Tables 6 and 7.
7. The fact that a large informal sector thrives in both these countries may explain part of this gap, but is unlikely to bring the difference into line with that of other European countries.
8. ISTAT data quoted in Banca d'Italia (1997), *Assemblea Generale dei Partecipanti* (Appendices, Table aB21).
9. With specific reference to the 1990s, for which comparable data from the Labour Force Survey is available, employment declined markedly in agriculture, manufacturing, construction, the distributive trades and transport, while it stagnated in banking and finance, as well as in public administration. With the exception of agriculture and retail and wholesale distribution (where the fall in employment has been larger for women, both in absolute and relative terms), all other sectors' job losses have been higher for men. While in the case of female employment, the downturn recorded by some branches of the service sector (retail and wholesale trade and public administration) has been offset by expansion in other branches (the outcome being a small positive expansion in services taken as a whole), in the case of male employment, the dramatic losses recorded in industry and agriculture have compounded the contraction in other service branches (with a few positive exceptions in hotels, business services, education and health).

REFERENCES

Banca d'Italia (1997): *Assemblea Generale dei Partecipanti*. Roma: Banca d'Italia.
Bettio, F. and P. Villa (1992): *Occupational Segregation. The Case of Italy*. EC Network of Experts on the Situation of Women in the Labour Market, UMIST Working Paper. Manchester: University of Manchester.
Bettio, F. and F. Mazzotta (1995): *Women and the European Employment Rate: Italy*. EC Network of Experts on the Situation of Women in the Labour Market, UMIST Working Paper. Manchester: University of Manchester.
Bettio, F. and P. Villa (1994): *Changing Patterns of Work and Working Time for Men and Women: Italy*. EC Network of Experts on the Situation of Women in the Labour Market, UMIST Working Paper. Manchester: University of Manchester.
(1996a): *Trends and Prospects for Women's Employment in Italy in the 1990s*. EC Network of Experts on the Situation of Women in the Labour Market, UMIST Working Paper. Manchester: University of Manchester.
(1996b): 'Un modello al bivio'. *DWF*, 4/32, pp.44–62.
Bagioli, M. (1998): Analysis of Wage Differentials Between and Within EU Countries Through the European Community Panel (ECHP) and the Structure of Earnings Survey (SES), University of Palma (mimeo).
Boje, T. (1996): *Trends and Prospects for Women's Employment in Denmark in the 1990s*. EC Network of Experts on the Situation of Women in the Labour Market, UMIST Working Paper. Manchester: University of Manchester.
Borzaga, C. (ed.) (1994): *Il mercato del lavoro femminile: aspettative, preferenze, vincoli*. Milano: F. Angeli.
Bulgarelli, A. and A. Ranieri (1994): 'L'efficacia della formazione nelle politiche attive del mercato del lavoro: una verifica empirica su base regionale'. *Economia e Lavoro*, 2, pp.47–68.
Colombino, U. and M. L. Di Tommaso (1996): 'Is the preference for children so low or is the price of time so high? A simultaneous model of fertility and participation in Italy with cohort effects'. *Labour*, 10/3, pp.475–94.
Crompton, R. and K. Sanderson (1990): *Gendered Jobs and Social Change*. London: Unwin Hyman.
Di Tommaso, M. L. (1998): 'A trivariate model of participation, fertility and wages: the Italian case'. Department of Economics, University of Torino and Centre for Business Research, Department of Economics, University of Cambridge (mimeo).
Erickson, C. L. and A. C. Ichino (1995): 'Wage differentials in Italy. Market forces, institutions and inflation'. In R. Freeman and L. Katz (eds.), *Differences and Changes in Wage Structures*, National Bureau of Economic Research Comparative Labor Market Series. Chicago and London: University of Chicago Press.
Eurostat (1996): 'Continuing vocational training in enterprises – an essential part of lifelong learning'. *Statistics in Focus. Population and Social Conditions*, No.7.
(1997) : 'Education in the European Union: opportunities and choices'. *Statistics in Focus. Population and Social Conditions*, No.4.
ISFOL (1993): *Rapporto ISFOL 1993*. Milano: F. Angeli.
ISTAT (1995): *Sistema educativo e mercato del lavoro nel contesto internazionale, Supplemento all'Annuario Statistico Italiano*. Roma: ISTAT.
(1997a): *Annuario Statistico Italiano*. Roma: ISTAT.
(1997b): *Rapporto annuale. La situazione del paese nel 1996*. Roma: ISTAT.
(various issues): *Annuario di Statistiche dell'Istruzione*. Roma: ISTAT.
(various issues): *Rilevazione delle forze di lavoro*. Roma: ISTAT.
OECD (1995): *Education at a Glance*. Paris: OECD.
Rubery, J. and C. Fagan (1993): *Wage Determination and Sex Segregation in Employment: the UK*. EC Network of Experts on the Situation of Women in the Labour Market,

UMIST Working Article. Manchester: University of Manchester.

Rubery, J., Smith, M. and C. Fagan (1996): *Trends and Prospects for Women's Employment in the 1990s.* EC Network of Experts on the Situation of Women in the Labour Market, UMIST Working Paper. Manchester: Manchester School of Management, UMIST.

Rubery, J., Smith M., Fagan, C. and Grimshaw, D.: Women and European Employment, London Routledge.

Spanò, A. (1995) : *Parità formativa, parità lavorativa e parità sociale: il contributo dell'istruzione alla definizione di una nuova condizione femminile.* Università di Napoli (mimeo).

Spence, A. M. (1973): 'Job market signalling'. *Quarterly Journal of Economics*, 87, 3, pp.355–74.

# Is the Male-Provider Model Still in Place? Partnership Formation in Contemporary Spain

## MARTA LUXÁN, PAU MIRET and ROCÍO TREVIÑO

We would like to begin by clarifying what we mean by 'male-provider model'. The ideal-type male-provider model would be a partnership constituted by a full-time employed man in a stable job and a woman not in the labour market. By contrast, we could have a dual-earner model, where both the man and the woman are involved in the labour force in stable full-time jobs. Of course, between these two poles we can find a wide range of other possible situations, for instance, a partnership where the each person works in an unstable job or where one of them is not in full-time employment. We must take into account the variety of labour-force involvement among adult family members.

Usually, patterns in the timing of male entry into marriage and its prevalence have been explained as a function solely of young men's economic characteristics with regard to their position in the labour market. The argument goes as follows. On the one hand, the more problematic it is for men to achieve economic independence, the later they will marry (and, vice versa, the better their economic conditions, the earlier they will be able to constitute a partnership). On the other hand, periods of critical economic difficulties will lead to an increase in the number of single males (while, on the contrary, the number of married men will increase during economic booms). Once young men have solved all possible economic problems, imbalances in the marriage market (that is, between the number of unmarried men and unmarried women) can obstruct their transition from being single to getting married. Thus, to consider the economic position of male young adults as a key factor for understanding marriage patterns has a long tradition in social analysis.

In consequence, within this model, the characteristics of young females, other than the relative number of unmarried women compared to unmarried men, played almost no role in explaining the timing and prevalence of marriage. It is a combination of the 'threshold hypothesis' and the 'marriage-market perspective', that is, young men in the early stages of their careers must, first of all, ensure that they have enough family support (basically, help from their parents) or enough earnings, or both, to set up an independent household. This is the 'threshold' they should pass in order to be able to constitute a family. As a second step, they had to find an appropriate partner (competing in the marriage market). Of course, higher socio-economic groups would have higher standards concerning the minimum necessary to get married and different opinions than other social classes about who could be considered a suitable partner.

One important example of how to achieve enough autonomy to get married was the so-called 'life-cycle servant' (Laslett 1972). In England, from the seventeenth century up to modern times, young men worked in a household other than their family home during the earlier stages of their lives in order to achieve economic independence and, consequently, establish their own household. Although this 'life-cycle servant' was not historically a common phase in the life course of young adults in other countries such as Spain, there have always been strategies through which a young men could reach the threshold necessary to get married. These strategies in Spain varied very much by region (see Reher 1997: Ch.3), but are basically related to family support (when it is available) and to involvement within the labour force.

We should note, nevertheless, that according to the 'West European Marriage Model' (which in some countries appeared from the seventeenth century), female marriage patterns were a social means of controlling fertility levels, that is, the more important it was socially to maintain low fertility, the more restricted and delayed was marriage for women (Hajnal 1965). As a consequence, the lower the pressure from community or family for having children (or the higher the pressure for having less), the greater female labour-force participation became. Thus, within western European culture, although the 'traditional' role within a married couple for men was to be a father-breadwinner, for women it was not being a full-time care-giver-mother, but to combine this role with their labour-force participation (especially in the earlier stages of family building). By contrast, if fertility was encouraged (that is, the pressure for having as many children as possible increased), society encouraged earlier and more widespread female marriages and, as a consequence, female labour-force participation was kept to a minimum (as women were forced to focus only on reproductive tasks).

Of course, setting up dual-earner household has always been a stronger strategy than relying for household income on just one member of the new family, especially during hard times. In fact, in the past, families relied on the work of their teenage and young adult children to create economic flexibility in the family household, although this is not the case any more in contemporary industrialized cultures (Oppenheimer 1994). In the same sense, female labour-force participation in the past was seen as a way of 'helping' the family get ahead in difficult situations, but it was not considered the 'normal' role for married women.

Indeed, most sociologists have pointed out from Emile Durkheim onward (1960, original edition in 1892) that the sexual division of labour within marriage was the source of interdependence between men and women in a family nucleus and as such was also the basis for social cohesion and stability. Talcott Parsons (1949) considered sexual role differentiation as the real foundation of any modern industrial society. This argument was mathematically formalized by Gary Becker (1987), who argued that both increases in female labour-force participation and progressively higher levels of female involvement in non-compulsory education systems leads to a rise in women's opportunity costs of having children and, consequently, women delay or avoid family formation. In other words, the higher the level of educational achievement for a woman, and the better and longer her labour-force career, the later she will marry and the stronger will be her desire to remain single and not have a family. However, there is only weak empirical support for this argument (Oppenheimer et al. 1997).

According to these approaches, the present low levels of cross-sectional first marriages registered in southern European countries should be explained by either (1) the present economic crisis, which does not allow young men to attain their traditional role of breadwinners or (2) the fact that women who are educated and highly involved in the labour force no longer accept their traditional role of care-givers as imposed by the conservative family culture of the region. Of course, a combination of both perspectives is perfectly possible in suggesting that the rate of marriage will decline if men and women do not accept and fully apply either the male-breadwinner or female-care-giver family model.

Yet there is a third possible explanation, which derives from the fact that the closer the marriage model comes to absolute gender role differentiation in western Europe, the lower is the level of first unions. Conversely, it appears that the more progress there has been toward gender equality within marriage, the greater is the intensity of cross-sectional family formation. Hence, the third hypothesis states that the present low levels of first unions in southern European countries are actually due to the difficulties in transforming partnership roles from a complementary model to a more egalitarian one (Cabré 1995; McDonald 1997).

We propose in this article to focus on trend changes in the male role in family formation in contemporary Spain. We will focus on comparisons between two different periods in the recent history of Spain which differ with regard to economic characteristics, political system and levels of cross-sectional partnership formation. Our goal is to find the key factors for understanding a particular pattern in marriage formation, especially for men. We will highlight the relevant changes observable in educational attainment and labour-market position for males and females and their possible association with the transition from single status to partnership. We will focus on how past economic booms and stability in family values in comparison with recent economic crises and changes in cultural values could maintain (even reinforce) or change (and even destroy) traditional roles in family formation. We will proceed by elaborating hazard rates by age and gender of entering into a first partnership, according to the level of educational attainment on the one hand and position within the labour market on the other.

## SOURCE OF DATA AND METHODOLOGY

The data used are drawn from the 1991 Socio-demographic Survey conducted by the Instituto Nacional de Estadística (Spanish Central Statistical Institute). The 1991 Survey consists of a sample of about 160,000 individuals, representative of the Spanish population resident in private households and aged over ten years (communal households are excluded). It is a retrospective survey and individuals were asked to report information about specific life-course events.

The survey asks respondents to give the date of their first partnership, if any. From that, we will build our dependent variable, that is, the transition from 'never in a partnership' to the 'constitution of a partnership'. We include marriage and cohabitation. In fact, it is not possible to differentiate clearly in the 1991 Survey between 'cohabitation outside wedlock' and 'marriage'. This is because only cohabitation which lasts for more than one year is recorded and, moreover, those partnerships which started in cohabitation but finished in marriage are considered as marriages from the very beginning. In any case, up to 1991 (when this survey took place), cohabitation outside wedlock in Spain was at a very low level and was usually considered as a 'trial' marriage (Cabré *et al.* 1995; Delgado 1993; Health and Miret 1996). Consequently, we will deal basically with family formation through marriage, and only cohabiting partnerships which are ongoing, ended in marriage or which lasted more than one year will be taken into account.

Of course, within a partnership, men and women define their roles in relation to one another. Unfortunately, the 1991 Survey is an individual data set and therefore does not provide us with longitudinal information concerning either educational attainment or the labour-market position of the interviewed partners. Hence, we have been forced to consider each sex separately, assuming that changes in gender roles within marriage will become evident by looking at the determinants for partnership formation for men on one hand and for women on the other.

We will employ discrete-time event-history methodology (Allison 1982; Yamaguchi 1991). For each year that an individual is known to be 'at risk', a separate observational record is created. Empirical analysis has shown that during the twentieth century in Spain there was no family formation before 17 years for males and 15 years for females (see, for women, Fernández 1978). In consequence, in our research, a man is considered to be at risk if he has never entered a partnership and is over 16 years old, and a woman is considered to be at risk if she has never been in a partnership and is over 14 years old. We refer to these observations in terms of 'person-years'. For each person-year, the dependent variable (that is, transition to first partnership) is coded one if a person becomes involved in his or her first partnership in that year. Otherwise it is coded zero (that is, he or she remains single during that particular year). Thus, a dummy variable is computed indicating whether a person begins a first partnership in any particular year. Individuals are followed from the minimum age considered (17 for men, 15 for women) up until the year they become involved in a partnership, or up to 50 years old if they never have a partnership.

Our goal is to check the influence of some selected explanatory variables on the hazard rates of changing from the state of 'never in a partnership' to the state of 'beginning in a first partnership'. As we noted, we will analyse independently each sex. We will use four time-dependent categorical variables: (1) age, (2) observational period, (3) educational attainment and (4) labour-force participation.

We have divided the age continuum into several age groups which came from a previous exploratory analysis: for men, the age groups are

17–19, 20–21, 22, 23, 24–26, 27–28, 29–32, 33–35, 36–38, 39–41, 42–44, 45–47 and 48–50 years; for women, they are 15–17, 18–19, 20, 21, 22, 23, 24–26, 27–28, 29–32, 33–35, 36–38, 39–41, 42–44, 45–47 and 48–50 years. Age as an independent variable shows to what extent differences in first-partnership hazard rates are due to timing but not to intensity, that is, the extent to which people in a specific period formed a first union earlier or later, but not more or less.

We will compare two periods: 1965–74 and 1981–90. Furthermore, we will illustrate the reason for choosing these two historical periods. The methodology is based on elaborating the hazard rates of entering into a first partnership registered by Spanish men and women during these two different periods of time, that is, 1965–74 (development period) and 1981–90 (crisis period).

Educational attainment has been classified into five categories: (1) compulsory education as a maximum, (2) high school (*bachillerato*), (3) vocational training (*formación profesional*), (4) three-year university degree (*diplomaturas*) and (5) five-year university degree (*licenciaturas* or *ingenierias*).

Lastly, the 1991 Survey categorizes labour-force participation according to the characteristics of the period each individual is experiencing. In other words, we can separate periods when the individual was (1) always at work in a continuous, full-time job (stable, full-time job), (2) in a continuous and full-time job, but with periods of unemployment (full-time job with unemployment), (3) always at work, but in a part-time or seasonal job (stable, but not full-time job), (4) experiencing a combination of periods of unemployment with either a seasonal or part-time job (unemployment with a job that was not full time) and (5) not in the labour force.

## CONTEXTUAL FACTORS SHAPING THE EVOLUTION OF PARTNERSHIP FORMATION IN SPAIN

In order to justify the choice of these periods, we need to present the historical context that has prevailed since 1939 (the end of the Civil War) until 1991 (the last year for which we have information from the data set).

After the Civil War, Spain experienced a severe set back in its economic development. Moreover, it was completely isolated from the rest of the world, even socially and culturally. Because of the political system, Spain did not undergo any kind of economic development or change in civil society's values up to the beginning of the 1960s. For instance, in terms of economic development, it was not until the early 1960s that Spain attained the same percentage of the population working in the industrial sector (Garrido 1992), GNP (Tamames 1986) and per capita income (Carreras 1988) that had existed in 1930. Moreover, the prevailing ideology was so-called 'National-Catholicism'.

Concerning demographic behaviour, from the end of the Civil War until the late 1950s, people experienced very delayed marriages, with a mean age at first marriage of almost 29 years for men and about 26 years for women. Consequently, fertility levels remained very low indeed (Fernández 1978). In Figure 1 we plot the hazard rates of entering a first partnership for men by age groups for different periods between the end of the Civil War and 1991. We can show how delayed the male marriage pattern was during the period from 1940 to 1959 in comparison with the other periods. The highest hazard rate during 1940–59 was for the age group 27–28 years (about 17 per cent), closely followed by the age group 29–32 (about 16 per cent) and the hazard rates of getting married were still quite significant at age 39–41 (at about 10 per cent, the rate was very similar to that for the 24–26 age group). We should note that we have no information for those who married after the age of 40, because they did not survive up to 1991, when the survey took place. For women (Figure 2), the period 1940–59 is characterized both by a delay in the first marriage and low intensity. Moreover, hazard rates in comparison with those of men were much more concentrated in a central age group, that is, 24–26 years (15 per cent) and 27–28 years (17 per cent).

But from the beginning of the 1960s, something changed inside the dictatorship, as the economy was liberalized and the country was opened to external influences. Therefore, the period 1960–64 should be considered as a transitional period from an isolated to a relatively open economy. In fact, as a consequence of these changes, although total employment grew only slightly in the mid-1960s, both men and women left the agricultural sector. The proportion of people in the labour market working in the agricultural sector fell by half, with men leaving to work in industry and women to work in services (Garrido 1992). As we can observe in Figure 1, regarding male family formation and comparing the two decades (1940–59), marriage during 1960–64 was timed earlier, as men were more likely to marry at any age before 32 years and were less likely to get involve in a first partnership over the age of 35. For women, this transitional period led to higher hazard rates right across the age range (Figure 2). But this 1960–64 period still did not reveal a completely

FIGURE 1
MALE FIRST-PARTNERSHIP HAZARD RATES BY AGE-GROUPS AND PERIODS

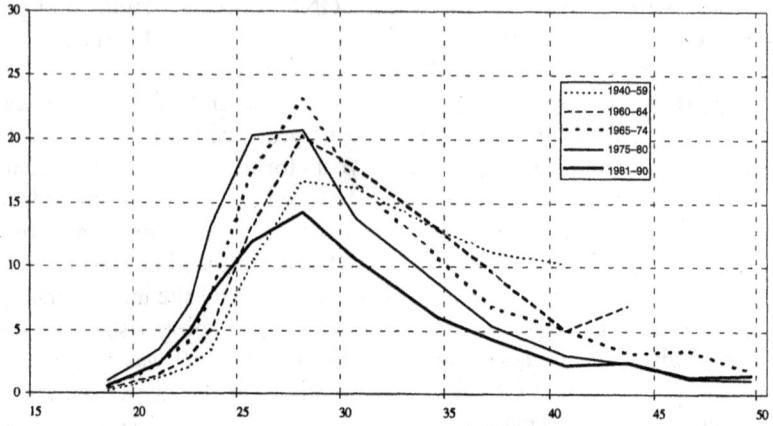

FIGURE 2
FEMALE FIRST-PARTNERSHIP HAZARD RATES BY AGE-GROUPS AND PERIODS

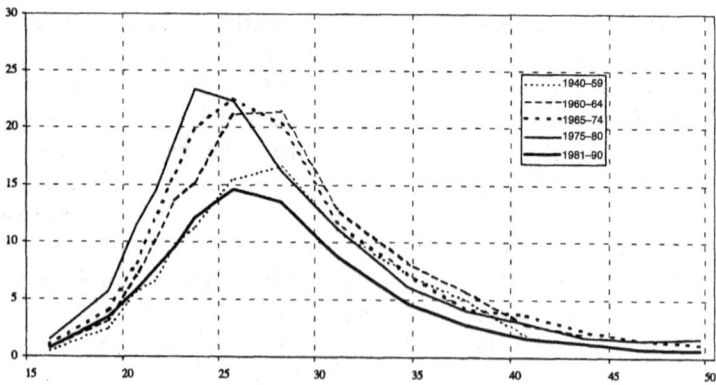

new pace in marriage rates as the hazard rates of getting married for males from 40 years on were still unusually high (Figure 1).

The period from 1965 until 1974 is called 'the economic development period', and is characterized by an increase in the number of employed people (Garrido 1994). The unemployment rate was close to zero, partly because almost all married women did not work outside the family home and because of enormous emigration from Spain, mainly to Germany and France, at that time. These ten years (from 1965 to 1974) are the first period to be subject to systematic comparison in this article.

To illustrate changes in the structure of the population for the periods we focus on, we will present the proportion of men and women by age who were 'at risk' of entering into a first partnership, first by educational attainment (Table 1) and second by labour-force participation (Table 2). So, in Tables 1 and 2 we observe the structure by age of never-married or never-cohabiting males and females according to educational attainment for the period 1965–74. During this period, a little over ten per cent of never-married men and around nine per cent of never-married women in their late twenties had finished high school, about the same percentage held a university degree and the rest had no more than compulsory education (more than 75 per cent of men aged 27–32 years and 80 per cent of women in the same age group). By contrast, for those over 30, the percentage with maximum primary school education was significantly higher (90 per cent for both men and women) and, consequently, the lower the number with a high school diploma or university degree. This cannot be other than a 'birth-cohort effect', because clearly the older people are, the less their involvement in the educational system.

Complementing this, we present in Table 2 the percentage of people 'at risk' according to the nature of their labour-force participation. In 1965–74, the proportion of 17–19 year old men not in the labour market and who had never married or had ever lived in cohabitation was 36 per cent (Table 2). We should remember that before 20 years of age, male hazard rates for entering a first partnership were not significant for the period 1965–74 (Figure 1). At the age of 23, however, 37 per cent of men who had never married or cohabited were not in the labour market (Table 2). We suggest that at this stage of their lives during the decade 1965–74, Spanish men who were not involved in partnerships were mainly in education. Furthermore, after 23 years of age, 70 per cent of men who had never married in 1965–74 were employed in full-time, continuous jobs. On the other hand, 35 per cent of women over 20 years

TABLE 1

PROPORTION OF NEVER-COHABITING AND NEVER MARRIED MEN AND WOMEN
ACCORDING TO THEIR EDUCATIONAL ATTAINMENT BY AGE, FOR 1965–74 AND
1981–90 PERIODS

| | | MEN | | | | | | | |
|---|---|---|---|---|---|---|---|---|---|
| | **1965-1974** | | | | | **1981-1990** | | | |
| | **Max. Primary** | **High school Vocational** | **University** | **Total** | | **Max. Primary** | **High school Vocational** | **University** | **Total** |
| 17-19 | 76.67 | 23.01 | 0.33 | 100 | 17-19 | 66.82 | 33.15 | 0.02 | 100 |
| 20-21 | 72.67 | 24.65 | 2.68 | 100 | 20-21 | 54.03 | 45.05 | 0.92 | 100 |
| 22 | 73.73 | 20.97 | 5.30 | 100 | 22 | 53.65 | 42.62 | 3.73 | 100 |
| 23 | 73.94 | 18.72 | 7.34 | 100 | 23 | 53.37 | 37.80 | 8.83 | 100 |
| 24-26 | 74.59 | 15.06 | 10.35 | 100 | 24-26 | 52.39 | 33.48 | 14.13 | 100 |
| 27-28 | 75.29 | 12.54 | 12.17 | 100 | 27-28 | 52.65 | 28.84 | 18.51 | 100 |
| 29-32 | 78.71 | 10.19 | 11.10 | 100 | 29-32 | 58.53 | 23.22 | 18.25 | 100 |
| 33-35 | 85.25 | 6.65 | 8.11 | 100 | 33-35 | 69.41 | 16.91 | 13.68 | 100 |
| 36-38 | 87.45 | 5.30 | 7.25 | 100 | 36-38 | 77.31 | 12.22 | 10.47 | 100 |
| 39-41 | 89.17 | 3.72 | 7.11 | 100 | 39-41 | 81.99 | 9.60 | 8.41 | 100 |
| 42-44 | 89.69 | 3.40 | 6.91 | 100 | 42-44 | 83.68 | 8.87 | 7.45 | 100 |
| 45-47 | 90.60 | 2.67 | 6.72 | 100 | 45-47 | 85.61 | 7.73 | 6.66 | 100 |
| 48-50 | 92.95 | 2.27 | 4.78 | 100 | 48-50 | 89.29 | 5.36 | 5.36 | 100 |
| Total | 76.70 | 17.65 | 5.65 | 100 | Total | 60.30 | 32.67 | 7.03 | 100 |

| | | WOMEN | | | | | | | |
|---|---|---|---|---|---|---|---|---|---|
| | **1965-1974** | | | | | **1981-1990** | | | |
| | **Max. Primary** | **High school Vocational** | **University** | **Total** | | **Max. Primary** | **High school Vocational** | **University** | **Total** |
| 15-17 | 93.74 | 6.17 | 0.10 | 100 | 15-17 | 91.72 | 8.26 | 0.01 | 100 |
| 18-19 | 81.85 | 17.01 | 1.14 | 100 | 18-19 | 52.98 | 46.99 | 0.03 | 100 |
| 20 | 81.45 | 15.29 | 3.26 | 100 | 20 | 46.66 | 53.02 | 0.32 | 100 |
| 21 | 81.79 | 13.16 | 5.04 | 100 | 21 | 45.64 | 49.10 | 5.26 | 100 |
| 22 | 81.90 | 11.66 | 6.44 | 100 | 22 | 44.80 | 46.57 | 8.63 | 100 |
| 23 | 81.67 | 9.90 | 8.43 | 100 | 23 | 43.24 | 39.83 | 16.93 | 100 |
| 24-26 | 82.38 | 8.71 | 8.90 | 100 | 24-26 | 41.97 | 33.07 | 24.96 | 100 |
| 27-28 | 82.45 | 8.62 | 8.92 | 100 | 27-28 | 42.50 | 27.80 | 29.71 | 100 |
| 29-32 | 85.72 | 7.27 | 7.00 | 100 | 29-32 | 50.17 | 22.40 | 27.43 | 100 |
| 33-35 | 88.24 | 4.51 | 7.26 | 100 | 33-35 | 58.51 | 19.16 | 22.32 | 100 |
| 36-38 | 89.84 | 3.40 | 6.76 | 100 | 36-38 | 63.31 | 16.74 | 19.95 | 100 |
| 39-41 | 90.35 | 2.46 | 7.19 | 100 | 39-41 | 68.42 | 14.37 | 17.21 | 100 |
| 42-44 | 90.63 | 2.04 | 7.33 | 100 | 42-44 | 73.22 | 11.55 | 15.22 | 100 |
| 45-47 | 90.86 | 1.81 | 7.33 | 100 | 45-47 | 79.78 | 8.77 | 11.44 | 100 |
| 48-50 | 90.04 | 1.71 | 8.25 | 100 | 48-50 | 84.79 | 5.99 | 9.22 | 100 |
| Total | 86.30 | 9.62 | 4.08 | 100 | Total | 60.84 | 30.48 | 8.68 | 100 |

of age who had never married or cohabited during 1965–74 were not in
the labour force, while 45 per cent were working in a full-time,
continuous jobs and 15 per cent were in the labour market in a part-time
job or experiencing periods of unemployment (Table 2).

Moreover, Figures 1 and 2 illustrate the relative early timing of the
hazard rates of getting married for the period 1965–74. Definitely, the

TABLE 2
PROPORTION OF NEVER-COHABITING AND NEVER MARRIED MEN AND WOMEN
ACCORDING TO THEIR LABOUR FORCE PARTICIPATION BY AGE, FOR 1965–74
AND 1981–90 PERIODS

**MEN**

|  | 1965-1974 | | | | |  | 1981-1990 | | | | |
|---|---|---|---|---|---|---|---|---|---|---|---|
|  | Stable job | Stop gap job | Non in lab. market | Others | Total |  | Stable job | Stop gap job | Non in lab. market | Others | Total |
| 17-19 | 43,78 | 18,97 | 35,92 | 1,33 | 100 | 17-19 | 15,92 | 15,34 | 66,14 | 2,59 | 100 |
| 20-21 | 32,24 | 12,98 | 53,82 | 0,96 | 100 | 20-21 | 19,28 | 15,31 | 62,74 | 2,67 | 100 |
| 22 | 29,23 | 9,41 | 60,20 | 1,16 | 100 | 22 | 36,90 | 23,28 | 36,89 | 2,92 | 100 |
| 23 | 47,70 | 13,89 | 37,20 | 1,21 | 100 | 23 | 45,74 | 26,84 | 24,54 | 2,89 | 100 |
| 24-26 | 67,60 | 19,52 | 11,72 | 1,16 | 100 | 24-26 | 53,14 | 28,87 | 14,83 | 3,16 | 100 |
| 27-28 | 72,35 | 21,79 | 4,43 | 1,42 | 100 | 27-28 | 58,27 | 30,51 | 7,46 | 3,76 | 100 |
| 29-32 | 70,35 | 24,63 | 2,90 | 2,12 | 100 | 29-32 | 60,83 | 29,29 | 3,95 | 5,92 | 100 |
| 33-35 | 68,07 | 26,40 | 2,15 | 3,38 | 100 | 33-35 | 61,12 | 28,55 | 3,40 | 6,92 | 100 |
| 36-38 | 67,49 | 26,45 | 1,96 | 4,10 | 100 | 36-38 | 62,22 | 28,45 | 3,29 | 6,05 | 100 |
| 39-41 | 68,50 | 24,83 | 2,46 | 4,20 | 100 | 39-41 | 62,98 | 26,77 | 3,47 | 6,77 | 100 |
| 42-44 | 68,53 | 23,29 | 3,45 | 4,73 | 100 | 42-44 | 62,49 | 25,98 | 3,67 | 7,86 | 100 |
| 45-47 | 69,15 | 20,99 | 4,95 | 4,91 | 100 | 45-47 | 59,27 | 26,59 | 4,78 | 9,36 | 100 |
| 48-50 | 70,57 | 17,38 | 5,05 | 7,00 | 100 | 48-50 | 57,63 | 25,89 | 5,90 | 10,58 | 100 |
| Total | 50,96 | 18,24 | 29,10 | 1,70 | 100 | Total | 37,64 | 22,38 | 36,32 | 3,66 | 100 |

**WOMEN**

|  | 1965-1974 | | | | |  | 1981-1990 | | | | |
|---|---|---|---|---|---|---|---|---|---|---|---|
|  | Stable job | Stop gap job | Non in lab. market | Others | Total |  | Stable job | Stop gap job | Non in lab. market | Others | Total |
| 15-17 | 21,13 | 11,95 | 63,02 | 3,90 | 100 | 15-17 | 4,41 | 6,25 | 86,39 | 2,95 | 100 |
| 18-19 | 34,66 | 16,70 | 45,34 | 3,31 | 100 | 18-19 | 14,66 | 16,41 | 65,54 | 3,39 | 100 |
| 20 | 39,45 | 17,64 | 39,80 | 3,11 | 100 | 20 | 20,53 | 20,94 | 54,74 | 3,79 | 100 |
| 21 | 41,54 | 17,94 | 37,71 | 2,81 | 100 | 21 | 23,75 | 22,82 | 49,42 | 4,01 | 100 |
| 22 | 42,73 | 18,13 | 36,37 | 2,76 | 100 | 22 | 27,72 | 23,68 | 44,45 | 4,15 | 100 |
| 23 | 42,87 | 18,14 | 36,00 | 3,00 | 100 | 23 | 31,02 | 25,40 | 39,33 | 4,25 | 100 |
| 24-26 | 43,42 | 19,07 | 34,34 | 3,17 | 100 | 24-26 | 38,28 | 26,68 | 30,17 | 4,87 | 100 |
| 27-28 | 44,07 | 17,91 | 33,98 | 4,04 | 100 | 27-28 | 47,53 | 26,50 | 20,96 | 5,01 | 100 |
| 29-32 | 42,82 | 17,04 | 34,68 | 5,47 | 100 | 29-32 | 51,57 | 24,09 | 18,87 | 5,46 | 100 |
| 33-35 | 43,27 | 14,74 | 35,58 | 6,40 | 100 | 33-35 | 54,98 | 20,45 | 17,39 | 7,18 | 100 |
| 36-38 | 45,08 | 15,46 | 34,30 | 5,15 | 100 | 36-38 | 52,04 | 21,67 | 18,79 | 7,50 | 100 |
| 39-41 | 44,36 | 15,55 | 34,94 | 5,15 | 100 | 39-41 | 52,04 | 19,62 | 20,84 | 7,51 | 100 |
| 42-44 | 45,78 | 14,10 | 35,46 | 4,66 | 100 | 42-44 | 47,68 | 19,86 | 24,73 | 7,73 | 100 |
| 45-47 | 46,66 | 13,48 | 35,68 | 4,17 | 100 | 45-47 | 42,59 | 19,60 | 30,20 | 7,62 | 100 |
| 48-50 | 48,74 | 13,62 | 34,66 | 2,98 | 100 | 48-50 | 43,86 | 16,48 | 31,94 | 7,72 | 100 |
| Total | 35,74 | 15,77 | 44,81 | 3,69 | 100 | Total | 23,56 | 17,61 | 54,68 | 4,15 | 100 |

main difference between this period and 1960–64 was the pace of marriage formation rather than the cross-sectional intensity, that is, people got married with similar intensity, but much younger than before. We should note that when the period of economic expansion came to an end, ushering in a period of economic crisis, it was ten years since the pre-war economic activity pattern had been restored. Furthermore, although some scholars place the beginning of the crisis in 1973, due to the euphoria caused by democratic transition, the effect of the crises was not noticed in Spain until 1977 (with The Moncloa Pacts) or, even later, until 1981, when a *coup d'état* occurred (Domingo 1997). Therefore, 1975–80 was a transitional period and from then until 1990 was a period of economic crisis. As we can verify in Figures 1 and 2, the trend in the timing of partnership formation in 1975–80 began to change in the early 1980s (Miret 1997). From 1975 onward, there was a continuous fall in the number of people in work and a complementary increase in unemployment rates. There were no differences by gender. We will take this 'crisis period' (1981–90) as our second period for comparison.

Table 1 reveals one of the key aspects of the 1980s in Spain, that is, the high level of involvement in non-compulsory education, especially for women. Some 45 per cent of men around 20 years of age who had never married or cohabited in 1980–91 had finished high school (compared to 20–25 per cent in 1965–74), as against 50 per cent of women (15 per cent during 1965–74). For 27–32 year olds in 1981–90, almost 19 per cent of males who had never had a partnership held a university degree (compared to 12 per cent in 1965–74) as against 30 per cent of women (9 per cent in 1965–74).

In 1981–90, compared with 1965–74, the proportion of men over 23 years old who had never married or cohabited and were working in an stable and full-time job decreased by ten percentage points (Table 2). Consequently, the impact of the economic crises affected single men uniformly across the whole age range. On the other hand, for women who had never married or cohabited, changes in labour-market participation were very much shaped by age. While a lower proportion of women aged less than 26 years old who had never had a partnership were working in a stable job in 1981–90 than in 1965-74, for women in their late twenties and early forties who had never married or cohabited the situation was the reverse (Table 2). That is, adult single women increased their involvement in the labour market.

Throughout this period, 1981–90, the total first nuptiality rate fell, while the age of marriage rose. Although there was a period of economic recovery from 1985 to 1990, the unemployment rate did not fall as might otherwise have been expected due to a parallel increase in the economically active population. Nuptiality levels experienced a little growth, but this ended suddenly due to the increase in rents and prices in the housing market, among other factors, following the removal of state controls on the market (Heath and Miret 1995; Miret 1997).

As we observed in Figures 1 and 2, the hazard rates of family formation are lower in 1981–90 than in 1965–74 for men over 25 years and for women at any age. For males, the age pattern for the 1981–90 period was significant for younger ages but male hazard rates over the age of 25 years were the lowest among all the periods analysed (Figure 1). For women aged under 25, the same age pattern is found in 1981–90 as in 1940–59; but women over 25 years of age experienced the lowest partnership-formation hazard rates of all the periods analysed during 1981–90.

## OPERATIVE HYPOTHESIS

We expect to find during the 'development period' (1965–74) in Spain that roles regarding the relationships between labour-market participation and educational attainment on the one hand, and family formation on the other, remained 'traditional', that is, fully separated by gender. Thus, during the period 1965–74, for a man, the age-group hazard rates for moving from 'never in a partnership' to 'in his first partnership' should be higher as (1) he becomes better educated and (2) he has a more stable involvement in the labour market. By contrast, during this first period (1965–74), for women we expect to find either that (1) there is no association between, on the one hand, educational attainment and labour-force participation and, on the other hand, the hazard rates by age-group for a woman to move from 'never in a partnership' to 'in her first partnership'; or that (2) there is a negative effect, that is, the age-group hazard rates for entering a first partnership were lower the more educated she was and the greater her labour-force participation. This would lead us to conclude that the ideal-type male-provider and female care-giver family-formation model was very much in place in Spain during the decade 1965–74.

Moreover, we suppose that between the period 1965–74 and the 1980s, gender roles regarding the relationship between labour-market participation and educational attainment on the one hand and family formation on the other changed a great deal, that is, during the 1980s, there were many more similarities between males and females regarding the effect of each independent variable on the hazard rates of entering a first partnership among the various age groups than during 1965–74. Assuming that we can find in this last period an evident male-provider model in family formation, this pattern would be eroded in the 1980s the more we find signs of a more egalitarian model. Nevertheless, we also expect to observe many more changes in female patterns of family formation than in males ones. That is, (1) we still suppose that men's first marriage hazard rates during the 1980s will be disproportionately higher for those men who were more highly educated and better connected to the labour market than for those who were less well-educated and who experienced job difficulties. But (2) for women, by contrast, we think we will find a very different model between the two periods analysed, with never-married or cohabiting women entering into partnerships more frequently the more highly educated and more involved in the labour market they become.

## EDUCATIONAL ATTAINMENT IN UNDERSTANDING THE PACE AND CROSS-SECTIONAL INTENSITY OF PARTNERSHIP FORMATION

Can we explain the differences in the timing and prevalence of partnership formation between 1965–74 and 1981–90 in terms of changes in the educational attainment of men or women during these periods? To answer this question, we present in Figures 3–6 the hazard rates for males and females by age group and for each historical period according to their educational attainment. For 1965–74, we have grouped university degrees because there was no difference during that period between three-year and five-year university degrees regarding first partnership hazard rates.

We discover from Figure 3 that during the period 1965–74, no matter which age group, male hazard rates for becoming involved in a first partnership were lower for men whose education had ended with primary school than for those with vocational training, and lower for those who had finished high school than for those who had finished primary school. Because it affected the whole age range (although it was more evident for young adult men), we can state that men with vocational training married more than those with maximum compulsory education and the latter more than men with high-school diplomas. Men with a university degree had timed their marriages later, but at a similar general intensity, than those with primary-school education. We can conclude that during the 'economic development period', for men to reach any level of non-compulsory education created a higher probability of marrying (with the exception of the high-school diploma, which we suppose was considered by the overwhelmingly majority of young Spanish men to be a step in their educational career), while attending university led to a postponement of marriage.

FIGURE 3
MALE FIRST-PARTNERSHIP HAZARD RATES BY AGE-GROUPS AND EDUCATIONAL
ATTAINMENT FOR 1965–74

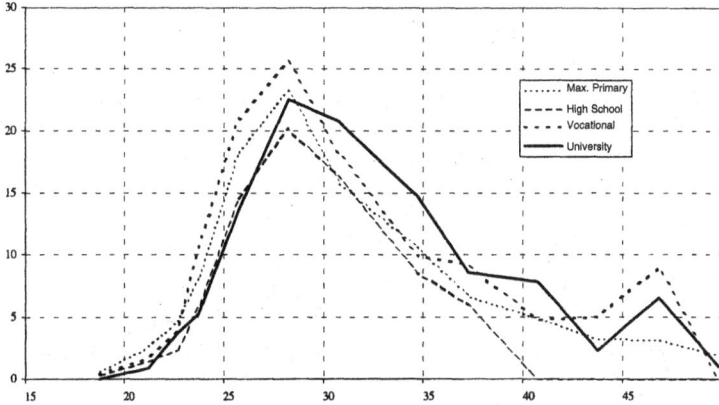

FIGURE 4
MALE FIRST-PARTNERSHIP HAZARD RATES BY AGE-GROUPS AND EDUCATIONAL
ATTAINMENT FOR 1981–90

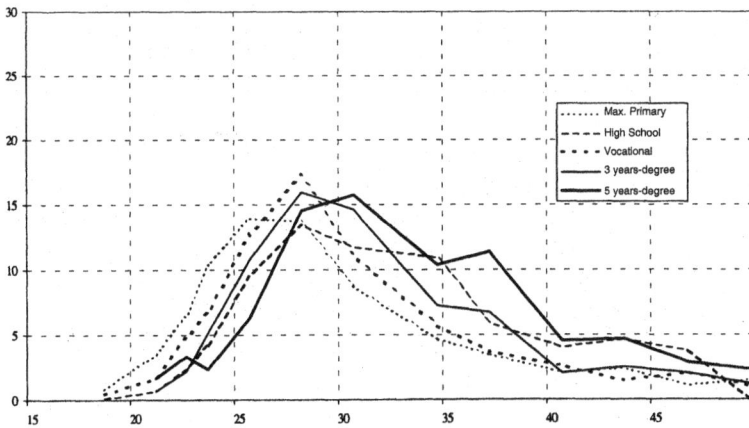

FIGURE 5
FEMALE FIRST-PARTNERSHIP HAZARD RATES BY AGE-GROUPS AND EDUCATIONAL
ATTAINMENT FOR 1965–74

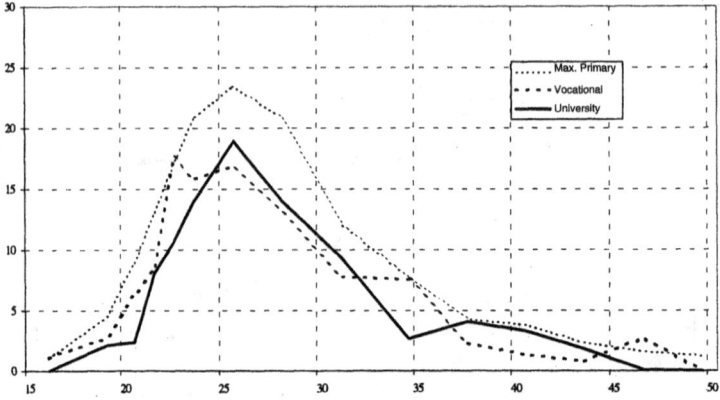

FIGURE 6
FEMALE FIRST-PARTNERSHIP HAZARD RATES BY AGE-GROUPS AND EDUCATIONAL
ATTAINMENT FOR 1981–90

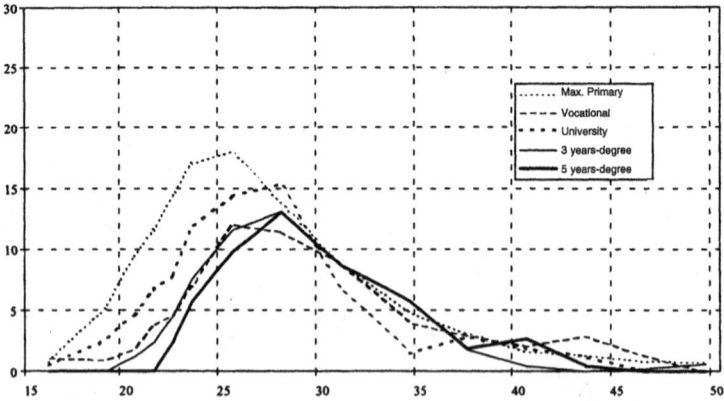

With our data for the 1981–90 period, we can divide university degrees into those which lasted three years and those which lasted five years. Figure 4 illustrates how during the 1980s economic crisis, Spanish men had different paths for entering a first partnership (which was clearly more delayed the longer was their chosen educational path), again with the exception of high school. But we cannot infer that men married or became involved in a partnership less frequently the less educated they were. In short, education in the period 1981–90 affected timing, but not intensity.

We turn now to Figures 5 and 6 to examine the relationship between educational achievement and first partnership formation for Spanish women. In contrast to men, during the period 1965–74 we can clearly see that young females with vocational training, a high-school diploma or a university degree were less likely to be involved in a partnership than those with primary-school education only, no matter which age group is chosen. That is, for women in 1965–74, there was a negative connection between education and partnership formation.

On the other hand, during the 1980s, younger females shared with their male counterparts later entry into partnership the more educated they were (Figure 6), although the difference between the educational categories are much more variable for women than for men. But, definitely, education affected cross-sectional general intensity, because more highly educated women over 30 years old did not register higher hazard rates (as was the case with men).

In brief, education during the economic crisis of the 1980s had differential effects by gender. While for men, higher education implied later marriage, but not less intensity, in partnership formation, for women, higher education led to both fewer and more delayed marriages. Thus, although for men we can state that educational attainment did not influence their nuptiality levels during the crisis, the behaviour of younger and more educated women was the reverse, that is, female education clearly did have a negative impact on partnership formation in Spain during the 1980s.

## LABOUR-FORCE PARTICIPATION IN UNDERSTANDING THE CROSS-SECTIONAL INTENSITY AND TIMING OF PARTNERSHIP FORMATION

Maybe labour-force participation will shed more light on changes in the partnership-formation process between 1965–74 and the 1980s. To begin with, we would like to note the classification of labour-force participation used in Figures 7–10. In these figures, we have elaborated the hazard rates of entering a first partnership for Spanish men by age group according to different levels of involvement in the labour force. First, we have the hazard rates for males who were occupied in a full-time and stable job (labelled 'Full-time Job & Stable Occupation' in Figures 7–10). Subsequently, in a second category, we find men who were in a full-time job, but had experienced unemployment ('Full-time Job & Unemployment'). The next ranks relate to those who were in a part-time or seasonal job and either without unemployment periods ('Non-full-time Job') or with periods of unemployment ('Non-full-time Job & Unemployment'). Lastly, we have those men who were 'Not in the Labour Force'.

The ideal-type, male-provider, family-formation model would show, at any specific age group, the highest first partnership hazard rates for men with a full-time job without unemployment, followed by those in a full-time job but with periods of unemployment, followed, in turn, by those in neither a full-time nor continuous job but never unemployed, those with neither a full-time nor a continuous job who experienced periods of unemployment and, lastly, those men not in the labour market. For women, the ideal-type, female-care-giver, family-formation model would present the opposite situation, that is to say, the highest first partnership hazard rates would be for women not in the labour market, followed by those for women in a stop-gap job with periods of unemployment, those for females in a stop-gap job but without periods of unemployment, those for women in a full-time job with employment gaps and, lastly, the lowest first partnership hazard rates would be for those women in a full-time, continuous job.

The combination of these situations for men and women would lead us to conclude that the ideal-type, male-provider and female-care-giver, first-partnership-formation model is strongly entrenched in Spain for a given period. Otherwise, we could state that the family-formation pattern in Spain during a particular period did not match with this ideal-type model. At the other extreme, a symmetric provider model would be illustrated by very similar first partnership hazard rates for men and women, showing quite equal hazard rates for different forms of involvement in the labour market, that is, for people with stable occupations, with stop-gap jobs and with or without periods of unemployment.

During the period of economic development (1965–74), only single men in their early and mid-thirties had higher first partnership hazard

FIGURE 7
MALE FIRST-PARTNERSHIP HAZARD RATES BY AGE-GROUPS AND LABOUR
FORCE PARTICIPATION FOR 1965–74 PERIOD

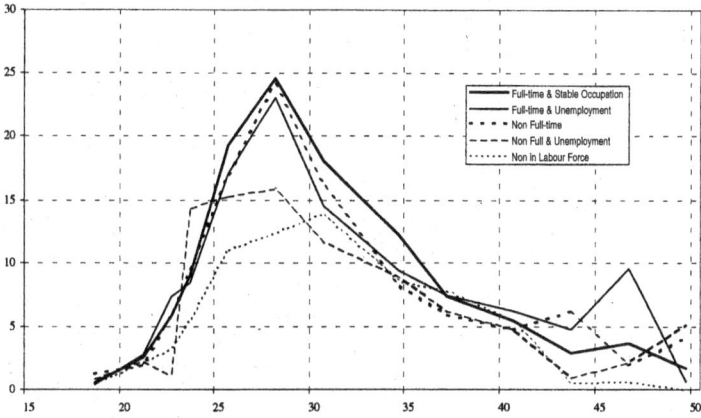

FIGURE 8
MALE FIRST-PARTNERSHIP HAZARD RATES BY AGE-GROUPS AND LABOUR
FORCE PARTICIPATION FOR 1981–90 PERIOD

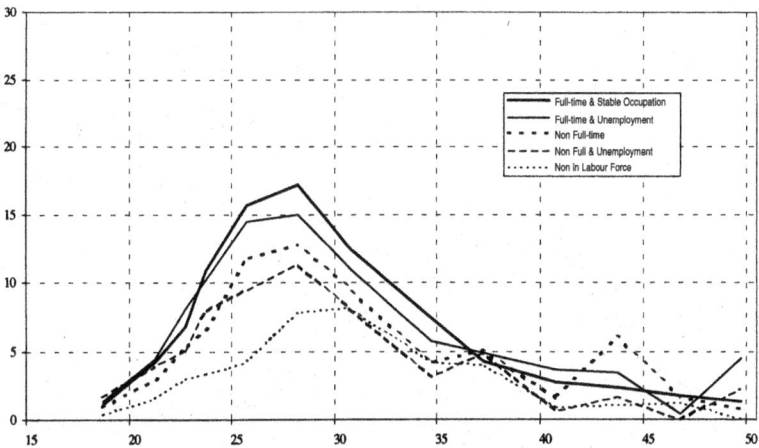

FIGURE 9
FEMALE FIRST-PARTNERSHIP HAZARD RATES BY AGE-GROUPS AND LABOUR
FORCE PARTICIPATION FOR 1965–74 PERIOD

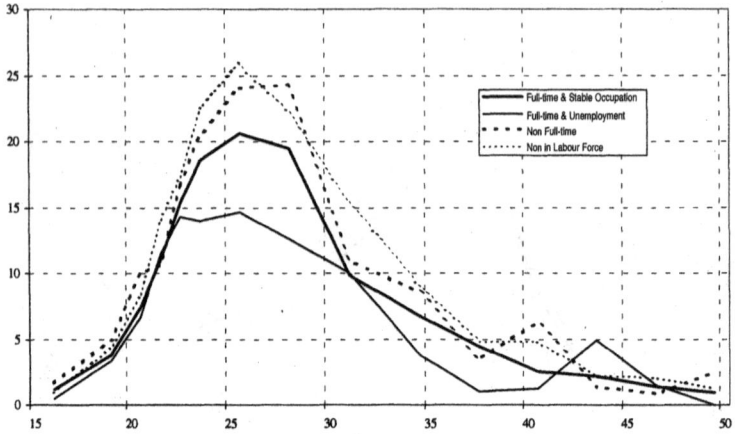

FIGURE 10
FEMALE FIRST-PARTNERSHIP HAZARD RATES BY AGE-GROUPS AND LABOUR
FORCE PARTICIPATION FOR 1981–90 PERIOD

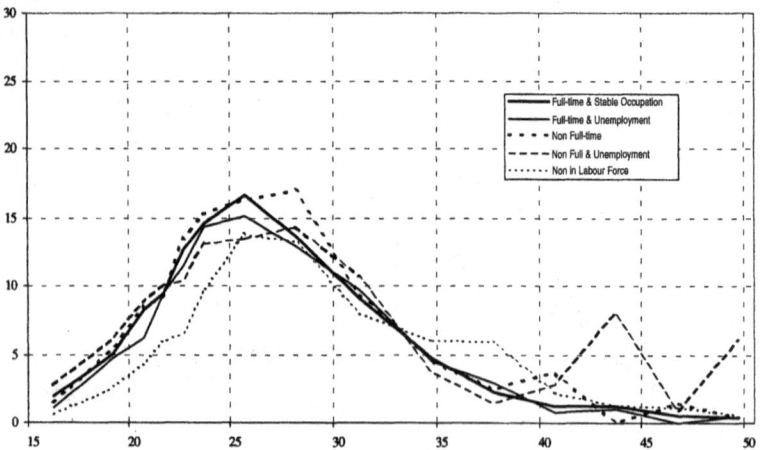

rates if their employment circumstances were better than for other men. Indeed, men in all forms of employment married at a very similar pace and intensity, with the exception of those men not working full time or working in seasonal jobs and with periods of unemployment (Figure 7). That is, in 1965–74, only men in more unstable jobs between 25 and 35 years of age experienced significantly lower hazard rates for entering their first partnership than other men of the same age but with more secure involvement in the labour market. Furthermore, as expected, first partnership hazard rates for those males not in the labour market were extremely low compared those in the labour market (Figure 7). Thus, to sum up, through the economic boom education played a more important role in explaining the differentials in the pace and intensity of first marriages among males (Figure 3) than did the nature of their employment (Figure 7).

By contrast, during the 1980s economic crisis, men entered their first partnership with less intensity the more precarious was their job (Figure 8): the hazard rates of marriage for men of any age group were lower the worse their link with the labour market. Moreover, during the 1980s, men not in the labour market had both a low intensity and later timing in family formation (Figure 8). Thus, we can conclude, in line with other analyses (Oppenheimer et al. 1997), that one of the causes of the low total first nuptiality rate in Spain during the 1980s was the employment crisis, a crisis which is still being experienced by young adult males. In summary, for men, being a 'provider' in family formation was much more important during 1980s economic crisis than during the 1965–74 period of economic development.

On the other hand, in the economic development period, the hazard rates of entering a first partnership for women not in the labour market and working in part-time jobs or seasonal occupations were quite similar. In addition, they were clearly higher than those for women who were working full time. Nevertheless, this does not reveal a threat to the care-giver model, as part-time work or seasonal occupations clearly allow for care-giver roles. Furthermore, part-time work in Spain was very unusual, as is still the case (Eurostat 1995; 1997). Women in part-time jobs or seasonal occupations who experienced periods of unemployment do not appear in Figure 9 because they are not significant. Another unexpected result in Figure 9 is the effect of unemployment on women working full time, as unemployment clearly discourages partnership formation among in this category. It seems that in 1965–74 women's behaviour was segmented: first, those single women not in the labour market or in stop-gap jobs had the highest probability of getting married (they were obviously well adapted to the 'care-giver model'); second, single women in more stable jobs had a lower probability of getting married but not remarkably so in relation to the first category; and, lastly, those who show clearly the lowest hazard rates were single women working full time but with periods of unemployment.

By contrast, during 1981–90, there were no significant differences in the pattern of partnership formation among the various female labour-force categories. Only women not in the labour force stand out, as they have a late timing in first partnership formation. We imagine this is due to the high proportion of students among women less than 25 years old who have never been in a partnership. Although, in comparison to the previous period, women were less likely to enter a first partnership whatever position they had in the labour market. This means that in 1981–90 women behave quite differently from what one would expect in the extreme care-giver, partnership-formation model.

## CONCLUSIONS

During the development period, for men any level of non-compulsory education led to higher partnership-formation hazard rates (high school was an exception, we imagine, because it was never considered by young men as the end of their educational career). However, a university degree implied a later entrance into marriage, but not a higher intensity. Regarding the labour variable, through 1965–74, only men in more precarious jobs or outside the labour market experienced lower partnership-formation probabilities across all age groups. The excellent economic circumstances did not force a strong relationship between labour stability and first marriage, as any job could be considered 'stable'. So, in 1965–74, education assumes much more importance in explaining differences in male partnership-formation patterns than labour-market position.

On the contrary, for women, we can confirm the hypothesis formulated for the period 1965–74, that is, that education diminishes a great deal the intensity of female partnership formation. In addition, in the same period, their was no clear direct relationship between the first marriage of a woman and her labour-force participation. On the one hand, as we expected, single women not in the labour market, and those with either part-time or seasonal jobs, registered the highest first partnership hazard rates. But, on the other hand, surprisingly, these rates contrasted strongly with those of single women working full time in a continuous job, unless they experienced periods of unemployment.

By contrast, in 1981–90, higher levels of education led to a more delayed pattern of partnership formation, but not to a low intensity. In short, for men, there has been a shift from a better education, higher first-nuptiality-rate model to another in which education makes a difference by age but not at the general level. Educational differences made much less difference in the past as regards male marriage behaviour. However, the importance of labour-force participation for the male-provider model increased during the economic crisis of the 1980s: the probability of marriage for single men increased the better their position in the labour market. On the whole, the main explanation for male partnership-formation patterns has shifted from education to labour-force involvement: while education only played an important role in timing, labour-force participation mainly explained differences in intensity.

For women, in 1981–90, higher levels of education led to a pattern of less and later female partnership formation. In summary, between the two periods, while education disappears as a significant independent variable for understanding the formation of first partnerships for males, its role in explaining female first marriages was strengthened. Furthermore, during that period, any sign of the care-giver-type model had disappeared: first partnership hazard rates were very similar regardless of the labour-force participation of single women.

Crises seem to affect family formation unequally by gender. While for men economic crises increased differences in partnership formation according to labour-market position, these were eliminated for women. That is, within the present economic crisis, a male's chances of first partnership formation are absolutely related to his involvement in the labour market. Thus, these results indicate that one explanation for the low levels of first partnership formation in the 1980s in Spain was the difficulties faced by young men in finding a stable job. However, we cannot find support for the hypothesis that the present higher level of female involvement in the labour market explains their low levels of marriage.

In conclusion, we cannot state that the male-provider model has disappeared, because the rules of family formation in Spain still encourage those men who are better situated in the labour market, that is, those who better fit the male-breadwinner model. However, there are important signs of change, especially for women.

We leave open the hypothesis that the present low levels of first family formation in Spain are due to the lack of a radical transformation in the male-provider model. Lastly, we should emphasize that we are analysing just one aspect of family life, that is, the formation of first partnerships. In order to really understand whether the male-provider model is still in place, we need to analyse the entire family life course.

## REFERENCES

Allison, P. D. (1984): *Event History Analysis in Quantitative Applications in the Social Sciences*, 46. Beverly Hills: Sage University Paper.

Becker, G. (1981): *A Treatise on the Family*. Cambridge: Harvard University Press.

Cabré, A. (1995): 'Notes sobre la transició familiar' ['Notes on familiar transition']. In *Jornades sobre la familia i canvi social*, pp.31–46. Barcelona: Servei de Documentació i Difusió de l'Associació per les Nacions Unides a Espanya.

Carreras, A. (1988): 'La renta y la riqueza'. In A. Carreras (ed.), *Introducción a las fuentes estadísticas de la historia de la España contemporánea*. Madrid: Banco Exterior de España.

Castro, T. (1992): 'Delayed childbearing in contemporary Spain: trends and differentials'. *European Journal of Population*, 8/3, pp.217–46.

Castro, T. (1993): 'Changing nuptiality patterns in contemporary Spain'. *Genus*, 49/1–2, pp.79–96.

Delgado, M. (1993): 'Cambios recientes en el proceso de formación de la familia'. *Revista Española de Investigaciones Sociológicas*, 64, pp.123–53.

Domingo, A. (1997 unpublished): 'La formación de la pareja en tiempos de crisis. Madrid y Barcelona, 1975–1995'. MA Thesis, Sociology Department, UNED.

Durkheim, E. (1960): *The Division of Labour in Society*. Glencoe, IL: Free Press.

Eurostat (1995): *Statistics in Focus. Population and Social Conditions*. Luxembourg: Eurostat.

——— (1997): *Labour Force Survey. Results 1996*. Luxembourg: Eurostat.

Fernández, J. A. (1978, unpublished): 'Nupcialité et fecondité en Espagne'. MA Thesis, Geography Department, University of Montreal.

Garrido, L. (1992): *Las dos biografías de la mujer en España*. Madrid: Ministerio de Asuntos Sociales, Instituto de la Mujer.

Hajnal, J. (1965): 'European marriage patterns in perspective'. *Population Studies*, II/2, pp.111–36.

Heath, S. and P. Miret (1996): *Living In and Out of the Parental Home in Spain and Great Britain: A Comparative Approach*. Cambridge Group for the History of Population and Social Structure, Working Paper Series, 2.

Laslett, P. (1972): *Household and Family in Past Times*. London: Cambridge University Press.

McDonald, P. (1997): 'Gender equity, social institutions and the future of fertility'. Women and Families Conference, Paris, UNESCO-CICRED.

Miret, P. (1997): 'Nuptiality patterns in Spain in the eighties'. *Genus*, 53/3–4, pp.185–98.

Oppenheimer, V. K. (1988): 'A theory of marriage timing'. *American Journal of Sociology*, 94, pp.563–61.

Oppenheimer, V. K. (1994): 'Women's rising employment and the future of the family in industrial societies'. *Population and Development Review*, 20/2, pp.293–337.

Oppenheimer, V. K., Kalmijn, V. and N. Lim (1997): 'Men's career development and marriage timing during a period of rising inequality'. *Demography*, 34/4, pp.311–30.

Parsons, T. (1949): 'The social structure of the family'. In R. Anshen (ed.), *The Family: Its Function and Destiny*, pp.172–201. New York: Harper.

Reher, D. S. (1997): *Perspectives on the Family in Spain, Past and Present*. Oxford: Clarendon Press.

Tamames, R. (1986): *The Spanish Economy: An Introduction*. London: C. Hurst.

Yamaguchi, K. (1991): *Event History Analysis*. Beverly Hills: Sage Publications.

# Separation and Divorce in Spain

## MONTSERRAT SOLSONA, RENÉ HOULE and CARLES SIMÓ

Separation and divorce as demographic events are poorly understood phenomena in Spain. The legislation on divorce is relatively recent. Even if the democratic transition dates from 1975, divorce was legalized only in July 1981.[1] Since then, the only published data on separations and divorces have come from the Annual Judicial Review[2] and this provides little information: only the total annual number of separations and divorces initiated each year, including information on the degree of agreement between spouses (with or without mutual consent) and the autonomous community of their residence. For this reason, the sociological studies interested in the topic are limited and only serve to highlight the growing importance of separations and divorces by mutual agreement of spouses (Alberdi 1995), and the strongest incidence of the phenomenon in some autonomous communities: the Canary Islands, Balearics and Catalonia (Treviño and Gil 1994). The absence of data also explains why the Spanish case is not included in comparative studies on divorce (see, for example, Monnier and Guibert-Lantoine 1993).

In this study, we approach the most recent reality of marriage disruption in Spain available from the retrospective Socio-demographic Survey (1991). Besides the recent evolution of marriage dissolution by separation or divorce, we have undertaken a first attempt to study some socio-economic characteristics related to the sociography of divorce, such as age at first marriage, educational attainment, participation in the labour market, custody of children and remarriage.

## HYPOTHESIS

We argue that union dissolution cannot be analysed independently from the specificity of the political and social conditions a country has experienced in recent decades. For explaining the incidence of the phenomenon and its determinant factors, it is not sufficient, albeit necessary, to analyse the individual characteristics influencing the propensity for divorce. A full understanding requires a three-level analysis: the individual or microlevel; the meso-level, or family and social level, and particularly the ideology of family as an institution in which individuals socialize; and, lastly, the macro-level, or those factors of social change that helped the democratization of family relations, making it possible, for example, for an unhappy marriage to end in divorce. The hypothesis we develop takes into account these three levels.

First, divorce in Spain is determined by the current legislation that was introduced in 1981. At that time, the most conservative and alarmist positions announced a wave of divorces that did not actually occur.[3] But as often happens, the new legislation only regulated a social practice that already recognized the right to dissolve a union in which relations between partners were in crisis. When the divorce law was implemented, existing *de facto* separations were already recognized before notary and these tended to be harmonized with the new law.

Second, we identify important generational factors. At the end of the 1960s and the beginning of the 1970s, the movement against the Franco dictatorship was very powerful. The left political parties not only rejected the political system, but also some features of the social system, particularly the patriarchal regime explicitly legitimized by Franco's legislation.[4]

We would expect to find the strongest incidence of separation and divorce among those generations that took part as young adults in this social movement. We refer to the generations born during the 1950s that were the first ones in Spain to benefit from the initial and massive opening up of the university system. Soon after that these same generations also benefited from the development of the welfare state during the first phase of the socialist government (1982–86), while many individuals got jobs in the public sector, with all the social protection generally associated with that. Subsequent generations, even if they were more educated than the preceding ones, were more numerous and their entry into the labour market coincided with a period of job losses (**Olano 1988**).

Third, it seems clear to us that the economic independence of individuals is a key factor in separation and divorce decisions. Indeed, since in Spain specific family allowances for the separated or divorced population are practically non-existent, we think that individual economic independence is a crucial explanatory factor in separation and divorce. If the development of the welfare state during the socialist period (1982–96) achieved its aims in terms of education, health and universal retirement pension schemes, it was not able, on the other hand, to lay the basis for individuals on the margins of the labour market to take decisions about their professional, personal and family life. For this reason, and taking into account the recent changes that have affected women in relation to their labour-market participation, we think that those generations and social groups that are more fully integrated in the labour market are also those most involved in marriage dissolution. The gender perspective is here essential because social practices differ according to work and reproduction, and this is reflected in divorce settlements, which generally concede the custody of children to women.

## DATA AND METHODOLOGY

The absence of a divorce register constitutes one of the most serious obstacles for studying the dissolution of marriages in Spain. The only source giving a direct estimate of the number of divorces and separations is the Annual Judicial Review. However, this document only reports separations and divorces initiated during the year, and does not indicate the actual outcomes.

In Spain, it is useful to distinguish between separation and divorce. Separations can be a *de facto* situation, but can acquire a legal character too, conferring a specific civil status (the status of a legally separated person). This legal status must always precede the eventual attainment of another legal category: the final divorce.

The separated population that appears in statistics (in censuses, for example) is the separated population legally defined as such. Only the 1991 Socio-demographic Survey allows us to identify the *de facto* separated population. In the national censuses of 1975 and 1981, the divorced and separated populations are classified in a single category. In the censuses of 1986 and 1991 (after the legislation of divorce in 1981), these categories are counted separately. On the other hand, annual deaths and marriages according to civil status published in **Vital Statistics publications** present the referring events for the two populations together.[5]

Lastly, the 1991 Socio-demographic Survey for Spain and its regions contains retrospective questions giving biographical information about union, education, economic activity and migration histories for more than 150,000 individuals. The union history module covers all the union of the respondent. This survey constitutes a very good quantitative source

FIGURE 1
HAZARD RATES OF UNION DISSOLUTION IN SPAIN BY UNION DURATION,
UNION COHORTS AND SEX OF RESPONDANT

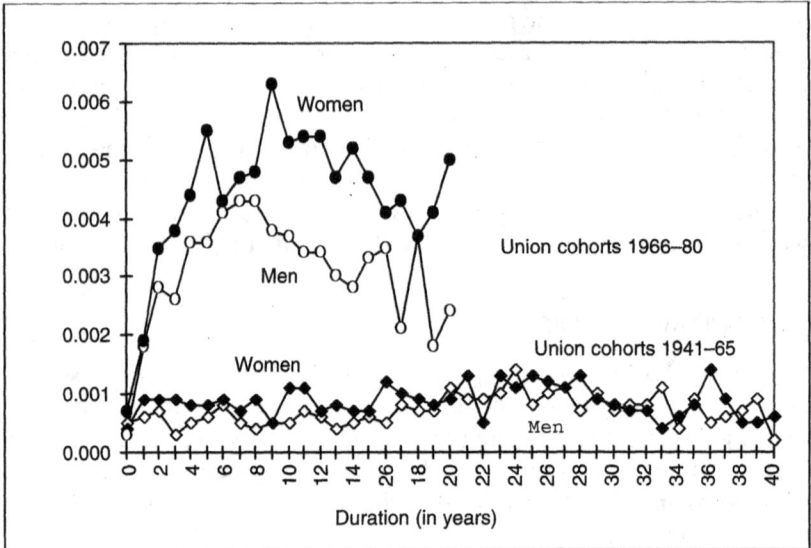

Source: INE, 1991 Spanish Sociodemographic Survey.

for this research as it includes more than 108,000 first union and 4,020 separations.

Most calculations were done using life-table analysis. The life-table technique consists of subdividing a period of observation (in our case, from the beginning of the marriage up to its dissolution by separation or death of partner, or up to the moment of the survey) into smaller time intervals (in our case, yearly intervals). For each interval, all those people who have been observed for at least a year are taken into account to calculate the probability of a terminal event (the separation) occurring in that interval. From this, probabilities of events occurring are estimated for each duration, which makes possible the calculation of cumulative survival and hazard rates (an estimate of the probability per unit of time) (SPSS 1994). We used data for women as well as for men for these calculations. Separations declared by men are underestimated, especially for recent marriage cohorts, as we can see from Figure 1. (This was also the case when applying vital statistics methods to the male population, as we did for women in Table 1.) But data for men and women are not

TABLE 1
DIFFERENT ESTIMATES OF DIVORCES AND SEPARATIONS IN SPAIN (1975–90)

| Vital Statistics Method (calculations from female data) | Divorcees | Divorcees and Legally Separated |
|---|---|---|
| Deaths | | |
| 1975–80 | | 202 |
| 1981–85 | 240 | 843 |
| 1986–90 | 584 | 1,957 |
| Remarriages | | |
| 1981–85 | 8,623 | 8,623 |
| 1986–90 | 23,308 | 23,308 |
| Populations | | |
| 1975 | | 70,758 |
| 1981 | | 146,397 |
| 1986 | 50,560 | 208,420 |
| 1991 | 96,986 | 274,821 |

| Net estimates of events | Divorces | Divorces and Legal Separations |
|---|---|---|
| 1975–80 | | 75,841 |
| 1981–85 | 59,423 | 71,489 |
| 1986–90 | 70,318 | 91,666 |
| 1981–90 | 129,741 | 163,155 |

| Annual Judicial Review | Divorces | Legal Separations |
|---|---|---|
| 1981–85 | 87,314 | 92,290 |
| 1986–90 | 109,263 | 162,890 |
| 1981–90 | 196,577 | 255,180 |

| Socio-demographic Survey | Divorces | De Facto Separations |
|---|---|---|
| 1975–80 | | 98,182 |
| 1981–85 | | 175,422 |
| 1986–90 | | 239,832 |
| 1981–90 | 216,823 | 415,254 |

Note: Deaths of divorcees are estimates from deaths among the separated and divorced population. For the estimates of numbers of divorces using the Socio-demographic Survey and vital statistics method, we assumed that the divorced population was zero (0) in 1981.

exactly comparable as some first marriages of respondents are marriages with a divorced partner (Bumpass *et al.* 1991), and in Spain it is more likely to happen to women than to men (see below). Unless otherwise indicated, in all the tables and figures we refer to all first union, irrespective of the legal form they may have taken after any disruption,[6] including cohabitations that lasted at least one year.

## RESULTS

Table 1 gives different estimates of the total number of divorces and separations in Spain between 1975 and 1991. The estimates vary from 130,000 to 217,000 divorces between 1981 and 1990, and the number of separations (legal or *de facto*) from 163,000 using the **vital statistics** method[7] (calculations with female data) to 415,000 using the Socio-demographic Survey over the same period. For calculations from the Socio-demographic Survey, separations of all ranks were taken into account, but cohabitation was excluded.

The estimates derived from the **vital statistics** method, which was developed to obtain estimates of net migrations between two censuses, suggest far fewer divorces than the other two sources. Considering the poor results given by the **vital statistics** method and the fact that the judiciary publishes only partial data (without marriage duration and other details), we came to the conclusion that only the Socio-demographic Survey allows us to study the evolution of union dissolution in Spain in its historical, geographical and socio-demographic perspective.

As a first approximation of the relative divorce intensity in Spain,[8] we calculated the total divorce rate or divorce period indicator (or more specifically a dissolution period indicator)[9] of first formal marriages using the Socio-demographic Survey. This indicator allows us to compare the Spanish situation with other European countries. As we can observe in Table 2, the incidence of divorce in Spain (13 dissolutions per 100 marriages) is similar to that of the other Mediterranean countries and the Balkan countries at the end of the 1980s. Nevertheless, the indicator for Spain refers to *de facto* separations and not only to divorces.

## THE EVOLUTION OF DIVORCE IN TIME AND SPACE

### *The Evolution of the Separated and Divorced Population*

We analyse, here, the importance of the separated and divorced population in the censuses of 1975,[10] 1981, 1986 and 1991. Tables 3 and

TABLE 2
TOTAL DIVORCE RATE IN EUROPEAN COUNTRIES (1990)

| Countries | Total Divorce Rate in 1990 (for 100 marriages) | Countries | Total Divorce Rate in 1990 (for 100 marriages) |
|---|---|---|---|
| Estonia | 46 | Moldova | 30 |
| Latvia | 44 | The Netherlands | 28 |
| Denmark | 44 | Germany | 27 |
| Sweden | 43 | Romania | 19 |
| England and Wales | 42 | Croatia | 17 |
| Finland | 41 | Bulgaria | 17 |
| Norway | 40 | Poland | 15 |
| Czech Republic | 38 | Slovenia | 14 |
| Luxembourg | 36 | Greece | 13 |
| Lithuania | 34 | Spain (1986–90) | 13* |
| Iceland | 34 | Portugal (1989) | 12** |
| Switzerland | 33 | Italy | 8 |
| Austria | 33 | Cyprus | 7 |
| France | 32 | Turkey | 6 |
| Hungary | 31 | Macedonia | 5 |
| Belgium | 31 | | |

\*    For Spain, the indicator refers to the dissolution of first marriages (excluding cohabitation) for the period 1986–90 (expressed annually). It obviously overestimates the indicator of divorce.
\*\*   For Portugal, see Monnier and Guibert-Lantoine (1993: 1,063).

*Source*: Conseil de l'Europe (1997: 41).

4 present the total size of these subpopulations and their intercensal growth rate. First, we observe that the separated or divorced population is one of weak numerical importance in absolute numbers. In fact, the separated and divorcees represented less than two per cent of the population aged 15 years and over in 1991. But its growth was rapid during the period 1975–91. Paradoxically, it was during the period preceding the divorce law that its growth was the most rapid. Its size doubled between 1975 and 1981. The growth rate decreased after that, but was still important. In 1986, and perhaps before, the divorced population increased more rapidly, nearly doubling between 1986 and 1991, whereas the separated population only rose by 15 per cent during the same period. Nevertheless, at 0.5 per cent, divorcees constituted a very weak fringe of the population aged 15 years and over in 1991.

Obviously, these figures must be considered with caution when one wants to deduce indicators of the incidence of separations and divorces. Indeed, these figures are underestimates because of the remarriage of divorcees, a recent and rapidly increasing phenomenon (see below). A

TABLE 3
SIZE AND INTERCENSAL GROWTH OF THE SEPARATED AND DIVORCED
POPULATION (1975–91)

|  | Size | | | Growth Rate (per cent) | | |
|  | Male | Female | Total | Male | Female | Total |
|---|---|---|---|---|---|---|
| 1975 | 40,351 | 70,758 | 111,109 | – | – | – |
| 1981 | 94,690 | 146,397 | 241,087 | 135 | 107 | 117 |
| 1986 | 134,034 | 208,420 | 342,454 | 42 | 42 | 42 |
| 1991 | 181,028 | 274,847 | 455,875 | 35 | 32 | 33 |

*Sources*: INE, 1975, 1981, 1986 and 1991 Spanish censuses.

TABLE 4
SIZE AND INTERCENSAL GROWTH OF THE SEPARATED AND DIVORCED
POPULATION (1986 AND 1991)

|  |  | Size | | | Growth Rate (per cent) | | |
|  |  | Male | Female | Total | Male | Female | Total |
|---|---|---|---|---|---|---|---|
| 1986 | Divorced | 30,807 | 50,560 | 81,367 | – | – | – |
|  | Separated | 103,227 | 157,860 | 261,087 | – | – | – |
| 1991 | Divorced | 59,325 | 96,986 | 156,311 | 93 | 92 | 92 |
|  | Separated | 121,703 | 177,861 | 299,564 | 18 | 13 | 15 |

*Sources*: INE, 1986 and 1991 Spanish censuses.

quite important number of these divorcees 'disappear' between censuses because of their remarriage. Some of the separated 'disappear' as well because of their transition to divorcee status.

Even though a separation or a divorce always involves a man and a woman, we observe a clear imbalance between the numbers of separated or divorced women and men in the different censuses. Part of the difference between the sexes can be explained by the different mortality levels of men and women, but the main factor is a differential propensity to remarry: remarriage is more frequent for men than for women. Another factor contributing to the imbalance between the levels of separated and divorced men and women comes from the undercounting of men in these two categories in censuses in comparison with women.

*Divorce by Union Cohorts, Duration and Period*

Particular groups and generations have led the evolution of divorce and separation since the 1970s. We can see the generational effects by examining dissolutions in the different union cohorts (Table 5). In the 1971–75 cohorts, constituted mostly by generations of men and women

TABLE 5
PERCENTAGE OF FIRST UNIONS ENDING IN SEPARATION OR DIVORCE AT THE
MOMENT OF THE SURVEY BY FIRST UNION COHORT

| 1941–45 | 1946–50 | 1951–55 | 1956–60 | 1961–65 | 1966–70 | 1971–75 | 1976–80 |
|---------|---------|---------|---------|---------|---------|---------|---------|
| 1.7 | 2.2 | 2.4 | 2.9 | 3.4 | 4.5 | 5.8 | 4.9 |

Source: INE, 1991 Spanish Socio-demographic Survey.

born in 1951–55, 5.8 per cent of first unions had dissolved at the time of
the survey (1991). The incidence of separation doubled in comparison
with the 1956–60 union cohort. The former generations took part in the
political changes that heralded the end of Franco's authoritarian regime
and at the same time were at the vanguard of new socio-cultural
behaviour, such as cohabitation, late marriage, the opening up of the
university system and increased female participation in the labour
market, linked to the second demographic transition in Spain (see
Lesthaeghe 1995; Solsona 1998a).

From Figure 2, we can observe how separation rates began to
accelerate from the 1951–55 union cohort onward. The survival curve
falls constantly between this union cohort and the more recent ones,
which means that the probability of keeping a union intact becomes
lower with time and the duration of a union.

In Table 6 and Figure 3, we can see the double effect of union cohort
and duration on hazard rates. In Table 6, the effect of union duration can
be read in the columns and the effect of the cohorts in the rows. This
double effect was mostly influenced by the behavioural changes that
began in late 1960s and appears clearly with the last cohorts, for which
the hazard rates increase with union duration. The **effect of a given
period** is visible in Figure 3, in the duration of unions; but it is far from
corresponding entirely to what was expected after the application of the
divorce law (1981). Cohort effects are more decisive factors in explaining
the recent evolution of separation rates (or union survival) than the **effect
of the period** linked to the legalization of divorce, even if there was an
effect produced by the interaction between both factors. In fact,
behavioural changes seem to have anticipated the divorce law.

## REGIONAL DIFFERENCES

In Spain, socio-cultural behaviour varies considerably by region, and
separation is no exception. In the 17 autonomous communities, the

FIGURE 2
PROPORTION OF SURVIVING FIRST UNIONS BY DURATION AND
FIRST UNION COHORT

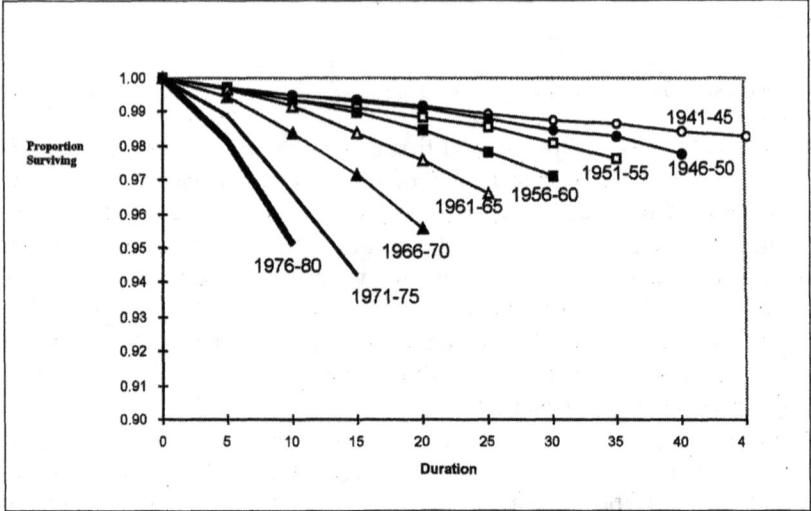

*Source*: as Table 6.

TABLE 6
FIVE-YEAR HAZARD RATES FOR THE DISSOLUTION OF FIRST UNIONS (FOR
10,000 UNIONS) BY UNION COHORT AND UNION DURATION

| Union Cohorts | 1941 –45 | 1946 –50 | 1951 –55 | 1956 –60 | 1961 –65 | 1966 –70 | 1971 –75 | 1976 –80 | 1981 –85 |
|---|---|---|---|---|---|---|---|---|---|
| Duration | | | | | | | | | |
| 5 | 6.0 | 7.0 | 7.0 | 6.0 | 7.0 | 11.0 | 23.0 | 38.0 | 50.0 |
| 10 | 4.0 | 4.0 | 6.0 | 7.0 | 11.0 | 22.0 | 46.0 | 62.0 | |
| 15 | 3.0 | 3.0 | 4.0 | 8.0 | 16.0 | 25.0 | 51.0 | | |
| 20 | 3.0 | 4.0 | 6.0 | 10.0 | 16.0 | 34.0 | | | |
| 25 | 5.0 | 7.0 | 6.0 | 14.0 | 20.0 | | | | |
| 30 | 4.0 | 6.0 | 9.0 | 14.0 | | | | | |
| 35 | 2.0 | 4.0 | 9.0 | | | | | | |
| 40 | 4.0 | 10.0 | | | | | | | |
| 45 | 3.0 | | | | | | | | |

*Source*: INE, 1991 Spanish Socio-demographic Survey.

FIGURE 3
FIVE-YEAR HAZARD RATES FOR THE DISSOLUTION OF FIRST UNIONS
(FOR 10,000 UNIONS) IN UNION COHORTS 1946–50 TO 1976–80 BY
DURATION AT THE CORRESPONDING PERIOD

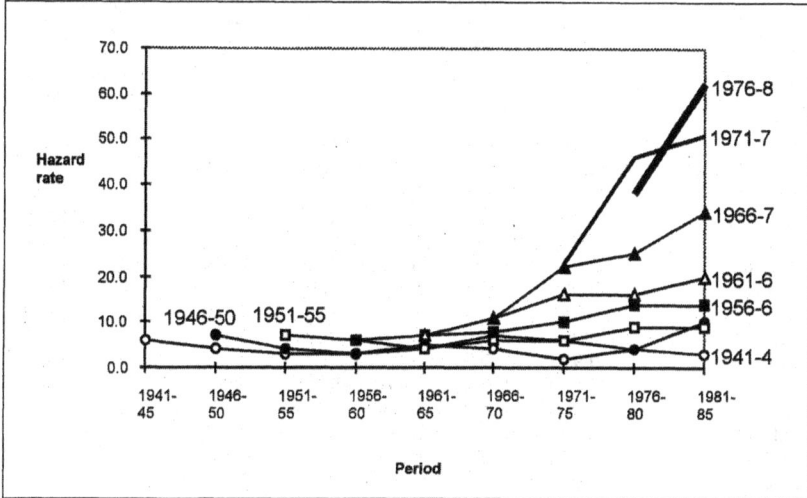

Note: Each line represents a union cohort and begins with a union duration of zero to four years in the corresponding period.

Source: Table 6.

percentage of all first marriages (excluding cohabitation) ending in a separation at the time of the 1991 survey varies between 1.5 per cent and 6.4 per cent, while the average for the whole of Spain is 3.6 per cent (see Table 7). The total dissolution rate calculated for the period 1981–90 confirms the regional trends in cohort behaviour: the highest rate of 20.6 per cent in the Canary Islands is four times that of the lowest, found in Extremadura (five per cent). In demographic terms, this differential behaviour can reflect the strength and nature of the diffusion of the second demographic transition across regions, since divorce is not an isolated phenomenon but part of recent family changes. The island periphery (the Canary Islands and Balearics) presents the highest rates, followed by the more urbanized regions, such as Catalonia (where the weight of the metropolitan area of Barcelona constitutes half of the population), and the autonomous community of Madrid. At the other end of the spectrum, we find central (except Madrid) and southern Spain: Andalusia, Extremadura, Castile and Aragon. Galicia, Asturias, the

TABLE 7
PROPORTION OF FIRST UNIONS SURVIVING TO SEPARATION, PERCENTAGE OF
FIRST MARRIAGES ENDING IN DISSOLUTION AT THE MOMENT OF THE SURVEY
(1991), AND TOTAL DISSOLUTION RATE FOR 1981–90 BY REGION OF RESIDENCE

| Union Cohorts | 1941–65 | | | 1966–80 | | First Marriages | |
|---|---|---|---|---|---|---|---|
| Autonomous Communities | 10 | 20 | 40 | 10 | 20 | Per Cent Ending in Dissolution | Total Rate 1981 –90 |
| Canary Islands | 0.980 | 0.969 | 0.938 | 0.938 | 0.879 | 6.4 | 20.6 |
| Balearics | 0.981 | 0.969 | 0.952 | 0.943 | 0.882 | 5.6 | 17.4 |
| Catalonia | 0.991 | 0.980 | 0.956 | 0.943 | 0.896 | 5.1 | 17.4 |
| Madrid AC | 0.990 | 0.981 | 0.957 | 0.954 | 0.908 | 4.4 | 14.6 |
| Asturias | 0.991 | 0.981 | 0.957 | 0.956 | 0.911 | 4.4 | 13.3 |
| Valencia | 0.996 | 0.988 | 0.973 | 0.960 | 0.926 | 3.4 | 12.2 |
| Spain | 0.994 | 0.986 | 0.969 | 0.965 | 0.928 | 3.6 | 12.0 |
| Basque Country | 0.996 | 0.991 | 0.978 | 0.958 | 0.927 | 3.4 | 11.5 |
| Cantabria | 0.995 | 0.985 | 0.967 | 0.962 | 0.933 | 3.9 | 10.8 |
| Galicia | 0.990 | 0.982 | 0.963 | 0.971 | 0.943 | 3.5 | 10.7 |
| Aragon | 0.997 | 0.990 | 0.980 | 0.967 | 0.943 | 2.4 | 9.6 |
| Andalusia | 0.993 | 0.986 | 0.969 | 0.970 | 0.942 | 3.0 | 9.5 |
| Navarre | 0.996 | 0.991 | 0.983 | 0.967 | 0.937 | 2.5 | 8.7 |
| Rioja | 0.997 | 0.996 | 0.990 | 0.971 | 0.953 | 2.1 | 8.2 |
| Murcia | 0.999 | 0.995 | 0.986 | 0.978 | 0.949 | 2.1 | 8.0 |
| Castile-León | 0.996 | 0.992 | 0.980 | 0.975 | 0.949 | 2.1 | 7.8 |
| Castile-La Mancha | 0.997 | 0.992 | 0.985 | 0.982 | 0.958 | 1.6 | 5.9 |
| Extremadura | 0.996 | 0.993 | 0.985 | 0.988 | 0.969 | 1.5 | 5.0 |

Note: The divorce period indicator is calculated as in Table 1 (only first marriages and
excluding cohabitation) for the period 1981–90.

Source: INE, 1991 Spanish Socio-demographic Survey.

Basque Country and Valencia are situated around the Spanish average.
Figure 4 displays first union survival up to a duration of 20 years in
different autonomous communities for the more recent union cohorts
(1966–85).

*Determinant Factors in Union Disruption*

Many efforts have been made by demographers in different contexts (the
USA, Sweden, Canada, Italy and so on) to classify the multiple
determinant factors for union dissolution according to their nature, for
example, Kellerhals *et al.* (1985) and Bumpass *et al.* (1991). Different
authors have grouped these factors according to four dimensions: family
background, individual characteristics, the characteristics of unions
(usually stressing **heterogamy**) and the economic autonomy of the

FIGURE 4
PROPORTION OF SURVIVING FIRST UNIONS BY DURATION IN THE 1966–85
COHORT FOR A SELECTION OF AUTONOMOUS COMMUNITIES

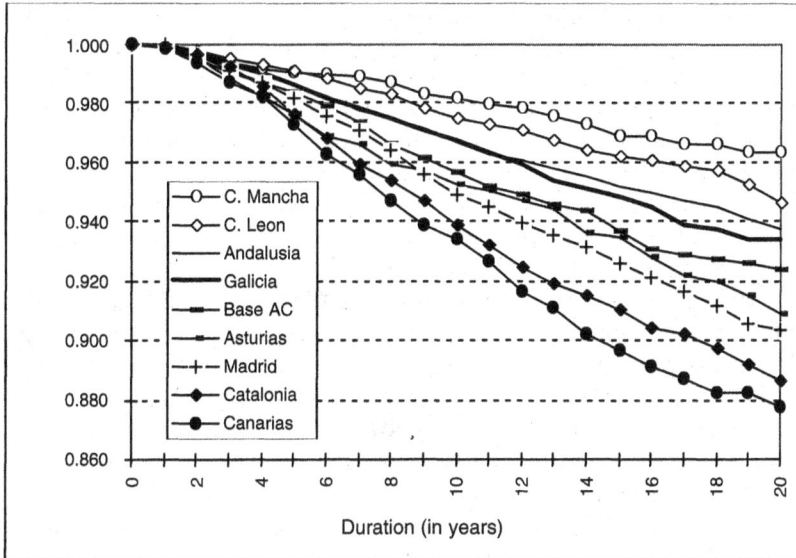

*Source*: INE, 1991 Spanish Sociodemographic Survey.

partners. In the formulation of our hypothesis, we have emphasized the effects of the last dimension because of the incipient development of the welfare state in Spain, but we also explore the other three dimensions.

In relation to family background, we considered only whether parents were separated or divorced. We expect a positive relationship with the propensity for separation and divorce. In fact, in a social context in which divorce is not yet normalized, having been socialized in a family in which a marital dissolution has occurred may remove the dramatism associated with such a decision.[11]

In relation to individual characteristics, and apart from those already analysed above (union cohort, union duration and region of residence), we also examine age at first union, educational attainment and occupational experience, the latter being related to economic independence. Studies done in very different regional contexts found a positive relationship between a very young age at first marriage and a propensity for union disruption: White (1990) and Castro Martin and Bumpass (1989) for the USA; Dharmalingan *et al.* (1998) for New

Zealand; Hoem and Hoem (1992) for Sweden; Pinnelli and De Rose (1997) for Italy, Germany and Canada; and Le Bourdais and Neill (1998) for Canada and Quebec. We expect the same result for Spain. Concerning the other factors (education, occupation and so on), the effects do not always go in the same direction. For instance, in the case of Italy and Germany, there is a positive relationship between the level of education and dissolution, but this is not the case for the USA, Canada and New Zealand. On the other hand, we can assume theoretically that women integrated into the labour market can better afford separation or divorce. But, it is more difficult to make comparisons among studies, as such comparisons depend on the point at which economic activity is measured, since it can either be a determinant factor or a consequence of divorce.

Lastly, in terms of characteristics of unions we consider the type of union (marriage or cohabitation) and, as a proxy for heterogamy, the age difference between partners, since it is the only variable of this kind available in the 1991 Survey, even if we are aware that it would be better to compare social characteristics between partners (education, income, professional status and so on). The main assumption is that marriage and **homogamy** reinforces the stability of the union (Tzeng 1992).

In a previous stage of this research, we have already explored, using another methodology, the effect of age at marriage, education level and occupation as determinant factors in union dissolution in Spain (Solsona *et al.* 1997). Here we use **life-table** analysis in order to give a more accurate measure of their effects.

### Family Background and Age at Marriage

The effects of family background on the propensity for dissolution are presented in Table 8. The results are presented by sex of the respondent and union cohort. Family background, here dichotomized between those individuals whose parents separated or divorced and those whose parents did not, is an important aspect in individuals' married life because it informs us about socialization, experiences and values in relation to the nature of marriage and the ideology of the family. What we see is that having parents who separated or divorced increases the probability that subjects themselves will experience separation. This result holds for both union cohorts observed and for both sexes.

### Individual Characteristics

As we have already discussed above, many studies have shown that age at marriage (or union) has a strong and consistent impact on the incidence

TABLE 8
FAMILY BACKGROUND IN TERMS OF THE DISSOLUTION OF PARENTS'
RELATIONSHIPS BY SEX OF RESPONDENT, UNION COHORT AND
DURATION OF UNION

| Sex and Union | Duration of Union (years) | All Groups | Parents Did Not Separate or Divorce | Parents Did Separate or Divorce |
|---|---|---|---|---|
| **Men** | | | | |
| 1941–65 | 10 | 0.995 | 0.995 | 0.969 |
| | 20 | 0.989 | 0.989 | 0.937 |
| | 40 | 0.972 | 0.972 | 0.857 |
| 1966–80 | 10 | 0.969 | 0.970 | 0.940 |
| | 20 | 0.940 | 0.940 | 0.909 |
| **Women** | | | | |
| 1941–65 | 10 | 0.992 | 0.992 | 0.958 |
| | 20 | 0.984 | 0.984 | 0.929 |
| | 40 | 0.966 | 0.966 | 0.929 |
| 1966–80 | 10 | 0.961 | 0.962 | 0.910 |
| | 20 | 0.917 | 0.918 | 0.824 |

TABLE 9
PROPORTION OF SURVIVING FIRST UNIONS AT DIFFERENT DURATIONS
OF UNION BY SEX OF RESPONDENT AND UNION COHORT FOR CATEGORIES
OF AGE AT FIRST UNION

| Sex and union cohort | Duration of union (in years) | All groups | Age at first union | | |
|---|---|---|---|---|---|
| | | | Early | Average | Late |
| **Men** | | | | | |
| 1941–65 | 10 | 0.995 | 0.991 | 0.996 | 0.995 |
| | 20 | 0.989 | 0.979 | 0.992 | 0.991 |
| | 40 | 0.972 | 0.947 | 0.979 | 0.977 |
| 1966–80 | 10 | 0.969 | 0.978 | 0.973 | 0.976 |
| | 20 | 0.940 | 0.954 | 0.947 | 0.953 |
| **Women** | | | | | |
| 1941–65 | 10 | 0.992 | 0.987 | 0.995 | 0.992 |
| | 20 | 0.984 | 0.972 | 0.987 | 0.986 |
| | 40 | 0.966 | 0.942 | 0.970 | 0.976 |
| 1966–80 | 10 | 0.961 | 0.941 | 0.969 | 0.977 |
| | 20 | 0.917 | 0.876 | 0.931 | 0.949 |

*Note*: Grouping of age at first union is different for men and for women. For men, young is 24 years old and less, average age is 25–29 years old, and old is 30 years old and over. (The overall mean age at first union for males is 27.) For women, young is 21 years old and less, average age is 22–26 years old, and old is 27 years old and over. (The overall mean age at first union for females is 24.)

*Source*: INE, 1991 Spanish Socio-demographic Survey.

of divorce or separation, especially for very young ages. Our study confirms these results, as can be seen in Table 9.

The results are presented by sex and union cohort. We grouped age at first union into three categories, though the age ranges differed for men and women (see note in Table 9). What should be noted is that a very young age at first union (21 and less for women and 24 and less for men) increases the probability that the union will break down if compared with other groups. For later age groups, there is no difference between the categories (that is, for an 'average' and a 'late' age of marriage), which is to say that those married at an average age or older have similar dissolution propensities. This pattern is true for legal unions as well as for cohabitation.

## The Educational Factor

The level of educational can be considered as a personal characteristic as well as an indicator of the capacity for economic independence. A positive relationship between educational level and the propensity to separate may show a selection effect in the sense that those individuals who can cope better with an eventual situation of separation are those who actually separate. In other words, the most educated men and women are those who may be able to accept and assimilate a dissolution better. This proposition seems to be supported by Table 10.

TABLE 10
PROPORTION OF FIRST UNIONS SURVIVING TO SEPARATION AT DIFFERENT DURATIONS OF UNION BY SEX OF RESPONDENT AND UNION COHORT, BY SECTOR OF ACTIVITY AT THE MOMENT OF THE UNION, UNION COHORT 1966-80

| Sex and Duration of union (in years) | All groups | Public sector | Private sector | Family sector | Other situation |
|---|---|---|---|---|---|
| **Men** | | | | | |
| 10 | 0.969 | 0.973 | 0.970 | 0.978 | 0.906 |
| 20 | 0.940 | 0.930 | 0.941 | 0.957 | 0.870 |
| **Women** | | | | | |
| 10 | 0.961 | 0.922 | 0.960 | 0.971 | 0.969 |
| 20 | 0.917 | 0.854 | 0.914 | 0.942 | 0.932 |

Note: The sector of activity corresponds to the first one held during the activity period which includes the moment of the union.

Source: 1991 Spanish Sociodemographic Survey.

## Economic Independence

In Spain, female participation in the labour market is one of the lowest in western Europe, even if in recent years a considerable increase has been observed. Because of the significance of economic activity in gender relations, and because male activity is much more stable, we focus here only on the female population.

Figure 5 shows the evolution of female activity rates from 20 to 64 years according to matrimonial status. Between 1977 and 1996, female activity has grown from 31 per cent to 50 per cent. Separated and divorced women have the highest activity rates, reaching 80 per cent in the last year we can observe, and exceeding slightly the rates for unmarried women. Nevertheless, the significant increase in the general activity rate of women can be explained mainly by the growing numbers of married women entering the labour market.

The relationship between matrimonial status and activity at a given moment, as collected by the *Encuesta de la Población Activa (Labour Force Survey)*, does not give us a clear idea about the relationship between separation or divorce as an event and women's occupations. Being active does not necessarily mean being employed. If a woman is

FIGURE 5
ACTIVITY RATE FOR WOMEN AGED 20–64 BY MATRIMONIAL STATUS, 1977–96

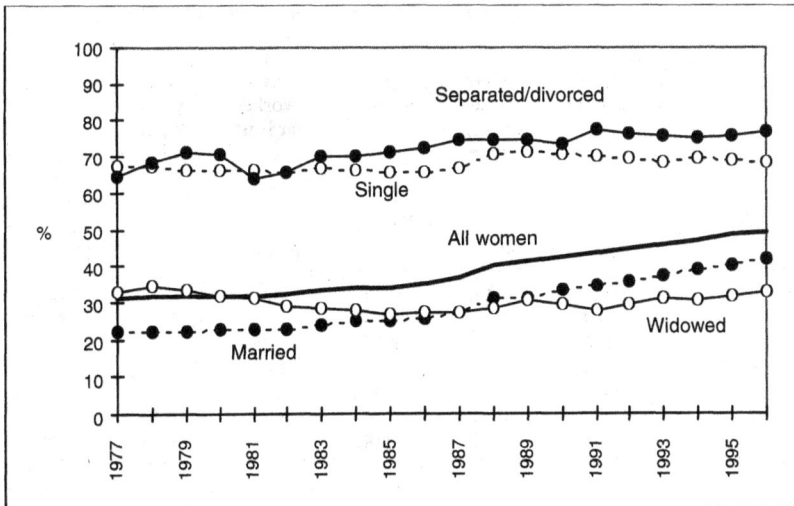

*Source*: INE, Spanish Labour Force Surveys (EPA).

searching for a job, she is considered to be an active person. We cannot therefore fully establish the relationship between separation and divorce and occupation. Does separation or divorce cause women to enter the labour market out of economic necessity? Or, are women already in the labour market better able to cope with their new personal situation after dissolution?

These questions led us to examine women's labour-market situation at the time of the first union dissolution and before dissolution, using the 1991 Spanish Socio-Demographic Survey. We classified separated and divorced women according to their experience in the labour market. We calculated two percentages referring to women who had been married: (1) the percentage of those having worked at least once, and (2) the percentage of those who had never worked (the two first columns of Table 11). We also distinguished between these two same categories for women who had dissolved their first marriage (columns three and four). Among women who have worked, we distinguished between those who had to work before their separation and those that began to work during the year of their separation or later (columns five and six).

TABLE 11
LABOUR-MARKET EXPERIENCE OF MARRIED WOMEN AND WOMEN WHO HAVE DISSOLVED THEIR FIRST MARRIAGE BY UNION COHORT OF FIRST MARRIAGE (AS A PERCENTAGE OF ALL WOMEN OF SURVEYED)

| First Union Cohort | Married Women | | Women who have dissolved their first marriage | | | |
|---|---|---|---|---|---|---|
| | 1 Never worked | 2 Have worked at least once | 3 Never worked | 4 Have worked at least once | 5 Have worked before separation | 6 Begin to work at the moment of the separation or after |
| | (per cent) | (per cent) | (per cent) | (per cent) | (per cent) | (per cent) |
| 1941–45 | 38.9 | 61.1 | 17.0 | 83.0 | 69.0 | 14.0 |
| 1946–50 | 36.9 | 63.1 | 18.3 | 81.7 | 70.0 | 11.7 |
| 1951–55 | 36.6 | 63.4 | 18.5 | 81.5 | 64.6 | 16.9 |
| 1956–60 | 34.0 | 66.0 | 13.8 | 86.2 | 74.5 | 11.7 |
| 1961–65 | 32.0 | 68.0 | 9.0 | 91.0 | 75.8 | 15.2 |
| 1966–70 | 26.7 | 73.3 | 7.4 | 92.6 | 78.8 | 13.8 |
| 1971–75 | 20.8 | 79.2 | 6.8 | 93.2 | 85.0 | 8.2 |
| 1976–80 | 16.3 | 83.7 | 3.7 | 96.3 | 84.9 | 11.4 |

Note: Cohabitants are excluded from this Table.
Source: INE, 1991 Spanish Socio-demographic Survey.

From Table 11 we can point to three major results. First of all, at the moment of the survey ten to 20 per cent more separated or divorced women have worked than married women (comparison of columns four and two). Second, the proportion of separated and divorced women who worked before separation is still higher than the proportion of married women who have never worked (comparison of columns five and two). But the difference is less, at five to ten per cent, except for the last cohort. By comparing these two columns, it should be noted that the duration of union for each cohort is shorter for separated and divorced women than for married women, but the proportion of the former who had never worked at this point of time (prior to the survey time, that is, 1991) is higher. This could be interpreted as the effect of labour-force participation on separation and divorce, in the sense that women's experience of the labour market seems to play a significant role, economically at least, in the decision to interrupt a union. Lastly, the proportion of separated and divorced women beginning to work in the year of their separation or later is quite high for all cohorts (around ten to 15 per cent), which means that separation or divorce is an important moment for women who decide to enter the labour market (column six). In fact, column six gives us a indication precisely of the effect of separation and divorce on women's entry into the labour market.

TABLE 12
PROPORTION OF SURVIVING FIRST UNIONS FOR COHORT 1966–80 OVER TIME BY SEX OF RESPONDENT AND SECTOR OF ACTIVITY AT THE MOMENT OF THE UNION

| Sex and Duration of union (in years) | All groups | Public sector | Private sector | Family sector | Other situation |
|---|---|---|---|---|---|
| **Men** | | | | | |
| 10 | 0.969 | 0.973 | 0.970 | 0.978 | 0.906 |
| 20 | 0.940 | 0.930 | 0.941 | 0.957 | 0.870 |
| **Women** | | | | | |
| 10 | 0.961 | 0.922 | 0.960 | 0.971 | 0.969 |
| 20 | 0.917 | 0.854 | 0.914 | 0.942 | 0.932 |

Note: The sector of activity corresponds to the first type of activity held during the period which includes the moment of union.

Source: 1991 Spanish Socio-demographic Survey.

In order better to understand the crucial question of the relationship between economic independence and separation, we introduced a proxy of occupational status into our life-table analysis, distinguishing men and women and taking into account only recent cohorts (1966–80 – see Table 12). The economic sector corresponds to that in which the respondent was employed in the year following the formation of the union. The four categories we created were as follows: public sector refers to salaried workers in that sector; private sector includes employers, salaried employees, independent workers and members of cooperatives; family workers refers to unpaid workers, that is, those people who work in a family enterprise without receiving any kind of monetary wage; and other situations includes unemployed people, housewives, students, pensioners and so on. This classification gives us some idea of the nature of the labour relations in which the population is involved. For instance, workers belonging to the public sector have, to a great extent, the most advantageous labour relations in terms of job security and social security benefits, while for family workers, the boundary between family relations and labour relations is not clear at all.

The results are clear for women when we look at the first three categories: there is a positive relationship between job security and union dissolution. In contrast, being a family worker is associated with union stability.

TABLE 13
PROPORTION OF FIRST UNIONS SURVIVING FOR DIFFERENT DURATIONS
BY SEX OF RESPONDENT, UNION COHORT AND TYPE OF UNION

| Sex and Union Cohort | Duration of Union (in years) | All Groups | Marriages | Cohabitations |
|---|---|---|---|---|
| **Men** | | | | |
| 1941–65 | 10 | 0.995 | 0.995 | 0.954 |
| | 20 | 0.989 | 0.989 | 0.906 |
| | 40 | 0.972 | 0.972 | 0.815 |
| 1966–80 | 10 | 0.969 | 0.971 | 0.764 |
| | 20 | 0.940 | 0.942 | 0.715 |
| **Women** | | | | |
| 1941–65 | 10 | 0.992 | 0.993 | 0.891 |
| | 20 | 0.984 | 0.984 | 0.789 |
| | 40 | 0.966 | 0.967 | 0.680 |
| 1966–80 | 10 | 0.961 | 0.963 | 0.738 |
| | 20 | 0.917 | 0.920 | 0.617 |

*Source*: 1991 Spanish Socio-demographic Survey.

## Characteristics of Union

Many studies have found that union instability is much more significant among cohabitants than married couples. Spain is no exception[12] (Table 13). Cohabitants have a higher probability of separating than married people. Why? The reasons are surely numerous, and here we give some of them. First, the level and nature of compromise for married couples is different from that of cohabiting couples. Roussel (1993) refers to the change in the nature of marriage in industrialized countries, such that marriage has lost its institutionalized form. In the case of Spain, it is clear that cohabitation is a framework for contingent relations between partners. A recent study done in the Barcelona Metropolitan Area provides empirical evidence of the different forms of compromise for marriages compared with cohabitations (Solsona 1998b): married people are more likely to be owners of their houses, to have children, to adopt more traditional gender divisions of productive and reproductive work, and not to be in hypogamic couples in terms of age, profession and education.

TABLE 14

PROPORTION OF SURVIVING FIRST UNIONS FOR DIFFERENT DURATIONS OF UNION BY SEX OF RESPONDENT, UNION COHORT AND AGE DIFFERENCE BETWEEN PARTNERS

| Sex and union cohort | Duration of union (in years) | All groups | Age difference between partners | | | |
|---|---|---|---|---|---|---|
| | | | m>>w | m>w | m=w | w>m |
| **Men** | | | | | | |
| 1941–65 | 10 | 0.995 | 0.994 | 0.995 | 0.997 | 0.993 |
| | 20 | 0.989 | 0.989 | 0.990 | 0.990 | 0.980 |
| | 40 | 0.972 | 0.969 | 0.975 | 0.976 | 0.959 |
| 1966–80 | 10 | 0.969 | 0.969 | 0.970 | 0.971 | 0.964 |
| | 20 | 0.940 | 0.939 | 0.942 | 0.942 | 0.928 |
| **Women** | | | | | | |
| 1941–65 | 10 | 0.992 | 0.994 | 0.993 | 0.992 | 0.984 |
| | 20 | 0.984 | 0.986 | 0.985 | 0.984 | 0.970 |
| | 40 | 0.966 | 0.967 | 0.967 | 0.968 | 0.947 |
| 1966–80 | 10 | 0.961 | 0.961 | 0.966 | 0.957 | 0.953 |
| | 20 | 0.917 | 0.927 | 0.923 | 0.904 | 0.901 |

Note: m>>w: man is older than the woman by five years or more; m>w: man is older by two to four years; m=w: indicates that the ages of the man and women are equal, the man is one year older or the woman is one year older; and w>m: that the women is older than the man by two years or more.

Source: INE, 1991 Spanish Socio-demographic Survey.

These differences are linked to the sociological explanation of the place of love in a couples' relationship (see, for example, Giddens 1992). In this sense, we may say that married people assume a stable and durable relationship, and they probably establish some kind of deal in which economic aspects also play an important role. Cohabitants, on the contrary, fit better with Gidden's idea of contingent love, that is, that erotism, love and friendship between partners are essential for maintaining the relationship.

Age difference between partners also constitutes a sensitive characteristic of divorce. In Table 13, unions are classified in four categories according to age difference between partners. Hypogamic couples (when women are older than men) are those which experience more dissolution at equal duration. We can conclude that it is a special kind of heterogamy, the hypogamic one that is the reverse of the conventional patriarchal pattern, which is associated with a higher probability of disruption.

### After Dissolution: Children and Remarriage

Divorce, as a demographic event, can be considered as the prelude to a new marriage or as the beginning of a new family form. If the separated couple had young children, the new family form is lone parenthood. In fact, socio-economic conditions leading to an eventual lone-parenthood situation can be very different from those that we find when a new union

TABLE 15
CHILD CUSTODY AFTER THE BREAKDOWN OF FIRST MARRIAGES,
IN PER CENT AND BY UNION COHORT

| Union cohort | Mainly the Mother | Mainly the Father | Other Situations |
|---|---|---|---|
| Before 1941 | 79.7 | 11.4 | 8.9 |
| 1941–45 | 85.9 | 12.7 | 1.4 |
| 1946–50 | 84.0 | 10.6 | 5.3 |
| 1951–55 | 84.8 | 6.9 | 8.3 |
| 1956–60 | 80.4 | 12.0 | 7.6 |
| 1961–65 | 89.8 | 6.3 | 3.9 |
| 1966–70 | 81.6 | 12.3 | 6.1 |
| 1971–75 | 85.7 | 9.4 | 4.9 |
| 1976–80 | 90.5 | 5.2 | 4.2 |
| 1981–85 | 90.3 | 7.0 | 2.8 |
| 1986–90 | 91.8 | 2.0 | 6.1 |

* Shared custody, or children with persons other than the parents.

Source: INE, 1991 Spanish Socio-demographic Survey.

TABLE 16
TOTAL NUMBER OF REMARRIAGES OF DIVORCEES IN SPAIN (1981–93)

|      | Men    | Women |
|------|--------|-------|
| 1981 | 38     | 34    |
| 1982 | 2,003  | 955   |
| 1983 | 4,030  | 1,911 |
| 1984 | 4,611  | 2,526 |
| 1985 | 5,760  | 3,197 |
| 1986 | 5,914  | 3,505 |
| 1987 | 6,441  | 3,872 |
| 1988 | 7,588  | 4,844 |
| 1989 | 7,809  | 5,262 |
| 1990 | 8,347  | 5,825 |
| 1991 | 9,479  | 6,733 |
| 1992 | 10,112 | 7,338 |
| 1993 | 10,148 | 7,712 |

*Source*: INE, Natural Movement of the Spanish Population, different years.

is settled. In order to begin to establish a relationship between the determinants and consequences of divorce, we have taken the first steps in an analysis of remarriage and lone parenthood.

Our results show how different are the conditions deriving from divorce in terms of gender relations. Lone parenthood, as an immediate consequence of separation, affects women much more than men. On the other hand, men's propensity to remarry is much higher than women's. Concerning the custody of children and remarriage, it is important to situate the analysis in a gender perspective. Indeed, as we see in Table 15, which refers only to dissolutions of first marriages, the percentage of children under 17 falling under the custody of the mother reaches 92 per cent (the highest proportion is observed for the last union cohort). These proportions are quite constant for all union cohorts. Only a small proportion of fathers obtain custody of their children. Mothers who obtain custody can also get alimony from their ex-partners. But when marrying again, women having obtained the right to receive alimony from their ex-partner, lose this right. In consequence, separated and divorced women do not approach the possibility of a new marriage in the same terms as their ex-consorts do.

Table 16 illustrates the development of remarriage in Spain, which is much more significant for divorced men. Observing the remarriage phenomenon as a whole, we can see **the effect** deriving from the application of the divorce law when a large number of divorced men had

FIGURE 6
REMARRIAGE RATES OF DIVORCEES IN 1986 AND 1991
(RATES PER 1,000 DIVORCEES)

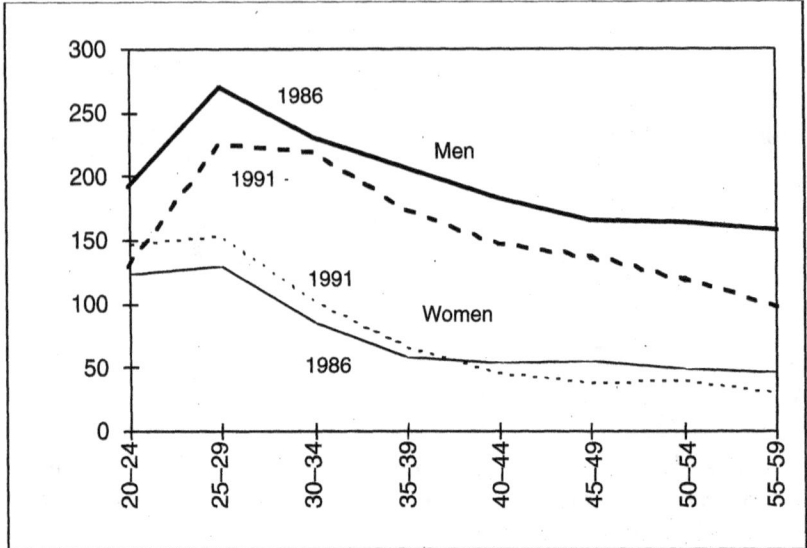

*Source*: Our calculations from INE, Spanish Censuses of 1986 and 1991, and Natural Movement of Spanish Population.

been waiting to remarry. Figure 6 shows remarriage rates for divorcees in 1986 and 1991. The differences between male and female remarriage are essential for understanding the phenomenon in Spain. Even if this difference has decreased during the most recent years observed, it still remains important.

The incidence of male remarriage has decreased significantly, while that of women has slightly increased, mainly at young ages and during the past two years. This different evolution can also be explained by the **period effect** resulting from the application of the divorce law. Two main effects can be noted: the fact that divorced men remarry much more than divorced women and the fact that men also remarry more quickly.

Lastly, we want to stress that the differences in remarriage in terms of gender relations reflect different socio-economic conditions resulting from a divorce. Lone parenthood constitutes one of the most difficult conditions that a divorcee has to cope with, and this affects mainly women.

## CONCLUDING REMARKS

In this article, we have explored recent trends in divorce in Spain and have confirmed the three hypotheses formulated at the beginning of the article regarding the period effect, the generation effect and economic independence. Furthermore our results concerning the determinant factors and consequences of union disruptions are consistent with other empirical evidence found in most western countries. In terms of determinant factors, we found a positive relationship between union dissolution and parental experience of divorce, a very young age at marriage, cohabitation, **heterogamy** (relation between partners) and economic independence. Regarding the consequences of divorce, our results show that the custody of children is mainly a mother's responsibility and that remarriage is more frequent and much quicker for men.

We highlighted an important period effect on marital disruption in Spain. On the one hand, this period effect is the result of legislative factors (the 1981 divorce law), but it is also part of the recent development of the second demographic transition in Spain.

At the microlevel, where individual factors have been analysed, our results show that these features play an important role in the explanation of divorce. We argue that research on divorce in western countries puts too much emphasis on individual characteristics (a young age at marriage, for example). Even though these factors are important, we explored other factors at the macro- and meso-level. We then demonstrated that contextual factors (regional cultures, generation and family background) are relevant too. Regional diversity is significant, and it is explained by cultural factors such as the persistence of regional patterns and the adoption of more 'modern' and differentiated behaviour. The generation effects were important and should continue to be evident within new nuptiality behaviour (delayed first age at marriage, a higher level of celibacy and the extension of cohabitation). Lastly, family background also appears to be an important factor, because it reflects the context in which individuals socialize.

Divorce affects the population selectively and it is more selective in countries where the phenomenon is recent. Spain and Italy are examples of recently experienced divorce and there it is still a very selective phenomenon. This context contrasts with other countries, such as Sweden and the USA, where divorce is normalized and appears to be a structural element in the current conception of couples' relationships. Educational level is a good example of this: in contexts in which the importance of divorce is weak, high levels of education correlate with a high proportion of divorce, but when divorce becomes more normalized the selective effect disappears.

In our results, economic independence turns out to be a selective effect as well. We observed that having some experience on the labour market before divorce is a factor positively associated with divorce; but, at the same time, we observed that divorce is a factor inducing women to enter the labour market (for economic reasons). On the other hand, job security also seems to be associated positively with the decision to separate. In conclusion, we want to note that the selective effect influences women more strongly than men. Perhaps an explanation for this can be found in the social status of women in relation to men. This points to the necessity of analysing divorce in terms of gender relations, with regard both to determinant factors and consequences.

## ACKNOWLEDGEMENT

This article is part of ongoing research which has benefited from a research grant from the Institut Català de la Dona of the Catalan government. The authors wish to thank this institution for its financial aid.

## NOTES

1. During the Second Spanish Republic (1931–36), divorce was the subject of a law which was recognized as one of the most progressive of that period. After the Civil War (1936–39), a new state based on Catholicism was created and the only form of marital dissolution officially allowed was canonical annulment. It permitted the establishment of a new marriage.
2. The absence of a specific divorce register has his own history. Since the legalization of divorce in 1981, some efforts have been directed toward the establishment of an agreement between the National Statistics Institute (INE) and the judiciary. In 1985, an agreement was signed between the two with the aim of introducing a brief form which must be filled in at the moment of the legal dissolution of a marriage in the corresponding Civil Register office. Nevertheless, many offices opposed the application of this agreement, reducing our capacity to understand the incidence of the phenomenon at the national level (see Communidad de Madrid 1990).
3. Alberdi (1995) discusses the political debate that took place during the Civil Code reform to allow the legalization of divorce.
4. Gender relations under this patriarchal regime were such that married women needed their husband's authorization to enter the labour market and the rape of a women was regarded as an offence to the honour of the father, brothers or husband. Lastly, female adultery was punished severely, while male adultery was not considered a crime.
5. Nevertheless, it is important to remark that only the divorced, and not the separated, as the publications curiously reveal, can remarry.
6. The survey shows the year of the disruption, but does not give data on the legal forms it may take over time. The legal form of the disruption was only asked for (at the moment of the survey, that is, 1991) at the point of the disruption.
7. The vital statistics method consists of calculating the number of events (divorces) between the two censuses using the following equation:

Divorced Population (1991) = Divorced Population (1986) – Divorcee Remarriages (1986–91) – Divorcee Deaths (1986–91) + Divorces (1986–91).

From this, the number of divorces can be computed as a residual by the following equation:

Divorces (1986–91) = Divorced Population (1991) – Divorced Population (1986) + Divorcee Remarriages (1986–91) + Divorcee Deaths (1986–91).

This calculation has the same kind of characteristics and problems as those identified for estimates of net migration (Wunsch and Termote 1978: 209–10). Among other things, it supposes that populations, deaths and remarriages are counted properly. It also supposes that international migrations do not affect the distribution of the population by civil status. Results in Table 1 show that these conditions do not seem to be respected.

  8. Alberdi (1995) and Treviño and Gil (1994) calculated the crude divorce rate, the ratio between the total number of events and the total population (or the married population). They showed that Spain has one of the lowest levels of crude divorce rate in western Europe, very close to that of Italy.
  9. The total divorce rate is the sum of duration-specific dissolution rates for a given period, and gives the proportion of first unions of a fictitious marriage cohort that would end in dissolution if its behaviour at different durations follows the pattern observed over the period being considered.
 10. The census of 1975 was carried out on 31 December of that year. Subsequent censuses were carried out during the first months of the year in which they were undertaken.
 11. Castro Martin and Bumpass (1989) have found the same positive relationship in the USA.
 12. The Socio-demographic Survey does not reveal, for marriages, those that lived for some time as cohabitants before marrying. We can only know those cohabitants still cohabiting. The differences in separation rates between the two groups are probably overestimated, since we miss in the cohabitant groups the most stable partnerships (that is, those that marry).

## REFERENCES

Agüero, I. and A. Olano (1988): 'Oferta de trabajo de jovenes: spectos demográficos y económicos'. *Revista de Economia y Sociologia del Trabajo*, 1–2.
Alberdi, I. (1995): *Informe sobre la situación de la familia en España*. Madrid: Ministerio de Auntos Sociales.
Bumpass, L. L., T. Castro Martin and J. A. Sweet (1991): 'The impact of family background and early marital factors on marital disruption'. *Journal of Family Issues*, 12/1, pp.22–42.
Castro Martin, T. and L. L. Bumpass (1989): 'Recent trends in marital disruption'. *Demography*, 26/1, pp.37–51.
Communidad de Madrid, Departamento de Estadística (1990): *Informe sobre la situación de la estadística de divorcios, separaciones y anulaciones*. Madrid: Conjeria de Economía.
Conseil de l'Europe (1997): *Évolution démographique récente en Europe. 1997*. Strasbourg: Éditions du Conseil de l'Europe.
Delphy, C. (1982): 'Matrimonio y divorcio: el doble atolladero'. *Cuadernos Inacabados*, 2–3, pp.65–76. Barcelona: Edicions La Sal.

Dharmalingam, A., I. Pool, S. Hillcoat-Nalletamby and N. McCluskey (1998): 'Divorce in New Zealand'. Paper presented at the 1998 PAA Conference, Chicago.

Giddens, A. (1995): *La transformación de la intimidad. Sexualidad, amor y erotismo en las sociedades modernas.* Madrid: Catedra.

Hoem, B. and J. M. Hoem (1992): 'The disruption of marital and non-marital unions in contemporary Sweden'. In J. Trussel, R. Hankibnson and J. Tilton (eds.), *Demographic Applications of Event History Analysis*, pp.61–93. Oxford: Clarendon Press.

Kellerhals *et al.* (1985): 'Statut social, projet familial et divorce'. *Population*, 6.

Le Bourdais, C. and G. Neil (1998): 'Are mom and dad married? and does it matter for the future of the family?' Paper presented at the 1998 PAA Conference, Chicago.

Lesthaeghe, R. (1995): 'The second demographic transition in western countries. An interpretation'. In K. Oppenheim Mason and A. M. Jensen (eds.), *Gender and Family Change in Industrialized Countries*. Oxford: Clarendon Press.

Monnier, A. and C. de Guibert-Lantoine (1993): 'La conjoncture démographique: l'Europe et les pays développés d'Outre-Mer'. *Population*, 4, pp.1043–67.

Oppenheimer, V. K. (1994): 'Women's rising employment and the future of the family in industrial societies'. *Population and Development Review*, 20/2, pp.294–338.

Pinnelli, A. and A. De Rose (1997): 'Micro and macro determinants of family formation and dissolution'. Paper presented at the twenty-third IUSSP General Population Conference, Beijing.

Roussel, L. (1993): 'Sociographie du divorce et divorcialité'. *Population*, 4, pp.919–38.

Solsona, Montserrat (1998a) 'The second demographic transition from a gender perspective.' *Innovation. The European Journal of Social Sciences*, 11/2, pp.211–25.

(1998a), 'Viure sol, viure en família'. In *Encuesta Metropolitana de Barcelona 1995.* Bellaterra (Barcelona): Institut d'Estudis Metropolitans.

Solsona, M., C. Simó and R. Houle (1997): 'Séparation et divorce en Espagne', Paper presented at the twenty-third IUSSP General Population Conference, Beijing. Published in *Papers de Demografia*, 129, Centre d'Estudis Demogràfics.

SPSS (1994): *SPSS Advanced Statistics 6.1*. Chicago: SPSS Inc.

Treviño. R. and F. Gil (1994): *La familia en cifras.* Barcelona: Centre d'Estudis Demogràfics, mimeo.

Tzeng, M. (1992): 'The effects of socioeconomic heterogamy and changes on marital dissolution for first marriages'. *Journal of Marriage and the Family*, 54/3, pp.6049–19.

White, L. K. (1990): 'Determinants of divorce: A review of research in the eighties'. *Journal of Marriage and the Family*, 52, pp.904–12.

Wunsch, G. and M. Termote (1978): *Introduction to Demographic Analysis. Principles and Methods.* New York: Plenum Press.

# Political Participation: Exploring the Gender Gap in Spain

## LAURA MORALES

### POLITICAL PARTICIPATION AND THE GENDER GAP

Political participation is one of the core features of democratic politics. Through different channels and mechanisms of participation, citizens are able to express their political preferences and attempt to influence the collective decision-making processes. The concept of democracy itself implies the participation of the demos in the government of political society and its institutions; this participation, moreover, is a right which defines the status of citizen.

Why, therefore, do some types of people participate in politics while others do not? What factors explain different patterns of political participation by social groups? There are several models in the literature that claim to explain individual motivations for participation and, hence, social differences: the instrumental, the communitarian, the educative and the expressive models (Parry *et al.* 1992). One strand of the instrumental interpretation is the social-psychological approach,[1] which is best represented by Verba and Nie and their colleagues. They stress the way in which civic attitudes (interest in and knowledge of politics, feelings of internal political efficacy, and a sense of obligation to participate) influence individuals' predisposition to participate. The development of these attitudes is strongly influenced by certain social circumstances as well as by socio-economic status: the individuals' upbringing and their socio-economic environment and resources condition their cognitive, evaluative and affective skills (Verba and Nie 1972).

In accordance with this approach (which emphasizes the relevance of various types of resources in explaining different patterns of political participation), along with education, income and race, gender has traditionally been considered to be one of the main sources of inequality in political participation. One of the first political scientists to analyse this gender gap was Duverger (1955); in the 1970s, it was also examined by Verba, Nie and Kim (1978), who showed the pervasive gender differences in political participation in seven countries (Austria, India, Japan, The Netherlands, Nigeria, the USA, and Yugoslavia). The magnitude of this gap varied across nations and political activities. It was, for example, smaller in the USA and The Netherlands when the activity considered was voting. Their findings were of some interest: neither educational differences nor the gap in institutional affiliation (party identification and organizational membership) could fully account for the gender gap in political participation. Although women were significantly less politically involved[2] than men, and political involvement strongly correlated with political activity, these differences could not account for the gender gap. The authors attributed the gender gap in political participation to a certain phenomenon of inhibition: '[women] care [about politics] but are held back by rules or norms or lack of opportunity' (Verba *et al.* 1978: 254). The existence of this phenomenon was confirmed by evidence for a different interaction between educational levels, institutional affiliation and political involvement with political activity.

This line of enquiry has been continued in a more recent study carried out by Verba, Burns and Schlozman (1997). Focusing on the case of the USA, they concluded that the gender gap in political participation can only be explained by the combined effect of gender differences in resources (education, income, organizational affiliation, civic skills and marital status) and in political engagement (interest, information and sense of efficacy). They argued, in turn, that the gender gap in political engagement cannot be explained by differences in resources, but rather that it seems to be due to the feeling women have that politics is a man's game. To support this conclusion, they offered some tentative evidence as to the positive effect that the presence of female politicians in the Senate elections has had on women's political engagement in the USA.

Nevertheless, there is no consensus that this type of explanation is the best for understanding gender inequalities in political participation. Rather, there are basically three alternative explanations for the gender gap in political participation and involvement: a structural one, a situational one and, lastly, one related to socialization in gender roles. These accounts are, in some sense, all related to the general social-psychological approach to motivations for participation. The structural explanation for gender differences in political behaviour and attitudes (Welch 1977; Togeby 1994) emphasizes the impact of the different levels of political resources available to men and women due to their different positions in society. Differences in income, education and occupational status are translated into differences in political behaviour and attitudes. The situational explanation is quite similar (Welch 1977), but puts more emphasis on the impact of women's roles as wives, carers and home-makers. The main consequence of women's situational position is the different interaction of structural factors with gender in terms of political behaviour, for example, education (see Sapiro 1983). Lastly, the socialization approach argues that gender differences in political behaviour and interest are rooted in childhood socialization into gender roles (Orum et al. 1974; Rapoport 1981; 1985), which leads young girls to believe that politics is incomprehensible and does not merit their interest. An intermediate position argues that while political resources, especially education, must be taken into account when explaining the gender gap in political behaviour and attitudes, political dispositions (psychological involvement, sense of internal and external political efficacy, partisanship, and so on) are the key factors (Bennett and Bennett 1989; Verba et al. 1997), and that since political dispositions cannot only be explained by structural or situational factors, the socialization hypothesis becomes more forceful.[3]

Lastly, it should be noted that recent studies show that the gender gap in political participation is narrowing in Western countries. Topf (1995a; 1995b) presents data from Western Europe which show that there are no significant gender differences in electoral turnout and that the gender gap in political activism decreased almost everywhere between 1959 and 1990. Verba, Burns and Schlozman (1997) demonstrate that the gender gap in electoral turnout has disappeared in the USA (it was already very low when Verba, Nie and Kim analysed it). On the other hand, Christy (1994) highlights the different rhythms and patterns of change in North America and Europe with respect to conventional political participation:[4] while in the 1950s and 1960s, the gender gap was smaller in the USA and Canada, it has narrowed more quickly in Europe. This finding is intriguing not only because it could point, as Christy notes, to the existence of a 'floor effect', but also because it is not linked to parallel changes in women's participation in the workforce; that is, changes in gender roles may not be directly tied to changes in women's political participation, since other institutional factors may also have a decisive influence. Other studies, such as the research carried out by Gundelach (1995), have also highlighted the shrinking gender gap in non-conventional participation[5] (or what he labels grass-roots activism), even if it is still rather significant.

The Spanish case is, in this sense, of empirical interest due to the fact that while gender differences in electoral turnout disappeared during the 1980s, there are still quite pronounced differences between Spanish men and women in other forms of political participation. On the other hand, few attempts have been made to analyse empirically the factors that might explain such differences in countries other than the USA or the Nordic countries, making the analysis of a southern European case potentially interesting for further comparative approaches. In addition, little use has been made of Spanish data for quantitative analyses in order to test theoretical models of political participation, which suggests that there is plenty of scope to contribute in this field.

This article offers an exploratory analysis of gender inequalities in political participation in Spain. First, I will consider the scale and the dimensions of the gender gap in terms of political participation and political attitudes. I will then use a multivariate analysis to explore the factors that might explain this gap in the Spanish case. The empirical analysis of Spanish survey data is, therefore, employed to verify which of the theoretical models under discussion best accounts for gender differences in political participation.

## POLITICAL CHANGE AND POLITICAL CULTURE IN SPAIN

In order to understand gender inequalities in political participation in Spain, it is first necessary to consider briefly the historical evolution of women's position in the political sphere, and then, to outline the patterns of continuity and change in Spanish political culture and political participation.

### Women and Politics in Spain

Even if the Spanish Constitution of 1931 was the first to establish the equal right of men and women to vote and to be elected[6] (Montero 1996), political rights were to be short lived. During the Second Republic (1931–36) women did enter parliament and hold political office: ten women were elected as deputies[7] (representing both left- and right-wing parties) and another, the anarchist Federica Montseny, briefly served as Minister of Public Health during the Civil War. Women's right to participate in politics in Spain ended with the Civil War (1936–39), when many women in the republican zone joined the militia, until the Republican government prohibited them from fighting at the front. After the end of the war, the dictatorship of General Franco sent women back to the home and reinforced traditional gender roles in the family, society and politics. The only role women could exercise in the public sphere during the authoritarian regime was linked to the activities of the Women's Branch of the single official party, which was responsible for the socialization of women in traditional roles (cooking, sewing, and religious faith and practice) and charitable activities. However, some women continued to participate in politics through the underground organizations of the opposition political parties and illegal trade unions. The feminist movement first appeared in the form of occasional meetings in the late 1960s, but it only really developed in organizational terms in the mid-1970s (Scanlon 1990; Threlfall 1996). One of the main features that distinguishes the Spanish feminist movement from its counterparts in Western Europe was its close connection to the left-wing political parties, especially the communists (PCE) and socialists (PSOE). This was explained by the peculiar political context in which the movement emerged: the period leading up to the transition to a democratic regime. Relations with the political parties were always a source of tension within the movement (Scanlon 1990; Threlfall 1996), since many feminist activists were also party members and the parties were accused of attempting to manipulate the movement for their own interests and purposes. The 1978 Constitution abolished many, but not all, of the discriminatory laws introduced during the dictatorship and guaranteed equal rights for men and women and full citizenship for the latter, but major reforms were still needed in the fields of work legislation, family rights, divorce, the economic rights of married couples, abortion, women's access to the army and legal procedures for cases of sexual discrimination and sexual harassment (Valiente 1997). The socialist governments in power between 1982 and 1996 introduced many of these reforms, although others are still pending. Some of the policy changes were pushed through by the Instituto de la Mujer (Institute of Women), created in 1983 to promote women's rights and equal opportunities, but deprived of all but the most limited executive functions (Valiente 1995; Threlfall 1996). The main tasks entrusted to this state-feminist institution have been to coordinate the implementation of equality policies, to run a variety of different programmes for women (health, social services, employment and training), to promote research and publications on women's issues, to produce media campaigns and to fund women's organizations and non-governmental organizations (NGOs).

Another important change with respect to the situation of women in politics in Spain has been the increasing presence of women in parliament, public office, and the political parties and trade unions (see Instituto de la Mujer 1994). In the national parliament, the level of women's representation has risen from around six per cent in 1977 to almost 22 per cent (Montero 1996), while in the regional parliaments, women have held an average of 14 per cent of all seats, a figure which has reached 29 per cent in the regional parliament of Madrid (Threlfall 1996; Montero 1996). More women are now gaining access to public office, both in elected and politically designated posts, and their presence is also increasing in the executives of political parties. One of the main reasons for the growing presence of women in political parties has been the introduction of gender quotas by the Socialist Party (PSOE) and United Left (Izquierda Unida) in the late 1980s, pushed through by their feminist members. Hence, even if full democratic parity has yet to be achieved in Spain, it is much closer now than just one or two decades ago.

## Political Culture and Political Participation in Spain

The recent evolution of Spanish political culture has been characterized by the presence of two overlapping processes: the resocialization of adults into democratic values and generational replacement. Even if there is some evidence that democratic values may have survived in certain sectors of the Spanish population through family transmission (Maravall 1978; 1981) and that some Spaniards did previously favour political change and democracy (López Pintor 1982), it seems clear that democratic values have spread among adults in Spain during the past 20 years (Montero and Torcal 1990; Morán and Benedicto 1995). However, Spanish political culture stands out in Western Europe for the strength of depoliticization, the lack of information, and the sense of distance from political objects, to the extent that it has been characterized as a political culture defined by the widespread political cynicism of its citizens (that is, very weak identification with political elites and institutions due to mistrust of politicians and their intentions)[8] as well as by high levels of dissatisfaction, disinterest and passivity (Maravall 1981: 91–7; Montero and Torcal 1990).

Several distinctive dimensions of Spanish political culture should be noted: first, the low sense of external and internal political efficacy, which should be considered a unidimensional feature in Spain (Torcal 1995), and the low levels of interpersonal confidence and confidence in political institutions and actors; second, widespread political moderation coupled with a significant level of reformist predispositions; third, low levels of psychological political involvement (interest in politics, discussion of politics and political information); fourth, low levels of participation, both conventional and non-conventional, including in all types of associations; and, last, the striking stability of this syndrome of political culture in spite of the major political and social changes that have taken place over the past two decades.

Political involvement in Spain rates among the lowest in western Europe, alongside countries such as Italy, Ireland, Belgium and Portugal, but contrary to what has happened in those countries, political involvement has not increased in Spain (Montero and Torcal 1990; Torcal 1995). Much the same is true of participation and interpersonal confidence, which conform to a pattern of political dispositions common to southern Europe (except Greece) and shared to some extent with Belgium and France. Lastly, the growing political moderation of the Spanish population has been seen as one of the main factors explaining the low levels of participation in politics and in associations in general (Torcal 1995).

Despite the essential stability of Spanish political culture, a number of changes can be identified. Even if levels of interest in politics have generally remained low over the past two decades, some effects of the political context can also be seen (Figure 1): interest increases at times of political innovation and change, only to decrease immediately afterwards (Montero and Torcal 1990; Morán and Benedicto 1995).

Nevertheless, there is no evidence for increasing levels of interest in the category referring to the strongest psychological involvement ('very interested'), which first drops and then stabilizes. Contextual effects are only noticeable in the other, weaker categories. There also seem to be some changes with respect to ideological moderation and attitudes toward political parties: in recent years, both ideological polarization and anti-partisan feelings appear to be intensifying (Torcal 1995). With respect to economic and social issues, reformist attitudes and anti-capitalist positions declined in strength during the 1980s, and there has been a redefinition of the role of the state in the economy, as state intervention is now believed to be appropriate in a narrower range of economic activities and sectors (Morán and Benedicto 1995).

One of the greatest forces for change is cohort replacement. Torcal (1995) applied cohort analysis to several dimensions of Spanish political culture and found that the youngest cohorts differ significantly from older cohorts in a number of respects: the younger cohorts are more moderate in ideological terms, attach more legitimacy to the democratic regime, have a greater sense of internal efficacy, and are less interested in

FIGURE 1
INTEREST IN POLITICS IN SPAIN

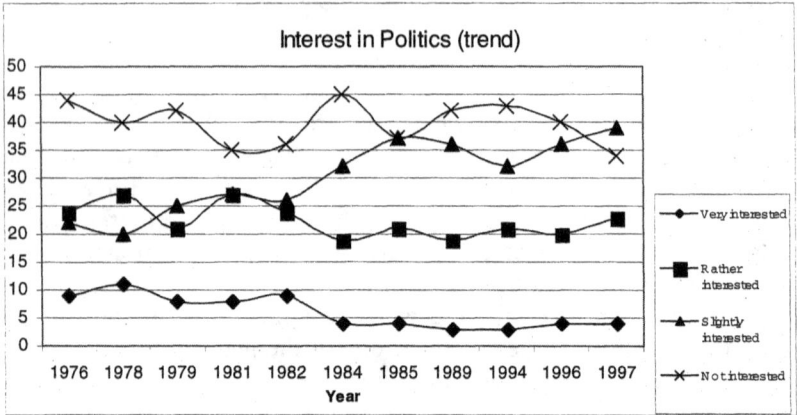

Interest in Politics (trend)

Source: Morán and Benedicto (1995) and Centro de Investigaciones Sociológicas 2105, 2107, 2212, 2240.

politics. Given the current political culture in Spain, this data provides few grounds for optimism with respect to a future increase in political participation. In this sense, further research might consider whether cohort replacement is having any effect on gender differences in political culture and participation.

## THE GENDER GAP IN SPAIN: POLITICAL PARTICIPATION AND POLITICAL ATTITUDES

As noted above, there is relatively little political participation in Spain. Few people feel psychologically involved in politics and even fewer are politically active. This has been a stable pattern in Spanish political culture, and one which shows no signs of changing in the immediate future. In this context, the existence of a gender gap in relation to participation in politics is not particularly surprising given that only 20 years have gone by since the end of a dictatorship which imposed a traditional role on women and excluded them from the public sphere. Of greater interest than the existence or otherwise of a gender gap, therefore, are the type of political activities and attitudes which continue to show strong gender differences and the factors that may explain these differences.

In this article, I will consider some data from 1994 and 1996[9] which throw light on some dimensions of the differences between men and women in terms of political behaviour and political attitudes. First, I will highlight the main features of this gender gap, distinguishing between various modes of political participation as well as between different types of political attitude. I will then discuss the results of a multivariate analysis and examine in some detail the factors that might explain the gender gap in Spain. This, in turn, will enable me to consider which model (the structural, the situational or the 'political disposition' model) best explains the Spanish case.[10]

### The Gender Gap in Political Participation and Attitudes: The Data

The following tables consider the different rates of political participation, psychological political involvement and political attitudes of Spanish men and women. Table 1 lists different forms of political participation. It should be noted that the figures on participation in organizations and social movements should be interpreted as figures of membership of these groups and not as indicators of activism within them. Having clarified this point, we can see that Table 1 reveals the existence of a significant[11] and generalized gender gap in political participation. The proportion of men who belong to at least one political organization or movement is double that for women. There is also a considerable gap in terms of belonging to social movements,[12] despite the fact that the latter are said to be more attractive to women and more women friendly all over Europe. The gender gap is greater in traditional political organizations, political parties and trade unions, where male participation is more than three times greater than that of women. The enormous difference in trade-union membership is hardly surprising in a country in which, in comparison to the rest of Western Europe, few women have entered the labour market and female unemployment is very high. In contrast, the smallest differences in male and female participation are found in the human-rights movement, followed by the peace movement, even if in the latter the proportion of men is still double that of women.

In terms of the various forms of political action, the relative differences are smallest with respect to the more conventional types of activity, such as signing a petition and participating in demonstrations or protest marches. Lastly, by constructing a simple additive index, it is possible to see the different scope of the average repertoire of political action by men and women: while, on average, men have taken part in

TABLE 1
GENDER DIFFERENCES IN VARIOUS FORMS OF POLITICAL PARTICIPATION
IN SPAIN (1994–96)

| Measures of Political Participation | Women (%) | Men (%) | |
|---|---|---|---|
| *Participation in Organizations and Social Movements (1994)* | | | |
| Participate or have Participated in: | | | |
| A Political Party | 2.0 | 7.7 | *** |
| Trade Unions | 5.5 | 17.4 | *** |
| A Human-rights Association | 3.0 | 4.5 | * |
| An Environmental Association | 3.2 | 6.0 | *** |
| A Feminist or Women's Group | 3.6 | 1.4 | *** |
| The Peace Movement | 1.4 | 3.0 | *** |
| Participation in at least one Social Movement | 5.6 | 9.1 | *** |
| Participation in at least one Political | | | |
| Organization or Movement | 12.6 | 25.6 | *** |
| | N ≅ 2,123 | N ≅ 1,994 | |
| *Unconventional Participation (1994)* | | | |
| Has Signed a Petition | 26.6 | 35.2 | *** |
| Has Participated in Demonstrations or | | | |
| Protest Marches | 22.5 | 34.9 | *** |
| Has Blocked the Traffic | 5.5 | 9.7 | *** |
| Has Occupied Buildings or Factories | 3.1 | 7.0 | *** |
| Has Painted Political Graffiti | 1.8 | 5.0 | *** |
| Has Damaged Things | 0.5 | 2.4 | *** |
| Has Used Violence | 0.8 | 2.3 | *** |
| Political Action Repertory (mean number of actions) | 2.25 | 2.99 | *** |
| | N ≅ 2,187 | N ≅ 2,044 | |
| *Conventional Participation (1996)* | | | |
| Have Often or Occasionally: | | | |
| Tried to Persuade Friends on Vote | 13.3 | 20.2 | *** |
| Worked With Other People in the City or | | | |
| Neighbourhood to Solve Local Problems | 18.2 | 23.8 | *** |
| Attended Political Meetings | 15.7 | 21.9 | *** |
| Taken Part in Demonstrations | 17.7 | 25.8 | *** |
| Spent Time Working for a Political Party or | | | |
| a Candidate | 5.5 | 6.5 | n.s |
| Voted in the National General Elections in 1996 | 71.0 | 70.8 | n.s |
| | N ≅ 1,286 | N ≅ 1,198 | |

*Note*: percentages were calculated as a percentage of all respondents for each of the items. The number of total cases varies for each item, therefore, an approximation is offered as the base.

*Significance*: * 0.05, ** 0.01, *** 0.001.

*Sources*: Survey 1994 (CIS 2105, CIS 2107), Survey 1996 (CIS 2212).

three of the actions mentioned, women have been involved in just over two. Thus, protest politics, especially in the form of violent political action, is relatively rare among Spanish women, who generally are or have been involved only in the more restrained forms of protest politics: demonstrating and signing petitions.

Conventional political participation gives a different image of the gender gap. In this case, the differences between men and women are much less significant, since in none of the activities is the proportion of men twice that of women. It is particularly interesting that there are no significant gender differences in two of the activities: voting in the last general election and spending time working for a political party or candidate. As was commented above, the gender gap in electoral participation disappeared long ago in the USA and has almost ceased to exist all over Western Europe. The strong and rapid tendency toward parity in women's electoral participation in Western countries has been attributed (Verba *et al.* 1978) to the minimal effort required to vote, as well as to the sense of civic duty that women feel toward electoral participation (Bennett and Bennett 1989). But this does not account for the absence of a gender gap with respect to spending time working for a political party or candidate.

What factors might explain the gender gap in political participation? Table 2 shows the gender differences in political involvement, which traditionally has been seen as a central factor in explanations of political participation. As noted above, the levels of political interest in Spain have consistently been rather low. The figures show that the gender gap is quite significant and consistent in each of the specific items of interest. However, it should be noted that the smallest differences are found in three specific areas: the activities of the local council, the activities of political parties, and electoral campaigns. Both men and women express most interest in the activities of the local council, thus confirming the well-known argument that the greater the proximity of the political unit, the greater people's interest and psychological involvement. But the smaller gender difference with respect to this item is also theoretically relevant, given the fact that this is a common pattern in other countries. In the USA, women are much more involved in local politics than at other levels, and are particularly active in school politics (Verba *et al.* 1997), thus showing that political involvement is domain specific.

On the other hand, the smaller gender difference with respect to interest in the activities of political parties and electoral campaigns is not only significant for this reason, but also because, when compared to the

TABLE 2
GENDER DIFFERENCES IN POLITICAL INVOLVEMENT

| Measures of Political Participation | Women (%) | Men (%) | |
|---|---|---|---|
| Interest in: | | | |
| Politics (1994) | 18.9 | 30.2 | *** |
| Politics | 18.0 | 30.3 | *** |
| What is Discussed in Parliament | 23.1 | 35.6 | *** |
| What the Government Does | 41.4 | 56.0 | *** |
| What the Regional Government Does | 43.8 | 55.9 | *** |
| What the Local Council Does | 59.0 | 67.5 | *** |
| The Activities of Political Parties | 18.2 | 24.5 | *** |
| The Activities of Trade Unions | 19.3 | 29.0 | *** |
| International Affairs | 29.6 | 43.0 | *** |
| Electoral Campaigns | 18.6 | 25.8 | *** |
| | | | |
| Considered Politics Important in their Lives (1994) | 22.1 | 25.7 | ** |
| Political Information: Frequently Read the Political Sections in Newspapers | 18.1 | 30.3 | *** |
| Frequently Comment On or Discuss Politics with Other People | 18.0 | 29.4 | *** |
| | N1994 ≅ 2,157 | N ≅ 2,027 | |
| | N1996 ≅ 1,272 | N ≅ 1,191 | |

Note: where not otherwise indicated, the item corresponds to the 1996 Survey.
Significance: * 0.05, ** 0.01, *** 0.001.
Sources: Survey 1994 (CIS 2105, CIS 2107), Survey 1996 (CIS 2212).

TABLE 3
GENDER DIFFERENCES IN POLITICAL ATTITUDES

| Political Attitudes | Women (%) | Men (%) | |
|---|---|---|---|
| *Approval of Social Movements (1994)* | | | |
| Ecologists | 91.8 | 88.3 | *** |
| Peace Movement | 84.9 | 79.2 | *** |
| Military Disobedience and Objection Movement | 48.8 | 46.3 | *** |
| Feminist and Women's Movement | 73.2 | 59.7 | *** |
| Gay and Lesbian Movement | 44.0 | 41.0 | * |
| Human Rights Movement | 92.0 | 90.0 | * |
| Pro-life (Anti-abortion) Groups | 57.9 | 50.8 | *** |
| | N ≅ 1,956 | N ≅ 1,933 | |
| | | | |
| Disposition Toward Political Parties (1996) | | | |
| | | | |
| Party Identification (strong + weak) | 41.3 | 41.6 | n.s |
| Valuation of Political Parties (mean on a scale of 1–10) | 4.4 | 4.3 | n.s |
| | N ≅ 1,150 | N ≅ 1,129 | |

Significance: * 0.05, ** 0.01, *** 0.001

figures for general interest in politics, women show equal interest in the activities of political parties and in electoral campaigns, while men show less interest in those two activities than in politics in general. This fact together with the absence of any significant gender gap with respect to attitudes toward political parties (Table 3) may help explain why there are no significant differences between women and men in terms of participation in electoral politics, voting and working for a party or candidate.

Another interesting question is the apparent incongruence between the indicators of political interest and of the importance attributed to politics. While the interest men show in politics is greater than the importance they attribute to it in their lives, the inverse is true of women: even though women consider politics to be important in their lives, that is, they are conscious of the effects it may have on them, they are less interested in it. This pattern is repeated for the other measures of political involvement, level of political information, and frequency of discussion of politics, in which the gender gap is the same as in political interest.

Lastly, it is also interesting to observe the lack of correspondence between men's and women's attitudes toward social movements and political parties (Table 3) and the gender differences in terms of political participation in these organizations (Table 1). Women are more favourably disposed than men to all social movements, and, as noted above, there are no significant gender differences in the case of political parties. This is perhaps not surprising, as attitudes of this type are seldom indicative of behaviour.

In short, a gender gap exists in Spain both in terms of political participation and political involvement. Gender differences in political membership are greatest with respect to participation in political parties and trade unions and insignificant with respect to voting in national general elections and spending time working for a political party or candidate. The gender gap is greater in non-conventional participation than in more conventional forms. Lastly, this gap in political participation is consistent with sharp gender differences in political involvement, but contrasts with Spanish women's greater approval of social movements.

*Explaining Political Participation and the Gender Gap*

Now that we know the dimensions of the gender gap, the question is to evaluate which model best explains the gender differences in political participation among Spanish citizens. Is this due to structural or situational factors or to gender differences in political disposition? In this section, I will examine these questions and I will try to offer a satisfactory answer for the Spanish case. To this end, various regression models will be offered in which the explanatory variables have been introduced in two steps in order to test the theoretical hypotheses: in the first step only socio-economic resources (education and cohort belonging) and situational variables (principal breadwinner and labour-market participation) were introduced, while, in the second step, measures of political disposition and attitudes were also included. The objective of the regression analyses presented in the following pages is not so much to obtain a strong predictive model of the different dependent variables (levels of political participation in several forms), as to control for the significance of gender in predicting participation. In this sense, when the introduction of other variables converts gender into a non-significant variable, we can assume that those variables account for the gender gap in political participation. In contrast, when gender remains statistically significant in each step of the regression model, we should conclude that the variables considered cannot account for gender differences in political participation. This might suggest either some fundamental explicative variable is missing or, hypothetically, that gender differences could be due to a latent cause such as differences in the socialization of men and women. Therefore, the strategy followed here attempts to test explicitly or implicitly the theoretical propositions outlined above.

Starting with the analysis of the empirical results, Table 4 shows the results of a logistic regression analysis of the dichotomous dependent variable, that is, participation in political organizations, which has been constructed by assigning a positive value to those individuals who have participated in at least one political organization (parties and trade unions) or social movement. The results are extremely interesting: socio-economic resources and situational variables alone cannot explain the gender gap in participation in political organizations. In this model of prediction, which moreover offers a poor fit, being a woman reduces by 24 per cent[13] the probability of participating in a political organization, while not being the principal breadwinner reduces that probability by 54 per cent.[14] Even if educational differences are very important for explaining participation in this model (having a university degree is the variable which has partially a greater correlation with the dependent variable (partial R = 0.1382)[15] and raises the probability of participating in political organizations by 157 per cent, compared to only having primary studies), they cannot account for gender differences. Therefore,

TABLE 4
MODELLING PARTICIPATION IN POLITICAL ORGANIZATIONS

| Dependent variable: Participation in political organizations | Predicting participation in political organizations on the basis of socio-economic resources and situational variables | | | Adding measures of political dispositions and attitudes | | |
|---|---|---|---|---|---|---|
| Variables | B | SE B | Partial R | B | SE B | Partial R |
| Constant | -.9851*** | .0984 | | -1.3209*** | .2279 | |
| Gender: woman (male) | -.3651 | .1371 | -.0492 | -.0363 | .1477 | 0 |
| Education | | | | | | |
| Secondary studies | .5154** | .1347 | .0775 | .1549 | .1498 | 0 |
| University studies | 1.0066*** | .1550 | .1382 | .3259 | .1767 | .0269 |
| (Primary studies) | | | | | | |
| Principal breadwinner | | | | | | |
| Not the interviewed | -.5711*** | .1598 | -.0716 | -.7709*** | .1726 | -.0964 |
| The interviewed and another person equally | -.2203 | .2361 | 0 | -.3781 | .2566 | -.0094 |
| (The interviewed) | | | | | | |
| Labour market participation: | | | | | | |
| Not working but has worked | -.2553 | .1658 | -.0133 | -.1818 | .1794 | 0 |
| Never worked | -.4365* | .1697 | -.0469 | -.4156* | .1825 | -.0406 |
| (Working) | | | | | | |
| Cohort | | | | | | |
| Born between 1964-74 | -.4887** | .1610 | -.0586 | -.5428** | .1767 | -.0621 |
| Born between 1953-63 | .0581 | .1485 | 0 | .0270 | .1626 | 0 |
| (Born 1942-52) | | | | | | |
| Interest in Politics | | | | | | |
| Interested | | | | .5157** | .1743 | .0591 |
| Indifferent | | | | -.0661 | .1630 | 0 |
| (Not interested) | | | | | | |
| Importance attached to Politics | | | | | | |
| Important | | | | .5395*** | .1414 | .0806 |
| (Not important) | | | | | | |
| Ideological self-placement: 1-10 | | | | -.1056** | .0313 | -.0697 |
| Confidence in people | | | | | | |
| Has confidence | | | | -.1262 | .1299 | 0 |
| Participation in social associations | | | | | | |
| Participates | | | | 1.3526*** | .1401 | .2175 |
| (Does not participate) | | | | | | |
| Political action repertory: 0-7 | | | | .2054*** | .0374 | .1208 |
| Cox & Snell R Squared | .087 | | | .199 | | |
| N | 1900 | | | 1900 | | |

Note: Between brackets appears the category used as the reference one.
Significance: *.05 **.01 ***.001
Source: Survey 1994 (CIS 2105, CIS 2107)

structural and situational variables are not only unable to explain gender differences in participation in political organizations, but they also offer a poor explanation for this type of political participation itself.

What happens when we add measurements for political disposition and attitude? First, the model improves substantially and gender differences disappear. Education is no longer a significant variable for predicting participation, but the other socio-economic resources that were significant in the previous step remain so and continue to have a similar impact on participation. The factor that stands out as having the greatest impact on the probability of participating in political organizations (partial $R = 0.2175$) is participation in social associations (religious, cultural, sports, youth, and charitable), thus confirming, in the Spanish case, the strong relationship noted by Almond and Verba (1989) between participation in civil society and political participation. Except for interpersonal trust, all the other measures of political disposition and attitude have a significant impact on the probability of participating in a political organization. Hence, structural and situational explanations do not seem to account for the Spanish gender gap in organizational participation.

Nevertheless, we have seen that there is also a gender gap in other forms of political participation. Therefore, the same type of analysis should be applied in these cases. Table 5 presents the results of an OLS regression analysis in which the dependent variable is the additive index of the political action repertory outlined in Table 1 above. Exactly the same variables have been entered in both steps. Neither of the two models are able to eliminate the gender differences in the scope of the political action repertory and, in this case, all variables have a significant impact on the prediction of the dependent variable, except the importance attached to politics and, again, interpersonal trust. The beta coefficients show the standardized impact of each variable or category on the dependent variable. Ideological self-placement on the left and membership of the youngest cohort seem to be the best predictors.

Once again, therefore, it can be seen that gender differences in political participation vary with the form of participation considered, since the model that best explains these differences in terms of participation in political organizations, that of political disposition, is not able to account for the variations in men's and women's repertoires of political action.[16] Hence, gender differences appear to be much more complex and to be conditioned by the type of participation considered in each case. It seems, therefore, that there is no single explicative model for

TABLE 5
MODELLING THE POLITICAL ACTION REPERTORY

| Dependent variable: additive index of the political action repertory (Table 1) Range: 0–7 | Predicting the political action repertory on the basis of socio-economic resources and situational variables | | | Adding measures of political dispositions and attitudes | | |
|---|---|---|---|---|---|---|
| Variables | B | SE B | Partial R | B | SE B | Partial R |
| Constant | 2.065 | .121 | | 2.422 | .150 | |
| Gender: woman (male) | .786 | .071 | .214*** .180*** | .661 | .067 | |
| Education | | | | | | |
| Primary studies | –.649 | .097 | –.174*** | –.426 | .095 | –.114*** |
| Secondary studies | –.153 | .104 | –.038 | –.0517 | .099 | –.013 |
| (University studies) | | | | | | |
| Principal breadwinner | | | | | | |
| Not the interviewed | | | | | | |
| The interviewed and | .421 | .083 | .113*** | .496 | .079 | .134*** |
| another person equally | .106 | .153 | .012 | .089 | .144 | .010 |
| (The interviewed) | | | | | | |
| Labour market participation | | | | | | |
| Not working but has worked | | | | | | |
| Never worked | –.297 | .081 | –.069*** | –.259 | .077 | –.060*** |
| (Working) | –.104 | .086 | –.028 | –.007 | .083 | –.002 |
| Cohort | | | | | | |
| Born between | | | | | | |
| 1964–74 | .628 | .080 | .155*** | .580 | .076 | .143*** |
| Born between | | | | | | |
| 1953–63 | .529 | .084 | .115*** | .357 | .080 | .077*** |
| (Born 1942–52) | | | | | | |
| Interest in Politics | | | | | | |
| Interested | | | | .503 | .081 | .124*** |
| Indifferent | | | | .208 | .068 | .054*** |
| (Not interest) | | | | | | |
| Importance attached to Politics | | | | | | |
| Important | | | | .110 | .072 | .026 |
| (Not important) | | | | | | |
| Ideological self-placement: | | | | | | |
| 1–10 | | | | –.186 | .014 | –.216*** |
| Trust in people | | | | | | |
| Has trust | | | | .022 | .062 | .006 |
| (Has no trust) | | | | | | |
| Participation in social movements | | | | | | |
| Participates | | | | .592 | .104 | .091*** |
| (Does not participate) | | | | | | |
| Participation in political parties or trade unions | | | | | | |
| Participates | | | | .564 | .086 | .109*** |
| (Does not participate) | | | | | | |
| R Squared | .122 | | | .218 | | |
| N | 3314 | | | 3314 | | |

Note: Between brackets appears the category used as the reference one.
Significance: *.05 **.01 *** .001
Source: Survey 1994 (CIS 2105, CIS 2107).

TABLE 6
MODELLING CONVENTIONAL POLITICAL PARTICIPATION

| Dependent variable: additive index of conventional forms of political participation (Table 1) Range: 0–6 | Predicting conventional political participation on the basis of socio-economic resources and situational variables | | | Adding measures of political dispositions and attitudes | | |
|---|---|---|---|---|---|---|
| Variables | B | SE B | Partial R | B | SE B | Partial R |
| Constant | 1.813 | .166 | | .430 | .196 | |
| Gender: male (woman) | .292 | .101 | .078** | -.028 | .091 | -.008 |
| Education | | | | | | |
| Primary studies | -.735 | .145 | -.191*** | .135 | .135 | .035 |
| Secondary studies | -.486 | .128 | -.129*** | .0045 | .116 | .001 |
| (University studies) | | | | | | |
| Principal breadwinner | | | | | | |
| Not the interviewed | -.055 | .116 | -.015 | -.054 | .103 | .015 |
| The interviewed and another person equally | -.136 | .194 | -.016 | -.008 | .173 | .173 |
| (The interviewed) | | | | | | |
| Labour market participation | | | | | | |
| Not working but has worked | -.151 | .109 | -.037 | -.033 | .097 | -.008 |
| Never worked | -.328 | .128 | -.079** | -.218 | .114 | -.053 |
| (Working) | | | | | | |
| Cohort | | | | | | |
| Born between 1964–74 | -.314 | .121 | -.076* | -.064 | .109 | -.016 |
| Born between 1953–63 | .035 | .123 | .008 | .039 | .110 | .008 |
| (Born 1942–52) | | | | | | |
| Ideological self-placement: 1–10 | | | | -.049 | .020 | -.050* |
| Political Involvement Scale: 1–5 | | | | .528 | .024 | .480*** |
| R Squared | .036 | | | .236 | | |
| N | 1944 | | | 1944 | | |

Note: Between brackets appears the category used as the reference one.
Significance: *.05  **.01  *** .001
Source: Survey 1996 (CIS 2212).

the gender gap in political participation.

Let us now test the models with respect to conventional political participation. In this case, the dependent variable is also constructed as a simple additive index of participation in the activities listed in Table 1. An OLS regression analysis has again been applied in two steps, but, in this case, the variables measuring political disposition and attitude vary because the data has been taken from a different survey in which some of the items previously considered were not included. However, ideological self-placement was included, along with a new scale of political involvement, which is an additive index of levels of interest in politics, information on politics, and discussion of politics. Thus, the only variables not present in this analysis are the importance attached to politics, interpersonal trust (which was found to be insignificant in the previous analyses) and participation in political organizations and social associations.

The results of the analysis are very similar to those obtained for participation in political organizations. The structural and situational model has a poor fit with the data and is not able to eliminate the gender differences. Education is the variable which has the strongest impact on the dependent variable, while income inequality within the home does not have a significant effect on conventional participation. Again, introducing measurements of political disposition and attitude proves to be a much more reliable predictor of participation, and also offers a proper account of the gender gap. However, in the case of conventional participation, the political disposition model has further implications: only ideological self-placement and the political involvement scale have significant effects on participation. But more importantly, political involvement accounts for almost half of the variance in the dependent variable. This almost overwhelming power of political involvement could not be properly tested in the previous models because the surveys contained no information about political information and political discussion.

If, therefore, political involvement is so important for explaining both conventional political participation and gender differences, what factors explain the different levels of political involvement in the Spanish population? Table 7 presents the results of an OLS regression analysis, in which the dependent variable is the index of political involvement (which is a simple additive index of political interest, political information and political discussion) and in which the independent variables have again been introduced in two steps in order to test the theoretical models under discussion.

The results are of considerable interest for the conclusions of this article, since neither the structural-situational nor the political disposition models are able to explain gender differences in political involvement, thus suggesting the plausibility of a socialization

TABLE 7
PREDICTING POLITICAL INVOLVEMENT

| Dependent variable: scale of political involvement (interest, information and discussion) Range: 1–5 | Predicting political involvement on the basis of socio-economic resources and situational variables | | | Adding measures of political dispositions and attitudes | | |
|---|---|---|---|---|---|---|
| Variables | B | SE B | Partial R | B | SE B | Partial R |
| Constant | 3.109 | .142 | | 2.892 | .172 | |
| Gender: male (woman) | .596 | .086 | .174*** | .600 | .084 | 1.76*** |
| Education | | | | | | |
| Primary studies | −1.684 | .123 | −.482*** | −1.697 | .120 | −.486*** |
| Secondary studies | −.957 | .1098 | −.279*** | −.961 | .106 | −.280*** |
| (University studies) | | | | | | |
| Principal breadwinner | | | | | | |
| Not the interviewed | −.024 | .099 | −.007 | .020 | .096 | .006 |
| The interviewed and another person equally | .261 | .166 | .034 | .247 | .161 | .033 |
| (The interviewed) | | | | | | |
| Labour market participation | | | | | | |
| Not working but has worked | −.228 | .093 | −.061** | −.223 | .090 | −.059** |
| Never worked | −.206 | .109 | −.055 | −.186 | .106 | −.049 |
| (Working) | | | | | | |
| Cohort | | | | | | |
| Born between 1964–74 | −.512 | .103 | −.135*** | −.424 | .101 | −.112*** |
| Born between 1953–63 | −.043 | .105 | −.010 | −.022 | .103 | −.005 |
| (Born 1942–52) | | | | | | |
| Ideological self-placement: 1–10 | | | | −.029 | .018 | −1.605 |
| Party Identification | | | | | | |
| Strong | | | | .895 | .116 | .164*** |
| Weak | | | | .677 | .076 | .188*** |
| (Not identified) | | | | | | |
| R Squared | .153 | | | .200 | | |
| N | 1946 | | | 1946 | | |

Note: Between brackets appears the category used as the reference one.
Significance: *.05 **.01 *** .001
Source: Survey 1996 (CIS 2212).

explanation. Moreover, given the fact that gender remains significant in the model for political involvement once all the variables considered relevant and available in the survey have been introduced, it could be argued that the explanatory power of the political disposition model with respect to gender differences in conventional participation might be rather limited. This would be the case because it is very likely that the effects of gender and of other structural variables on conventional participation would be masked by the strong effect of political involvement, since gender and education have significant and important effects on political involvement. It is also very likely that we would find a similar pattern with respect to participation in political organizations, since participation in social organizations and the index of political action correlate closely to gender and other variables such as education.

It is also interesting to identify the other factors which have a significant impact on the level of political involvement. Both structural-situational and political disposition measurements help account for the degree to which Spanish citizens are involved in politics. Education, party identification, and gender are the best predictors of psychological political involvement. The only variables which do not appear to be significant are income inequality within the home and ideological self-placement.

To sum up, the results of the multivariate analysis suggest a clear conclusion: even if structural and situational factors are not the main causes of gender differences in conventional and organizational political participation, they certainly have a decisive impact on participation through political involvement. Thus, while there is no direct causal connection between structural and situational variables and political participation, they are linked by the strong effect of the former on political involvement. We cannot, therefore, dismiss the explanatory power of any of the three theoretical approaches to gender differences in political participation and involvement that have been considered here, but more encompassing models should be introduced in order to understand gender inequalities in politics. On the other hand, any conclusion about the Spanish case should be tentative, since survey data on political participation are scarce and the relevant variables for analysis are not always found in the same survey as the items on the diverse forms of political participation. Further research should, therefore, be carried out in order to obtain more reliable conclusions.

## CONCLUDING REMARKS

Gender inequalities with respect to political participation are quite significant in Spain, although they have disappeared in domains such as electoral participation. This gender gap in political participation is quite pervasive and is present in almost all types of political participation: in organizations and social movements, as well as in conventional and non-conventional modes of political action. The data also support the contention that gender differences in political participation vary in accordance with the form of political participation considered, and thus, current approaches to the subject are not able to grasp all the key causal relations that might explain this gender gap.

Although gender differences in levels of political participation in Spain are partly due to structural and situational factors, these cannot fully account for the gap. Political dispositions and attitudinal variables offer a better explanation of gender inequalities in conventional political action and participation in political organizations and social movements. The gender gap in political participation seems to be deeply rooted in gender differences in the levels of psychological political involvement, and the latter is largely, but not totally, explained by structural and situational factors. To the extent that the three theoretical accounts considered in this text (that is, the structural, the situational, and the political disposition models) do not provide a completely satisfactory explanation for the gender gap in political participation, it seems reasonable to think that there could be some latent factor behind that gender gap that cannot be identified through survey data. Probably, greater credibility should be given to the socialization accounts of gender inequalities in politics, and an effort should be made to integrate this line of research into our understanding of the gender gap in political participation.

ACKNOWLEDGEMENTS

The author would like to thank Justin Byrne, Pablo González, Teresa Jurado, José S. Martínez, José Ramón Montero, Mª Luz Morán, Luis Ramiro, and José Ignacio Sánchez-Cuenca for helpful comments on earlier drafts of this article.

NOTES

1. The other main approach within the instrumental model is the strictly 'economic' one, which emphasizes the role of interests and issues in the explanation of individual motivations for political participation. The other three models (communitarian, educative and expressive) are not discussed in this paper since survey research has failed to incorporate them, but they are analysed in Parry, Moyser and Day (1992).
2. Political involvement is defined by Verba, Nie and Kim (1978: 71) as psychological involvement in politics: awareness of politics, interest in politics, information, attention to the media, and so on.
3. The empirical and theoretical approaches considered here limit their analysis of political participation to the individual level. However, I think that a proper account of both political participation in general and of inequalities in political participation should also consider other non-individual factors. In this sense, the analysis of gender

differences in political participation should include some consideration of factors such as the mobilizational role of the women's movement and feminism and macro-changes in values, roles and institutions (see Katzenstein 1987; Togeby 1994; 1995).

4. Conventional political participation is that which, traditionally at least, political science has considered to be democratic and legitimate: voting, campaign activity, community activity and contacting officials. These are the main types of political participation considered by Verba and Nie (1972). Each one of these dimensions was then considered in more detail as the authors specified the concrete forms of participation: convincing other people to vote in a certain way, attending political meetings, working for a party or candidate, working in groups to solve local problems, contacting public officials, and so on. The study coordinated by Barnes and Kaase (1979) was the first to offer a quite different approach to political action and political protest: conventional and non-conventional political activities are not mutually exclusive, but are used jointly by people as part of their repertoire of political action. Since the appearance of this study, the analysis of political participation has included both conventional and non-conventional political action.

5. The forms of non-conventional participation analysed by Barnes and Kaase and their colleagues are: signing petitions, supporting slogans, attending lawful demonstrations, participating in boycotts, participating in unlawful strikes or demonstrations, occupations of buildings, damaging property and involvement in violent action.

6. Some 24 countries gave women the right to vote before Spain did, but this right was defined in electoral laws rather than constitutional texts. In terms of southern Europe, women obtained the right to vote in Italy in 1945, Greece in 1952 and Portugal in 1976 (Montero 1996).

7. Two of these women deputies, Clara Campoamor and Victoria Kent, were appointed to head the Departments of Social Assistance and Charity, and Prisons, respectively. Dolores Ibárruri would later become the head of the Communist Party in exile (1944–60).

8. Interestingly enough, this political cynicism has always been accompanied by strong support for the democratic regime.

9. The three surveys from which the data have been obtained were designed and carried out by the Centro de Investigaciones Sociológicas (CIS) and were made available by its Data Archive. The following surveys were used: studies 2105 and 2107, carried out in June 1994 for the Intergenerational Values and Dynamics project from a representative sample of 2,530 Spaniards aged 15–24 and another representative sample of 2,491 people of other age groups. Both surveys were merged into a single file and the resulting sample was weighted by age in order to obtain a representative sample of the entire adult population. The third survey used was number 2212, carried out in April 1996, with a sample of 2,499 people aged 18 or over. I have used two different time points, not in order to carry out a longitudinal analysis, but because one survey contains information on conventional political participation and the other on non-conventional participation and participation in organizations.

10. For an overview of the Italian and Greek cases, see Corbetta and Parisi (1994); Hayes and Bean (1993); Bimbi (1992); Vianello et al. (1990); Christy (1984); Weber (1981); Vianello (1982); Dobratz (1992a), (1992b) and (1986); and Papageorge-Limberes (1988).

11. The marks of significance shown in the following tables are related to the corresponding chi-square tests.

12. Of course, the exception is participation in the women's or feminist movement, in which women are more active.

13. A simple formula has been applied to calculate the percentage by which one category of a variable increases or decreases the probability of the event happening: 100 (odds ratio −1). The increase or decrease in the likelihood should be interpreted with respect to the category of reference of the variable considered, in this case, being a man. Thus, being a woman reduces the probability of participation by 24 per cent with respect to that of being a man. The percentages cannot be compared for different variables.

14. It should be remembered that the interpretation of increases and decreases in the likelihood of participation must be related to the reference individual, and all other variables held constant.
15. The Partial R statistic measures the partial correlation between the dependent variable and each of the independent variables. A positive value indicates that as the variable increases in value, so too does the likelihood of the event occurring. Small values for R indicate that the variable makes a small partial contribution to the model.
16. It should be noted that the sense of political efficacy could not be entered in any of the models because it was not available in any of the surveys used here.

## REFERENCES

Almond, G. A. and S. Verba (1989) [1963]: *The Civic Culture*. Newbury Park: Sage.
Barnes, S. H. and M. Kaase (1979): *Political Action. Mass Participation in Five Western Democracies*. Beverly Hills: Sage.
Bennett, L. L. and S. Earl Bennett (1989): 'Enduring gender differences in political interest. The impact of socialization and political dispositions'. *American Politics Quarterly*, 17/1, pp.105–22.
Bimbi, F. (1992): 'La cittadinanza delle donne. Trasformazioni dell'economia del dono e culture del welfare State in Italia'. *Inchiesta*, 22/97–98, pp.94–111.
Christy, C. A. (1984): 'Economic development and sex differences in political participation'. *Women and Politics*, 4/1, pp.7–34.
(1994): 'Trends in sex differences in political participation: a comparative perspective'. In Marianne Githens, Pippa Norris and Joni Lovenduski (eds.), *Different Roles, Different Voices*. New York: Harper Collins College Publishers.
Corbetta, P. and A. Parisi (1994): 'Smobilizazione partitica e astenzionismo elettorale'. *Polis*, 8/3, pp.423–43.
Dobratz, B. A. (1986): 'Sociopolitical participation of women in Greece'. *Research in Politics and Society*, 2, pp.119–46.
(1992a): 'Differences in political participation and value orientations among Greek men and women'. *International Journal of Sociology and Social Policy*, 12/8, pp.59–92.
(1992b): 'The political involvement and participation patterns of Greek men and women'. Paper presented to the American Sociological Association Congress.
Duverger, M. (1955): *La Participation des Femmes á la Vie Politique*. Paris: Unesco.
Gundelach, P. (1995): 'Grass-roots activity'. In Jan W. Van Deth and Elinor Scarbrough (eds.), *The Impact of Values*. New York: Oxford University Press.
Hayes, B. C. and C. S. Bean (1993): 'Gender and local political interest: some international comparisons'. *Political Studies*, 41/4, pp.672–82.
Instituto de la Mujer (1994): *Women in Figures. A Decade, 1982–1992*. Madrid: Ministerio de Asuntos Sociales.
Katzenstein, M. F. (1987): 'Comparing the feminist movements of the United States and western Europe: an overview'. In Mary F. Katzenstein and Carol M. Mueller (eds.), *The Women's Movements of the United States and Western Europe. Consciousness, Political Opportunity and Public Policy*. Philadelphia: Temple University Press.
López Pintor, R. (1982): *La Opinión Pública Española del Franquismo a la Democracia*. Madrid: CIS.
Maravall, J. M. (1978): *Dictadura y Disentimiento Político. Obreros y Estudiantes bajo el Franquismo*. Madrid: Alfaguara.
(1981): *La Política de la Transición, 1975–1980*. Madrid: Taurus.
Montero, J. Mª. (1996): *Mujeres Públicas: La Segunda Representación*. Madrid: Fundación Dolores Ibárruri.
Montero, J. R. and M. Torcal (1990): 'La Cultura política de los españoles: pautas de Continuidad y Cambio'. *Sistema*, 99, pp.39–74.
Morán, Mª L. and J. Benedicto (1995): *La Cultura Política de los Españoles. Un Ensayo de*

*Reinterpretación*. Madrid: CIS.

Orum, A., R. Cohen, S. Grasmuck and A. W. Orum (1974): 'Sex, socialization and politics'. *American Sociological Review*, 39, pp.197–209.

Papageorge-Limberes, Y. (1988): 'Conventional political involvement of Greek women'. *Journal of Political and Military Sociology*, 16/1, pp.31–41.

Parry, G., G. Moyser and N. Day (1992): *Political Participation and Democracy in Britain*. Cambridge: Cambridge University Press.

Rapoport, R. B. (1981): 'The sex gap in political persuading: where the structuring principle works'. *American Journal of Political Science*, 25, pp.32–46.

(1985): 'Like mother, like daughter'. *Public Opinion Quarterly*, 49, pp.198–208.

Sapiro, V. (1983): *The Political Integration of Women*. Urbana: University of Illinois Press.

Scanlon, G. M. (1990): 'El movimiento feminista en España, 1900-1985: Logros y Dificultades'. In Judith Astelarra (ed.), *Participación Política de las Mujeres*. Madrid: CIS/Siglo XXI.

Threlfall, M. (1996): 'Feminist politics and social change in Spain'. In Mónica Threlfall (ed.), *Mapping the Women's Movement*. London: Verso.

Togeby, L. (1994): 'Political implications of increasing numbers of women in the labor force'. *Comparative Political Studies*, 27/2, pp.211–40.

(1995): 'Feminist attitudes in times of depoliticization of women's issues'. *European Journal of Political Research*, 27, pp.47–68.

Topf, R. (1995a): 'Electoral participation'. In Hans-Dieter Klingemann and Dieter Fuchs (eds.), *Citizens and the State*. New York: Oxford University Press.

(1995b): 'Beyond electoral participation'. In Hans-Dieter Klingemann and Dieter Fuchs (eds.), *Citizens and the State*. New York: Oxford University Press.

Torcal, M. (1995): 'Actitudes políticas y participación política en España. pautas de cambio y Continuidad'. Universidad Autónoma de Madrid. Ph.D. thesis.

Valiente, C. (1995): 'The power of persuasion: the Instituto de la Mujer in Spain'. In Doroty M. Stetson and Amy G. Mazur (eds.), *Comparative State Feminism*. London: Sage.

(1997). *Políticas Públicas de Género en Perspectiva Comparada: La Mujer Trabajadora en Italia y España (1900–1996)*. Cantoblanco: Universidad Autónoma de Madrid.

Verba, S., N. Burns and K. Lehman Schlozman (1997): 'Knowing and caring about politics: gender and political engagement'. *The Journal of Politics*, 59/4, pp.1051–72.

Verba, S. and N. H. Nie (1972): *Participation in America: Political Democracy and Social Equality*. New York: Harper & Row.

Verba, S., N. H. Nie and J. Kim (1978): *Participation and Political Equality*. New York: Cambridge University Press.

Vianello, M. (1982): 'Indicators concerning political participation of women in Italy'. Paper presented at the International Sociological Association Congress.

Vianello, M., R. Siemienska, N. Damian, E. Lupri, R. Coppi, E. D'Arcangelo, S. Bolasco and C. F. Epstein (1990): *Gender Inequality: A Comparative Study of Discrimination and Participation*. Newbury Park: Sage.

Weber, M. (1981): 'La partecipazione politica femminile in italia: evoluzione, Determinanti, Caratteristiche'. *Rivista Italiana Di Scienza Politica*, 11/2, pp.281–311.

Welch, S. (1977): 'Women as political animals? A test of some explanations for male-female political participation differences'. *American Journal of Political Science*, 21, pp.711–30.

# ABSTRACTS

### Introduction: Interpreting the Transformation of Gender Inequalities in Southern Europe
### MARÍA JOSÉ GONZÁLEZ, TERESA JURADO and MANUELA NALDINI

This introduction identifies the main features of change (new patterns of gender equality) and continuity (legacies of traditional gender orders) in the labour market, the family, the welfare state and in political participation. The authors reject foreign models of gender equality to assess the notion of change. Instead, they use a normative ideal-type, the Universal Care-giver Model, to which gender inequalities in different areas of southern European societies are compared. They conclude that the main requirements for approaching the Universal Care-giver Model are twofold: first, women have to renegotiate gender contracts within the family according to a more egalitarian gender division of labour; and, second, they have to push for the implementation of family-friendly policies (such as an employee- and family-oriented flexibility of working time).

### Women's Flexible Work and Family Responsibilities in Greece
### NOTA KYRIAZIS

The main purpose of the article is to examine flexible working in Greece in the context of family responsibilities and family roles, focusing on the subjective interpretations of workers themselves. The results reported are derived from a broader study carried out in the Greek commercial sector in 1997. The analysis draws on the experiences of men and women of flexible work schedules as they were recounted in the course of in-depth interviews. In general, the results indicate that flexibility is almost exclusively employer induced and is therefore at odds with the special needs of women with caring responsibilities. Moreover, the promotion of equal opportunities for men and women, either directly or indirectly, has not been met through the implementation of flexibility, except in the most general sense of facilitating women's entry into paid employment.

### Development and Equality between Women and Men in the Portuguese Labour Market
### ISABEL MARGARIDA ANDRÉ and PAULO AREOSA FEIO

The rapid economic development of Portugal over the past decade has brought with it a considerable degree of social exclusion and a deepening of social cleavages. The vulnerabilities of the female population are serious handicaps in their success and professional progress. At certain points and under certain circumstances in the past three decades, conditions were created for an important promotion of female employment. Economic modernization led to relative political liberalization and an increase and enlargement in scholarization, both contributing to greater equality of opportunities. With the revolution of April 1974, the general improvement in labour conditions was much more favourable to men than to women: a major increase in female unemployment in the second half of the 1970s was accompanied by a stabilization of male unemployment at very low levels. Equality between men and women in the labour market increased, although it was an equalization based on negative terms. In the 1980s, both groups became subject to greater instability, an increasing precariousness of contracts and decreases in real wages.

### The Family Paradigm in the Italian Welfare State (1947–96)
### FRANCA BIMBI

This article tries to explain why, in Italy, in spite of the moral and ideological emphasis on the family, there is a general lack of family policies, something which has been a persistent feature of the postwar period. Italy is a useful case in that it illustrates that it is possible to have important innovations in welfare policies without any significant change in the dominant modes of representation of the care of children and in the gender division of labour. The traditional family paradigm' went largely unchallenged in the political discourses of the major political parties until the late 1980s and 1990s. Nevertheless, during the 1990s, the debate on the nature of the family and women's choices seems to have reopened deep political conflicts.

### Social Rights of Women with Children: Lone Mothers and Poverty in Italy, Germany and Great Britain
### ELISABETTA RUSPINI

This article focuses on lone mothers' poverty in the familistic Italian welfare regime. In order to appreciate its peculiarities, the study of the Italian situation is developed comparatively by taking into account two other European settings: Germany and Great Britain. What comes out of this analysis is that lone mothers' poverty is a very complex phenomenon, since women's risks of poverty are strongly connected to the close interaction of gendered processes in the labour market, domestic circumstances and welfare systems that can substantially vary from one country to the next. In Italy, there is a specific arrangement between family, the labour market and the welfare state, and, within this triad, it is the family that plays the most crucial role.

### Gender in the Reform of the Italian Welfare State
### ELISABETTA ADDIS

This article examines the gender relations upheld by the Italian welfare state, and argues that recent reforms in the area of cash transfers reinforced the male breadwinner-female housekeeper model. It describes recent changes in family allowances, unemployment benefits, and old-age, retirement and survivors' pensions, and other forms of mean-tested cash transfers for low-income families. It analyses the gender effects of new forms of means-testing, and the implications for the labour supply, participation, and care work within the family. It argues that the misalignment between an old model of gender relations and the reality of women's activity within and outside the household is the source of commonly acknowledged problems in the Italian welfare system, and should be addressed as such in order to reform it.

## To What Extent Does it Pay to be Better Educated? Education and the Work Market for Women in Italy
### FRANCESCA BETTIO and PAOLA VILLA

Italian women are doing progressively better than men in terms of educational attainment. While, however, this has not fully materialized as overall employment gains for women, it is contributing to the enhancement of differences among them. Female participation is low mainly because poorly educated women are disproportionately excluded from the (official) labour market. Also, female unemployment remains high and the puzzling association between rising educational attainment and rising unemployment reflects a contradiction between strong incentives to invest in education at the microlevel and the possibility that more education swells the ranks of the unemployed at the macrolevel. We can make sense of this seeming contradiction only if we recognize the different roles that education performs in different institutional contexts, over and above that of augmenting human capital.

## Is the Male-Provider Model Still in Place? Partnership Formation in Contemporary Spain
### MARTA LUXÁN, PAU MIRET and ROCÍO TREVIÑO

In this article, we examine the influence of some explanatory variables related to educational attainment and labour-market position for males and females on the hazard rates of entry into a first partnership in two historical periods in contemporary Spain. Our goal is to highlight the causes of the present low level of first unions in Spain and to assess different approaches to the interpretation of changes in first partnership formation. Some changes have been observed between the development period (1965–74) and the crisis period (1981–90) in gender patterns of family formation: on the one hand, for males, the positive relationship between the probabilities of entering into a first partnership and educational attainment and labour-market position has been strengthened; on the other hand, for women, the negative relationship between the labour market and first partnership formation has disappeared.

### Separation and Divorce in Spain
#### MONTSERRAT SOLSONA, RENÉ HOULE and CARLES SIMÓ

In this article, we approach the most recent evidence concerning union breakdown in Spain using mainly the retrospective Spanish Socio-demographic Survey (1991). Life-table analysis was used as the main statistical methodology. We examine three basic aspects. First, we present the evolution of the phenomenon across generations and regions, taking into account the duration of first marriages. Second, we make a first attempt to study the determinant factors of marriage dissolution, considering for this purpose four dimensions: family background (parents' experience of divorce), individual characteristics (age at first marriage and educational level), economic autonomy of the partners, (occupation and socio-professional status), and characteristics of marriages (type of marriage and heterogamy). Third, we study the consequences of marital disruption for the custody of children and remarriage.

### Political Participation: Exploring the Gender Gap in Spain
#### LAURA MORALES

Based on data from the 1990s, this article analyses the gender gap in political participation in Spain and the factors which explain it. Three alternative theoretical models are empirically considered: the structural, the situational, and the 'political disposition' models. Two-step regression analyses show that these three theoretical accounts are needed to understand gender differences in political participation, but, even then, some of these differences remain unexplained. Lastly, reference is made to the importance of considering the effects of latent factors such as socialization processes in gender roles.

# BIOGRAPHICAL NOTES

María José Gonzáles is currently completing her Ph.D at the European University Institute (Florence, Italy) on 'The Interplay between Professional Career and Family in Spain: Demographic Evidence and Social Policy Implications'. Her recent publications include Do Modern Welfare States Foster Democratic Family Arrangements? Comparative Case Studies of Britain and Spain", *South European Society & Politics*, 2(3) Winter 1997.

Teresa Jurado has a Ph.D. in Political and Social Sciences from the European University Institute in Florence. Her thesis analysed the patterns of young people leaving home in France and Spain. She has published various comparative articles on labour market, family and social policy issues in Southern Europe and is currently programme officer at the Freudenberg Foundation in Weinheim, Germany where she works on the social exclusion of immigrants in Europe.

Manuela Naldini is a researcher in the Social Sciences department of the University of Turin. Her main areas of interest are comparative social policy and family policy, sociology of the family and women's studies. She has written various articles on the issues of social policy, women's labour market participation and social services for families with children in Italy and Spain.

Nota Kyriazis is Professor of Sociology at Panteion University, Athens. She is the author of *Sociological Research, a Critical Survey of Methods and Techniques* (1998); with Jane Lambiri-Dimaki (eds) *Greek Society at the end of the Twentieth Century* (1995); *Population Reproduction, Theoretical Approaches and Empirical Research* (1992), as well as numerous articles mainly in the area of social demography as well as on gender issues.

Isabel Margarida André is Auxiliary Professor in the Department of Geography and a researcher in the Centre of Geographical Studies both at the University of Lisbon. She is also partner of Geoideia (a consulting firm). She is specialist on employment and gender issues and the co-ordinates projects on public policies evaluation. She is author and co-author of books and articles in the area of family and gender and women employment in Portugal.

Paulo Areosa Feio is an assistant in the Department of Geography and a researcher in the Centre of Geographical Studies both at the University of Lisbon. He is also partner of Geoideia (a consulting firm). He is specialist on economic geography and regional development policies and co-ordinates projects about those themes, namely on services development in the perspective of employment. He has published a book on industrial competitiveness in Portugal and articles on economic geography.

Franca Bimbi is Associate Professor of Social Politics at the University of Padova. She has written a book and several articles and she is co-author of many books on the Mediterranean welfare regime, women citizenship, lone parent families, gender and the use of time and the social construction of motherhood and fatherhood. She is Delegate of the Rector of the University of Padova for the Equal Opportunities and Women's Studies and she is representative for her University in the Athena Programme, a Socrates network of the European Commission.

**Elisabetta Ruspini** is Post-Doctoral Research Fellow of the Department of Sociology, University of Padova. Her research interests include gender issues, comparative welfare research, social and family policies, poverty and the study of living conditions. She has published a number of articles and contributed conference papers on longitudinal research and gender issues on poverty.

**Elisabetta Addis** is an Assistant Professor at the University of Rome la Sapienza. She has published on changes in the Italian banking system in the 1980s and on European Monetary Union, articles on wage differentials, fiscal equity and women's employment, and books on female .soldiers and on economic and gender differences.

**Francesca Bettio** is Associate Professor of Economics at the University of Siena. She is the current co-ordinator of the 'Gender and Employment' network of experts working for the European Commission. She has written a book and several articles on theoretical and applied issues relevant to female labour, fertility patterns, labour market organisation and gender economics in Italy and from a comparative perspective.

**Paula Villa** is Professor of Industrial Economics at the University of Trento. She is the author of numerous studies on labour economics. Since 1984 she has been involved in the EC network of experts on situation of women in the labour market.

**Marta Luxán** has been a research assistant at the Centre d'Estudis Demogràfics (Barcelona) since 1994, participating in several projects on nuptiality, fertility and the family. She is supported by a grant from the Basque government.

**Pau Miret** is currently Research Fellow at the Centre d'Estudis Demogràfics (Barcelona) and lectures at the Universitat Oberta de Catalunya. Previous appointments include the Cathie Marsh Centre for Census and Survey Research, University of Manchester (1994-1995 and 1999) and the Department of Social Statistics, University of Southampton (under the European Commission's "TMR" programme), working on family dynamics in Europe.

**Rocío Treviño** has been a researcher in the Centre d'Estudis Demografics in Barcelona since 1989. She has also participated in the international research network on Family Change and the Welfare State in Europe, co-ordinated by the University of Mannheim's Zentrum fur Europaishe Sozialforschung (MZES).

**Montserrat Sosona** is a lecturer on Demographic and Gender at the Autonomous

University of Barcelona. She is associate researcher at the Demographic Studies Center where she is the chair of the research group 'Gender, Family and Work' and she is an active member of the Working Group on Geography and Gender at the same university.

**René Houle** is associate researcher at the Demographic Studies Center in Barcelona where he is responsible for data base management and the WEB site. His research interests focus on ethnic and linguistic demography, demographic projections, age-sex structures and historical demography.

**Carles Simó** is associate researcher at the Demographic Studies Center in Barcelona. His research interests focus on biodemography, historical demography, data collection, divorce. He is also member of the editorial board of the Boletin de la Asociación de Demografía Histórica, the review of the Spanish and Portuguese Historian Demographers. He teaches in the Demography program at the Demographic Studies Center and also in the department of Geography (Autonomous University of Barcelona).

**Laura Morales** received a degree in Political Science at the Universidad Complutense de Madrid, and is a researcher at the Center for Advanced Study in the Social Sciences of the Instituto Juan March where she obtained an MA in Social Sciences. She is currently a PhD candidate in Sociology at the Universidad Complutense de Madrid and is doing her PhD research on political participation in Western countries. She is also involved in research on the electoral gender gap in Europe.

# INDEX

*Information in notes is indexed in the form
114 (n9), e.g. note 9 on page 114*

abortion 18
  Italy 77–8, 84
Austria, lone mothers 114 (n9)
Azores, women in labour market 61

*Bank of Italy Survey of Household Income
  and Wealth* (SHIW) 91, 98, 114 (n6)
birth rates, extramarital 21, 22
*British Household Panel Survey* (BHPS) 91,
  98, 114 (n6)
Brueckner, H. 100

care-giver model, women 129–30, 191–2
Care-giver Parity Model 10
Catholic Church, family values 74, 75–6,
  77, 83–4
childcare
  Greece 46–7, 52 (n6)
  state provision 27–8
children's rights, Italy 83, 86 (n5)
citizenship rights, women 74–5
City Time Programmes, Italy 81–2, 86 (n4)
cohabitation
  non-marital 21, 174–5
  Spain 174–5, 215–16, 222 (n12)
Communism, women's role 74, 77
continuing vocational training (CVT) 168
  (n4)

division of labour, domestic work 22–3
divorce
  age at marriage 208–10
  determinant factors 206–16, 219–20
  economic independence of women
    211–14
  educational factors 210
  Europe 201
  family background effects 208, 209
  Italy 77
  remarriage 201–2, 216–18
  Spain 195–220
domestic work
  division of labour 22–3
  Italy 129–31

dual-earner household 173

earnings differentials 25
education
  factor in divorce 210
  Italian women 152–7
  and labour market 158–68
  and marriage 184–7
  as a 'parking lot' 151, 157
  Portugal 57–60, 62
  Spain 184–7, 210
  of women 12, 17, 152–7
elderly
  care provision 28
  Greece 48
employment
  flexible 35–52
  gender imbalance 162–7
  *see also* labour market; unemployment
equivalence scales, poverty 101, 115 (n18)
Esping Andersen, G. 9–10
Europe
  divorce rates 201
  lone mothers 91
*European Community Household Panel
  Survey* (ECHP) 91, 98, 99, 113–14
  (n5), 115 (nn14,15)
European Regional Development Fund
  (ERDF) 56
European Social Fund (ESF) 56
European Union
  flexible working 37
  lone parents 91, 93, 114–15(nn 9,10)

family allowances, Italy 127, 132–5
family hierarchies, relaxation of 20–1
family paradigm, Italy 6, 72–85, 90
family responsibilities, Greece 46–50
family wage 7
feminist movements 29
  Italy 76–80
  Spain 227
fertility rates 17, 19
  Italy 85(n1)
financial dependency on men 23–5
flexible work
  Greece 35–52
  types of 36–9

Franco, General F. 196, 226–7
Fraser, N. 9

gender contracts 30
gender equity 7–10
gender gap, political participation 223–6, 230–44
gender order
  changes in 11–21
  traditional 21–9
*German Socio-Economic Panel* (GSOEP) 91, 98, 114 (n6)
Germany, lone mothers 95, 102–13
Great Britain
  lone mothers 95–6, 102–13
  poverty trap 93—4, 103—4, 116 (n22)
Greece
  childcare 46–7, 52 (n6)
  education and labour force 161–2
  employment legislation 39–40
  family responsibilities 46–50
  female labour force 13, 15
  flexible work 35–52
  retail sector 40–52

heterogamy 208, 216
household finances, Greece 48–9

Italy
  abortion 77–8, 84
  *assegni familiari* 133–5
  care-giving work 129–30
  *Cassa Integrazione Guadagni* (CIG) 127, 136–7
  Catholic Church influence 74, 75–6, 77, 83–4
  children's rights 83, 86 (n5)
  citizenship rights 74–5
  City Time Programmes 81–2, 86 (n4)
  constitutional compromise on family policies 73–5, 86 (n2)
  demographic trends 85 (n1)
  divorce 77
  education and labour force 158–62
  education of women 152–7
  family allowances 127, 132–5
  family paradigm 6, 72–85, 90
  family policies 72–4, 82–3
  female labour force 13, 15, 123–5, 158–62
  feminist movement 76–80
  financial dependency 125–7, 147 (n2)

gender imbalance in employment 162–7, 168 (n9)
gender relations 145–6
ideological conflict 73–4
*Indicatore della Situazione Economica* (ISE) 131
labour market 158–68
lone mothers 85 (n1), 94–5, 102–13
pensions 127, 137–44
reforms to pension system 139–44, 146–7
trade unions 78–9
unemployment 89, 113 (nn1,2,3), 162–7
unemployment benefits 127, 136–7
vocational training 155–7
welfare state 76–7, 90, 123–47
women in labour market 158–68

labour force
  and marriage 176–83, 187—922
  women's participation 12–17, 24–5, 60–5, 158–62, 172–3, 211–14
labour market
  and education 158–68
  Portugal 54–6, 60–5
  *see also* employment
*latifundios* 25
legislation, Greece 39– 40
leisure time 147 (n3)
Lewis, J. 8
life-cycle servant 172
lone mothers
  Europe 91
  Germany 95
  Great Britain 95–6, 102–13
  Italy 85(n1), 94–5, 102–13
  and poverty 92–6, 102–13
  researching 96–9
  Spain 216–17
  welfare benefits 93–4, 102–13

Maastricht treaty 146
male provider, decline of 11
male-provider model 7, 171
  Spain 188, 191
male roles, inflexibility 22–3
marriage
  age of women 17, 18
  and education 184–7
  timing of 171–2, 177
  *see also* divorce
maternity policies 18–20

Greece 39
means testing, Italy 131–2
motherhood, effect on labour participation
    159–61

night-work, Greece 37

overtime work, Greece 36

parental rights, Greece 39–40
partnership formation, Spain 174–94
part-time work
    Great Britain 116 (n22)
    Greece 37–8, 42–6, 50–1
paternity leave 20
patriarchal regime, Spain 196, 220 (n4,14)
Pedersen, S. 8
pensions 26
    Italy 127, 137–44
political apathy
    Spain 228–30
    women 28–9
political participation
    analysis 244–5(n4)
    gender gap 2236, 230–44
    non-conventional 245 (n5)
    women 28–9
Portugal
    economic development 56
    educational equality 57–60, 62
    employment quality 65–9
    labour force 14, 16
    labour market 54–6
    lone mothers 114(n9)
    polarisation in labour market 63–5
    women in labour market 60–5
post-Fordism 11
poverty
    definition 99–102
    duration of 105–8
    lone mothers 92–6, 102–13
poverty trap
    Great Britain 93–4, 103–4, 116 (n22)
    Italy 130, 135

regional differences, childcare 28
regression analysis, political participation
    236–43
remarriage of divorcees, Spain 201–2,
    216–18
retail sector
    flexible employment 40–1
    Greece 40–52

riccometro 131, 147—8 (n4))

Scandinavia, women-friendly state 8
shift work, Greece 37
single parents see lone mothers
social policies 17–20
Spain
    Annual Judicial review 195, 197
    cohabitation 174—5, 215—16,
        221(n12)2)
    determinant factors in divorce 206–16
    divorce 195–220
    divorce rate 221 (nn8,9)
    economic independence of women
        211–14
    education and divorce 210
    education and marriage 184–7
    feminist movements 227
    gender gap in political participation
        230–44
    labour force 14, 16
    labour force and divorce 211–14
    labour force and marriage 176–83,
        187–92
    lone mothers 216–17
    male-provider model 188, 191
    marriage age 177–83, 208–10
    partnership formation 174–94
    patriarchal regime 196, 220(n4), 226–7
    political apathy 228–30
    political participation 226–44
    post-Civil War 176–7
    regional differences in marriage
        separation 203–6
    remarriage of divorcees 201–2, 216–18
    separation of marriages 197–8
    Socio-demographic Survey (1991)
        174–6, 195, 197–8, 212
    women as care-givers 191–2
    women and politics 226–8
state, role of 8–9

taxation 17–18
temporary work
    Greece 38–9
    Portugal 68–9
trade unions, Italy 78–9

unemployment
    gender gap 123, 125, 162–7
    Italy 89, 113(nn1,2,3), 162–7
    Portugal 65–7
    state benefits 24, 26

*see also* employment
unemployment benefits, Italy 127, 136–7
United States, political participation
    gender gap 224, 225
Universal Breadwinner Model 9–10
Universal Care-giver Model 10, 29–31
university education, Italy 152—55

vital statistics method, divorces 200,
    220–1(n7)
vocational training, Italy 155–7

weekend work, Greece 36
welfare benefits
    duration of use 108–10
    lone mothers 93–4, 102–13

welfare state
    gender equity 128–44
    gender gap 25–8, 122–3
    Great Britain 95–6
    Italy 76–7, 90, 123–47
women
    as care-givers 129–30, 191–2
    citizenship rights 74–5
    education of 12, 17, 152–7
    financial dependency on men 23–5
    labour force participation 12–17, 24–5,
      60–5, 158–62, 172–3, 211–14
    political apathy 28–9
    political participation 226–8
    unemployment 89, 113(nn1,2,3),
      162–7

For Product Safety Concerns and Information please contact our EU
representative  GPSR@taylorandfrancis.com
Taylor & Francis Verlag GmbH, Kaufingerstraße 24, 80331 München, Germany

www.ingramcontent.com/pod-product-compliance
Lightning Source LLC
Chambersburg PA
CBHW070355270326
41926CB00014B/2564

9 780714 680842